Language Shifts Among the Scheduled Tribes in India

A Geographical Study

M. Ishtiaq

MOTILAL BANARSIDASS PUBLISHERS
PRIVATE LIMITED • DELHI

First Edition: Delhi, 1999

ISBN: 81-208-1617-x

Also available at:
MOTILAL BANARSIDASS
41 U.A. Bungalow Road, Jawahar Nagar, Delhi 110 007
8 Mahalaxmi Chamber, Warden Road, Mumbai 400 026
120 Royapettah High Road, Mylapore, Chennai 600 004
Sanas Plaza, 1302, Baji Rao Road, Pune 411 002
16 St. Mark's Road, Bangalore 560 001
8 Camac Street, Calcutta 700 017
Ashok Rajpath, Patna 800 004
Chowk, Varanasi 221 001

PRINTED IN INDIA
BY JAINENDRA PRAKASH JAIN AT SHRI JAINENDRA PRESS,
A-45 NARAINA, PHASE I, NEW DELHI 110 028
AND PUBLISHED BY NARENDRA PRAKASH JAIN FOR
MOTILAL BANARSIDASS PUBLISHERS PRIVATE LIMITED,
BUNGALOW ROAD, DELHI 110 007

Dedicated to my
Parents

PREFACE

The present work is a geographer's attempt to study the phenomenon of language shift among the lesser-known languages of India.

Language shift has long been a focus of research in anthropology sociology, and linguistics. Such studies require not only spatial explanations but also linguistic and social descriptions. In geography, the focus on language shift is a recent phenomenon-though linguistic geography, which owes its origin to the comparative method evolved by Bopp (Bottiglioni, 1954) and his successors, has been dealing with language shift for more than a century.

Geographers view this phenomenon diachronically in time and synchronically in space. The primary concern here is to determine the patterns of regional variation of language shift and to study the mechanism through which it occurs. Such study helps in understanding and analysing the social and political dimensions of the shifting linguistic identity of a population. In our study we found that the higher the degree of language contact, the higher was the rate of language shift. Such a study can also become a basis to understand language dynamics-just as it might have implications for language planning in a multilingual society like India (Breton, 1971).

I would like to express my sincere thanks to my teacher, Professor R.C. Sharma, School of International Studies at the Jawaharlal Nehru University, New Delhi for encouraging and helping me in completing this book. Without his able guidance, it would have been impossible for me to complete this book in time. Special thanks are due to Professor Anvita Abbi, Chairperson, Centre of Linguistics and English, Jawaharlal Nehru University, New Delhi for going through the draft and providing me with valuable suggestions which have improved the quality of the manuscript. I am grateful to Professor Prem Singh of Delhi University for having given me his critical comments on parts of this work.

I am also thankful to Prof. Ramakant Agnihotri, Head, Department of Linguistics, University of Delhi, to Professor Aslam Mahmood, Jawaharlal Nehru University and to Dr. M. Firoz Khan, Jamia Millia Islamia for sparing their valuable time to go through the statistical sections. I am also thankful to Professor S. Sajid Husain, Mr. Mazhar Ali Khan and Dr. Mary Tahir for their valuable comments and suggestions and also helping me in proof reading the text. Thanks are due to Mr. N.K. Saini and

Mr. Bikram Kumar Dutta for preparing maps and diagrams for this book.

I am indebted to my University, Jamia Millia Islamia, New Delhi for granting me study leave to pursue this research. The cooperation received from Dr. Devinder, K. Awana, Hafiz Tauseefuddin and Mr. Fazlur Rahman is gratefully acknowledged.

It is my pleasure to extend thanks to the respondents in the 16 villages and 3 towns of Bihar, Madhya Pradesh and Rajasthan who responded my probing questions with patience and dignity.

I would fail in my duty if I do not extend my hearty thanks to Saba for the support and encouragements which she extended during the completion of this work.

New Delhi M. Ishtiaq

CONTENTS

PREFACE vii
LIST OF TABLES xi
LIST OF FIGURES xiii

1. INTRODUCTION 1

2. LANGUAGE SHIFT: CONCEPTUAL FRAMEWORK
2.1 Introduction 7
2.2 Directions of Language Shift 10
2.3 Processes of Language Shift 12
2.4 Overview of Literature 16

3. TRIBAL LANGUAGES OF INDIA
3.1 Introduction 19
3.2 Distribution of Austric Languages 20
3.3 Distribution of Sino-Tibetan Languages 23
3.4 Distribution of Dravidian Tribal Languages 26
3.5 Distribution of Indo-Aryan Tribal Languages 27

4. AUSTRIC LANGUAGES : DISTRIBUTION AND PATTERNS OF LANGUAGE SHIFT
4.1 Introduction 29
4.2 Major Austric Languages 30
4.3 Minor Austric Languages 44
4.4 Changing Linguistic Identity 51

5. TYPOLOGY OF LANGUAGE SHIFT AND MAINTENANCE
5.1 Decadal Variations and Language Shift 61
5.2 Patterns of Language Shift and Maintenance : Case Studies 76
5.2.1 The Bhils 76
5.2.2 The Korkus 77
5.2.3 The Mundas 79
5.2.4 The Santals 80
5.3 The Empirical Evidence 82
5.4 Typology of Language Shift and Maintenance 83

6. DETERMINANTS AND CORRELATES OF LANGUAGE SHIFT
6.1 Introduction 97
6.2 Linguistic Diversity 98
6.3 Linguistic Exposure 99
6.4 Bilingualism/Multilingualism 101
6.5 Correlates of Language Shift 107
6.6 Explaining the Unexplained 116

7. LANGUAGE SHIFT: IMPLICATIONS AND EXPLANATIONS
7.1 Introduction 119
7.2 Development and Language Shift 120
7.3 Urbanisation and the Process of Language Shift 127
7.4 Language Regionalism 131

8. PLANNING FOR THE PRESERVATION OF TRIBAL LANGUAGES 139

9. SUMMARY AND CONCLUSIONS 145

APPENDIX 151

REFERENCES 173
INDEX 180

LIST OF TABLES

1. Language Shift among the Tribal Population 9
2. Major Austric Languages of India 23
3. Major Tibeto-Burman Languages of India 25
4. Major Dravidian Tribal Languages of India 26
5. Distribution of Santali Speakers 33
6. Distribution of Mundari Speakers 36
7. Distribution of Ho Speakers 37
8. Distribution of Khasi Speakers 39
9. Distribution of Korku Speakers 41
10. Distribution of Kharia Speakers 43
11. Distribution of Savara Speakers 44
12. Distribution of Bhumij Speakers 46
13. Distribution of Korwa Speakers 46
14. Distribution of Gadaba Speakers 47
15. Distribution of Koda/Kora Speakers 50
16. Lesser-Known Austric Languages 51
17. Austric Tribes Declaring Their Own Mother Tongue 54
18. Austric Tribes Declaring Languages of Other Tribal Groups 55
19. Austric Tribes Declaring Regional Languages 57
20. Austric Tribes Declaring Non-Regional Non-Tribal Languages 60
21. Growth of Major Tribal Languages 70
22. Population Growth of Some Major Tribal Groups 71
23. Correlation Matrix 75
24. Language Shift and Maintenance among the Bhils 77
25. Language Shift and Maintenance among the Korkus 79
26. Language Shift and Maintenance among the Mundas 80
27. Language Shift and Maintenance among the Santals 82
28. Typology of Language Shift and Maintenance among the Bhils 85
29. Typology of Language Shift and Maintenance among the Korkus 89
30. Typology of Language Shift and Maintenance among the Mundas 90
31. Typology of Language Shift and Maintenance among the Santals 93
32. Areas of Linguistic Diversity 99
33. Illustration for Calculating Exposure Index 100
34. Exposure Index 101
35. Percentage of Bilingual Tribal Population- 1981 106
36. Correlation Matrix (Based on District Level Data) 112

37. Correlation Matrix (Based on Household Level Data) 115
38. Levels of Development 124
39. Degree of Language Shift 125
40. Relationship Between Percentage of Tribes, Development and Language Shift 127
41. Districts with High Level of Urbanisation 129
42. Districts with Medium Level of Urbanisation 129
43. Correlation Matrix 131

LIST OF FIGURES

1. Location of Study Area 3
2. Distribution of Tribal Languages in India 21
3. Distribution of Santali Speakers 32
4. Distribution of Mundari Speakers 34
5. Distribution of Ho Speakers 38
6. Distribution of Khasi Speakers 40
7. Distribution of Korku Speakers 40
8. Distribution of Kharia Speakers 42
9. Distribution of Savara Speakers 45
10. Distribution of Bhumij Speakers 48
11. Distribution of Korwa Speakers 48
12. Distribution of Gadaba Speakers 48
13. Distribution of Koda/Kora Speakers 49
14. Austric Tribes Declaring Their Traditional Languages 52
15. Austric Tribes Declaring Languages of Other Tribal Groups 56
16. Austric Tribes Declaring Regional Languages 58
17. Austric Tribes Declaring Non-Tribal Non-Regional Languages 59
18. Major Tribal Languages of India- 1961, 1971, 1981 68
19. Growth of Major Tribal Languages During 1961-71 72
20. Growth of Major Tribal Languages During 1971-81 74
21. Typology of Language Shift and Maintenance among the Bhils 87
22. Typology of Language Shift and Maintenance among the Korkus 88
23. Typology of Language Shift and Maintenance among the Mundas 92
24. Typology of Language Shift and Maintenance among the Santals 94
25. Bilingual Tribal Population in India- 1981 104
26. Rural Bilingual Tribal Population 105
27. Levels of Development 126
28. Language Shift among the Tribal population 126
29. Stages of Language Shift 134
30. Unidirectional Language Shift 134

Chapter 1

INTRODUCTION

The present work aims to identify the nature and the magnitude/ extent of language shift among the lesser-known languages of India. It studies the dynamics of language shift and identifies their spatial parameters. The nature of language shift among males and females in various age groups has been analysed to understand the age and sex differentials. An assessment of linguistic exposure for the four linguistic groups i.e., the Bhils, the Korkus, the Mundas and the Santals has been made to evaluate the levels of exposure to Hindi. A typology of language maintenance and language shift of these groups has been developed in order to determine the linguistic combinations as well as to delineate the areas of high, medium and low grades of the shift. Levels of bilingualism, linguistic diversity and decadal variations of some of the lesser-known languages of the country have been discussed. An attempt has been made to examine the relationship between language shift and a set of socio-economic variables. The relationship between language shift and the levels of urbanisation and regional development has been studied to examine the impact of these developmental activities on the linguistic behaviour of the Austrics.

The study revealed that language shift occurs throughout the country, although its extent varies from region to region depending upon the degree of exposure to exogenous influences and other locational factors. Languages belonging to the Austric and the Tibeto-Burman families have shown a higher degree of retention than the Dravidian and the Indo-Aryan languages. On the other hand, languages spoken on the margin of the major languages, have shown a greater tendency of shifting linguistic identity. Besides literacy, per capita income, non-primary economic sectors (i.e., secondary and tertiary work-force), change of traditional belief, etc., have also been found to be positively correlated with language shift.

The present study helps to remove certain misformed notions about language shift. It also rejects the claim that language shift indicates the process of integration; rather it shows the process of assimilation of people into the majority culture group(Doshi,1972). In fact, language shift among these societies occurs more often due to social and political compulsions (Burdhan,1973). It, therefore, may be considered as the loss of linguistic identity among them. It has been found that the developmental activities have repulsed the wave of such a shift and have led to the emergence of language consciousness and language regionalism among many linguistic groups of the lesser-known languages. The study also emphasises the need for promoting and preserving these languages.

Database and Methodology

The study is based on both field data and the secondary data. The field/primary data have been collected from the field work at the household level for the Bhils, the Korkus, the Mundas and the Santals. Data were collected not only on socio-economic conditions, but also on linguistic behaviour, including mother tongue, language choice, recognition of their language at regional, national and local levels and, their past and present language. To test the degree of linguistic exposure of these people to Hindi, a set of 50 common Hindi words had been included in the informations schedule. These words are baag, motor, aspatal, chaand, kursi, almari, chappal, dukan, suraj, jahaz, kela, kitab, machli, namak, mandir, pita, chadar, murgi, dakia, bank, thana, cycle, rocket, juta, kapda, ghari, cup, kalam, roti, dacter, ghar, aam, doodh, dahi, neembu, dhoti, kurta, kuan, pani, samundra, pahar, ladka, kutta, bhains, car, shareer, mota, lamba, master, mahal.

Four districts were selected for the field work. These districts include East Nimar of Madhya Pradesh, Banswara of Rajasthan, and Santal Parganas and Ranchi of Bihar (Fig. 1). The basis for the selection of these districts was the dominance of the Bhils in Banswara, the Korkus in East Nimar, the Mundas in Ranchi and the Santals in Santal Parganas. The selection of the Tehsil/Block was made on the above criterion while the villages were selected on the basis of different levels of tribal concentration. Keeping the above criteria in mind, Bagidora Development Block of Banswara; Punasa and Khalwa Development Blocks of East Nimar, Bundu and Murhu Development Blocks of Ranchi and Littipara Development Block of Santal Parganas were chosen. Altogether, 16 villages and 3 towns were selected. Of these, 4 villages (i.e., Wanera Para, Regania, Nai Abadi, Umedgarhi) were from Bagidora Tehsil, 7 villages (i.e., Mirpur, Kutbi, Punasa, Pangra, Udaipur, Richhi, Kalamkala) from Khalwa and Punasa Blocks, 4 villages (i.e.,Bande, Litingdih, Kula Buru, Murhu) from Murhu and Bundu Blocks, and Suraj Beda from Littipara Block; and the 3 towns were Banswara, Ranchi, and Dumka. These towns are the district headquarters. It is to be noted that Khandwa, the district headquarter of East Nimar, was excluded from the field survey as the town did not have the Korku population in its notified urban area (Appendix - I).

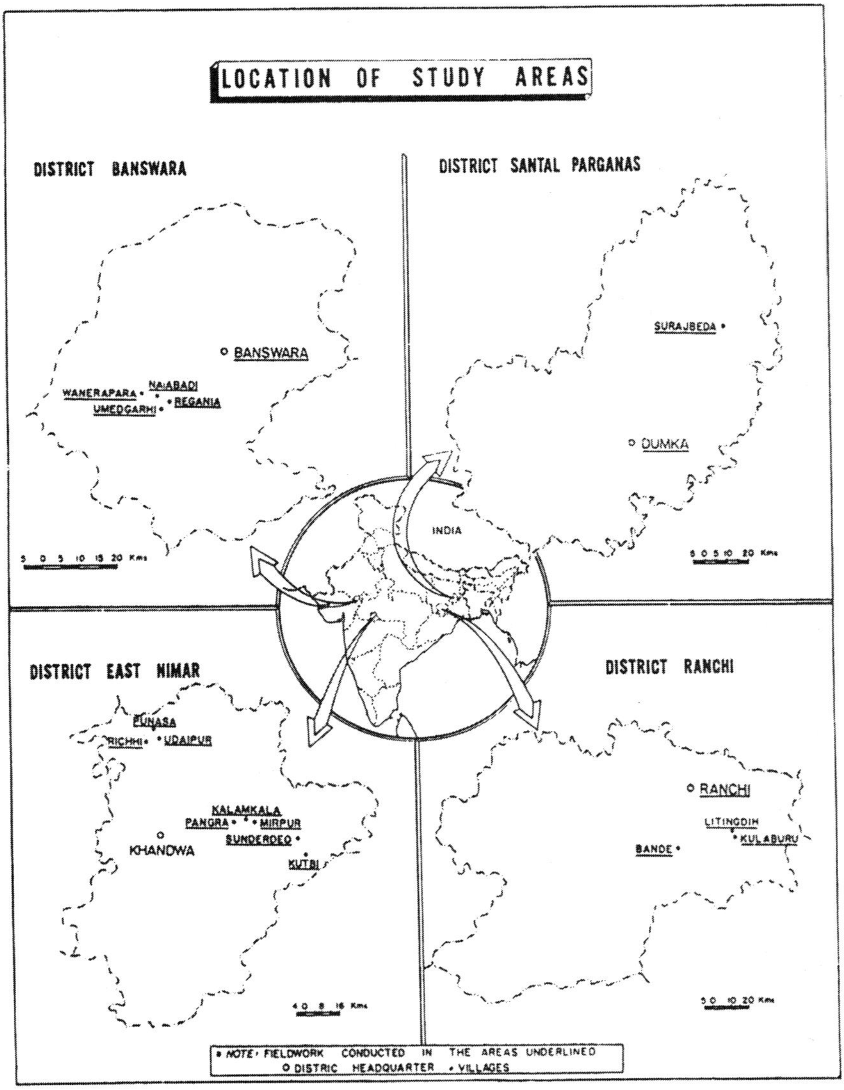
LOCATION OF STUDY AREAS
DISTRICT BANSWARA
BANSWARA
WANERAPARA
NAIABADI
UMEDGARHI
REGANIA
DISTRICT SANTAL PARGANAS
SURAJBEDA
DUMKA
INDIA
DISTRICT EAST NIMAR
PUNASA
RICHHI
UDAIPUR
KALAMKALA
PANGRA
MIRPUR
SUNDERDEO
KHANDWA
KUTBI
DISTRICT RANCHI
RANCHI
LITINGDIH
KULABURU
BANDE
* NOTE: FIELDWORK CONDUCTED IN THE AREAS UNDERLINED
O DISTRIC HEADQUARTER • VILLAGES

Fig. 1

The field work was conducted by the author himself during October 1989 and January 1990. I spent about three and a half months among them. Altogether 397 households were surveyed and 754 persons interviewed. The Santals were more hostile to the outsiders. Thus, I could spend lesser time among them than among the Bhils, the Korkus and the Mundas. Consequently, we had a lesser number of respondents from the Santals. In Suraj Beda, I was allowed to conduct the survey only when the interpreter-cum-security personnel had convinced the head of the village (Mukhia) that I was a teacher and did not belong either to any political party or to the government's office. But I had to throw a refreshment party for some senior persons of the village to avoid any untoward situation. I also had to pay two thousand rupees to them. The security man, who had managed to smuggle me safely out of the village, asked me to leave the village immediately. On the other hand, the Santals of Dumka town were comparatively less hostile; therefore, I could spend about a fortnight among them.

It is interesting to note that the Korkus of Punasa, Udaipur and Richhi villages under Punasa Block (Khandwa Tehsil) have completely switched over to Nimadi, a regional dialect of Hindi. These people consider themselves superior to those Korkus who have retained their traditional linguistic identity and live in Khalwa Block (Hersud Tehsil).

Such a superiority complex on grounds of language identity does not exist among the Bhils, the Mundas and the Santals. But the Mundas and the Santals were more conscious of their languages and wanted them to be included in the VIIIth Schedule of Indian Constitution.

However, the Korkus of the Khandwa Block (East Nimar) who have already switched over to Nimadi, had shown no urge to revive their traditional language.

The secondary data have been derived from the following tables of the Census of India:

a. Census of India, 1981, Sr. 1, INDIA
Households and Household Population by Language Mainly Spoken in the Household.

b. Census of India, 1981, Sr. 1, INDIA
Special Table for Scheduled Tribes on Mother Tongue and Bilingualism, pt. IX (ii).

c. Census of India, 1971, Sr. 1, INDIA
Special Table for Scheduled Tribes, Pt. V-A(ii).

d. Census of India, 1971, Sr. 1, INDIA
Social and Cultural Tables, Pt. II C(i).

e. Census of India, 1961, Vol. 1, INDIA
Language Tables, Pt. II C(ii).

The data from the above census tables have been collected for the following linguistic groups :

Austro-Asiatic Languages	Dravidian Languages
Ho	Gondi
Kharia	Kondh/Khond
Khasi	Kisan
Korku	Koya
Munda/Mundari	Kui
Santali	Kurukh/Oraon
Savara	Tulu

Indo-Aryan Languages	Tibeto-Burman Languages
Bhili/Bhilodi	Adi
Halabi/Halbi	Ao
Khandeshi	Bodo
	Garo
	Lushai/Mizo
	Mikir
	Nissi/Dafla
	Tripuri

Chapter Scheme

This work is divided into nine chapters. The first chapter deals with the objectives of the study, database and methodology, and chapter scheme. The second chapter deals with language shift, its nature and processes. Language shift among the tribes may occur either towards the non-tribal languages-including regional and non-tribal non-regional-or towards the other tribal languages (as a result of various socio-economic and political changes). The last section of this chapter is an overview of the sporadic researches on linguistic shifts conducted in India and abroad.

The third chapter deals with the spatial distribution of the tribal languages of India. These languages have been discussed under the Austric, Sino-Tibetan, Indo-Aryan and Dravidian famiiies. The chapter is descriptive in nature.

The Austric speaking tribal population of India accounts for about 1.6 per cent of the total population and is spread over central India from east to west. Their dialects are considered to be the oldest in the Indian sub-continent (Roy, 1970). An effort has been made in the fourth chapter to find out the patterns of distribution of the Austric languages under the major and the minor groups and also to evaluate the magnitude of the changes in their linguistic identity. For this purpose, two methods-Index of Concentration and Degree of Language Shift have been applied. The chapter is analytical in nature.

The fifth chapter presents a typology of language shift and maintenance among the selected tribal communities from central India. For this purpose, the Bhils, the Korkus, the Mundas, and the Santals, have been selected. Typology of language shift and language maintenance have been calculated through statistical techniques and the coefficient of variance has been calculated to find out the magnitude of regional variations of language shift and maintenance. The chapter is analytical and based on secondary data.

Since language shift is a cultural phenomenon, it may often follow cultural change. A number of socio-economic variables affect language shift. Thus, an attempt has been made in the sixth chapter to find out the determinants and correlates of language shift. Linguistic Diversity, Linguistic Exposure, Bilingualism / Multilingualism and a set of other socio-economic variables have been analysed and statistically tested to examine the degree of language shift attributable to these factors. Correlation and Regression have been used in this chapter. The chapter is based on both primary and secondary data.

A number of implications may be associated with language shift and its maintenance. These are cultural assimilation and integration, regional development, urbanisation and growth of language regionalism, etc. An attempt has been made in the seventh chapter to study and evaluate the above mentioned implications of language shift and maintenance among the tribal population of India.

There is an urgent need to preserve these languages because they are the cultural heritage of India. The eighth chapter suggests what steps need to be taken to promote and to develop the lesser-known languages of India.

The last chapter presents a summary and conclusions. The chapter also highlights the problems commonly faced by the researchers in studying language shift among the tribal communities in India-specially in dealing with the census data.

Chapter 2

LANGUAGE SHIFT: CONCEPTUAL FRAMEWORK

2.1 Introduction

Language shift, a universal phenomenon, may occur either consciously or sub-consciously. Linguistic researches have revealed that language shift is a continuous, though slow, process. Rubenstein (1957:283) believes that such shifts are normally gradual and not abrupt. A high degree of language shift may occur in the areas of high cultural mobility and social instability. On the other hand, such shifts tend to slow down where cultural change is relatively slow (Milroy and Milroy, 1985: 380). It is also believed that rapid cultural change may be followed by rapid changes in the linguistic system (Hoijer, 1948: 340). The shift is faster in urban areas than in rural as the insulacity and rigidity of rural life reduce the acceptability of change (Fishman, 1976: 315). The degree of language shift also varies at the individual level mainly with regard to the age, sex and educational attainments. In general, children, women and illiterates comprise the lower levels of language shift both in rural and urban societies.

Language shift may be either natural (divergent) or non-natural (convergent). Natural/divergent shift refers to the shift occurring in all languages in due course of time and thus, it is a process of historical change. Such a shift is not dependent on inter-communication between different linguistic groups-rather, it operates within the system and produces a systematic shift between two historical stages in the same language. The growth of daughter languages descending from the proto-language is an example of such a change. On the other hand, non-natural shift (convergent) takes place when different linguistic groups interact. This results in the transfer of elements from one language to another by the process of borrowing or diffusion. Thus, language contact leads to a systematic change which involves merging of two separate systems (Diebold, 1964: 495-96).

The process of language shift among tribal communities has been noticed throughout India, although its extent and magnitude varies according to region and tribe. The tribals, after having lived in varying degrees of isolation for many centuries have now constantly been interacting with the non-tribal population on the periphery of the tribal homelands. The process of interaction between the tribes and the non-tribes acquired a new dimension in India after independence with the introduction of adult franchise and community development programmes (Gupta, 1977: 162). Intensive exploitation of mineral resources,... and, consequently, the establishment of industrial plants and development of urban centres in the tribal regions provided suitable ground for many changes, among which language shift is an important one. A higher degree of language shift may be noticed among those who had been interacting with the non-tribal groups in the surrounding areas than among those living in the tribal heartland. The degree of shift depends upon the degree of exposure to the exogenous influences and other locational factors. For example, the tribals of the sub-Himalayan region have shown least inclination to such a shift due to limited interaction with the outsiders as the region is relatively isolated.

The tribes of central India, on the other hand, present a varied degree of continuity in their linguistic identity. The majority of these tribes have shown their willingness to switch over to the non-tribal languages. The Austric tribals, however, have posed resistance to this shift, and continuing to communicate in their own traditional languages. Unlike the sub-Himalayan tribes, the tribes of western and southern India could not continue their traditional/ancestral languages due to the pressure exerted by non-tribals. Raza and Ahmad(1990) estimated that a little less than half of India's tribal population have, already, lost their linguistic identity and have adopted regional languages as their mother tongue. The magnitude of the loss of linguistic identity was exceptionally high (i.e., above 90%) in the states of Kerala, Tamil Nadu and Gujarat, and very high in Karnataka (74%), Maharashtra (69%), Andhra Pradesh (66%), and Madhya Pradesh (65%). On the other hand, almost all the tribes of Manipur, Arunachal Pradesh, Mizoram and Andaman and Nicobar Islands have maintained their linguistic identity. The degree of language retention was exceptionally high in the states of Meghalaya (97%) and Tripura (92%) followed by Bihar (85%), Himachal Pradesh (79%), Nagaland (74%) and Rajasthan (73%).

Table - 1 LANGUAGE SHIFT AMONG THE TRIBAL POPULATION

State/UT	% of L.Shift	Major Tribal Languages
Andhra Pradesh	66.24	Gadaba, Savara (AA); Gondi, Khond, Koya, Kui(D)
Arunachal Pradesh	<1	Adi, Mishmi, Mopna, Nissi/Dafla, Nocte, Wancho (TB)
Assam	39.62	Bodo, Garo, Lushai/Mizo, Mikir, Miri/Mishing(TB); Santali(AA)
Bihar	14.53	Kurukh/Oraon(D); Bhumij, Ho, Kharia, Mundari, Santali (AA)
Gujarat	92.86	Bhili/Bhilodi, Khandeshi(IA)
Himachal Pradesh	21.18	Bhotia, Kinnauri, Lahuli(TB)
Jammu & Kashmir	1.02	Balti, Ladakhi(TB)
Karnataka	74.21	Tulu, Coorgi/ Kodagu (D)
Kerala	98.31	Tulu(D)
Madhya Pradesh	65.31	Bhili/Bhilodi, Halbi(IA);Gondi, Kolami, Kurukh/Oraon (D); Korku (AA)
Maharashtra	68.78	Bhili/Bhilodi, Khandeshi,Halbi (IA); Gondi(D); Korku(AA)
Manipur	<1	Hmar,Kabui, Kacha Naga, Kuki, Mao, Paite, Tangkhul, Thado(TB)
Meghalaya	2.74	Bodo,Garo(TB); Khasi(AA)
Mizoram	<1	Lushai/Mizo, Tripuri(TB)
Nagaland	26.43	Ao, Angami, Chang,Lotha,Konyak, Phom, Sangtam, Sema(TB)
Orissa	49.66	Bhumij, Ho, Kharia, Mundari, Savara, Santali(AA); Gondi, Kurukh/ Oraon, Khond, Kisan, Kui, Koya(D)
Rajasthan	26.98	Bhili/Bhilodi(IA)
Sikkim	<1	Bhotia, Lepcha, Sherpa(TB)
Tamil Nadu	94.90	Coorgi/Kodagu, Tulu(D)
Tripura	9.16	Mogh, Garo, Tripuri(TB)
West Bengal	20.71	Kurukh/Oraon(D); Bodo(TB); Mundari, Santali(AA)
Andaman & N. Isls.	<1	Kharia, Nicobarese(AA)
Dadra & N. H.	18.21	Bhili/Bhilodi(IA)
Lakshdweep	82.98	

Source: 1. Raza,M. and A. Ahmad (1990) **An Atlas of Tribal India,** Concept, New Delhi.
2. Census of India 1981 Sr.1 INDIA, **Households and Household Population by Language mainly spoken in the Household**.

AA = Austro-Asiatic IA = Indo-Aryan
D = Dravidian TB = Tibeto-Burman

2.2 Directions of Language Shift

Language shift to social scientists means switching over from one's traditional/ ancestral language to the non-traditional language. Traditional languages are those which have been spoken by one's ancestors. The non-traditional language refers to that language which was acquired through contact with the surrounding people. Such a language may be the regional or national language or the language of the majority culture group. For example, if the Santals, whose traditional language is Santali, declare Hindi as their mother tongue, this is indicative of a shift in their traditional language. The basic idea behind the word 'shift' is a change which occurs in two points of time. But language shift can be studied both in apparent and in real times (Chambers and Trudgill, 1980:80). The shift is apparent if it is realised in one particular point of time. On the other hand, real change refers to the shift in more than one time. The former is known as synchronic study of a language while the latter is known as diachronic study (Crystal, 1971:158).

The directions of language shift among the tribal people of India, as has already been mentioned, indicated multidimensional shifts from non-tribal to the other tribal languages. Some of the probable directions of the language shift are as follows :

From	To
	to other tribal language
own mother tongue	to own regional language
	to other regional language
	to national/international language

By selecting the Munda tribe as an example, the above may be illustrated as follows :

From	To
	Santali
Mundari	Hindi
	Bengali/Oriya
	Hindi/ English

It is necessary to mention here that the above example may be true only when the Munda tribe is selected from the Hindi region. On the other hand, if the same tribe be selected from the non-Hindi region, the shift to the regional language and other regional languages will change accordingly. Language shift to the other tribal languages results mainly due to long association between a small tribal group and the majority tribal group. In order to find a place in the tribal social order as well as to feel more secure, the smaller group adopts the language of a major tribal group. A group of the Oraons, the Mundas, the Bhumijs, the Hos, etc. in the Chotanagpur region, for example, have also declared Santali, the language of the major tribal group, as their own mother tongue.

The largest share in the degree of language shift among the tribal population of India goes to regional languages. These are, invariably, the languages of the non-tribal population and the official language of some state of the Indian Union. Since education in India is imparted through regional languages, the tribals have no option but to study using the non-tribal languages as media. This has led them to abandon their mother tongue in favour of the regional language. The tribals who shift to other regional languages or international languages constitute an insignificant proportion of the total population. Relative to other regional language, Hindi is gaining momentum and has become popular over the years. As a result, tribal population is gradually drawn to the mainstream of national culture. Today, the tribal people of India may be identified as belonging to one of the following groups on the basis of their linguistic affiliations.

a. tribes declaring a language with which they are traditionally identified;
b. tribes adopting a language of other tribal groups with whom they have come in close contact;
c. tribes declaring regional language as their own mother tongue; and
d. tribes adopting non-tribal non-regional language.

It is easy to understand the above classification of the tribes into various linguistic groups. Linguistically, group 'a' refers to those tribal groups who remained loyal to their traditional language and have declared it as their mother tongue. On the other hand, groups 'b', 'c' and 'd' are cases of language shift. Group 'b' refers to those tribals who have adopted the language of other tribal groups. For example, a group of the Mundas who have declared Santali as their mother tongue may be classified under group 'b'. Group 'c' refers to those who have declared regional language, i.e., Hindi in Bihar, Telugu in Andhra Pradesh, Oriya in Orissa, etc. as their mother tongue instead of their traditional language. There are also cases on the periphery of tribal areas and along the borders of different states where some tribal groups have declared non-tribal non-regional language as their mother tongue. It was found, for example, that the Santals of Bihar living along the Bihar and West Bengal border, declared Bengali as their mother tongue. And those living along the Bihar-Orissa border, declared Oriya as their mother tongue. Both these languages are non-tribal and non-regional in character, and they may be classified under group 'd'. Tribes declaring foreign languages, i.e, English, French, etc. as their mother tongues may also be grouped under group 'd'.

2.3 **Processes of Language Shift**

A number of processes bring about language shift, although all of them do not function simultaneously. Some of them are active in some regions whereas others are dominant in others depending upon the socio-economic and cultural conditions. The degree of language shift differs in different time periods. Thus, the time factor has been regarded as an important aspect to examine the process of language shift (Prabhoo, 1980: 262 and Weinreich, 1953: 103). Language Contact, Colonization and Cultural Change are some of the important processes to bring language shift.

Language Contact

Contact provides dramatic instances of language shift. It also leads to extensive re-arrangement of languages. For example, the Finnish-American language is an outcome of the long contact between Finnish and English in the United States (Blount and Sanches, 1977: 16). In India too, Sadari/ Sadani, a language developed through contact, is spoken in the Chotanagpur region mainly by the tribal people. Though Sadari, according to the census report, has been classified under the group of the Indo-Aryan languages, many linguists question this classification. Nevertheless, it is a fact that Sadari presents a composite linguistic mosaic of all the three language families, i.e., the Indo-Aryan, the Dravidian and the Austric. It is assumed that Sadari has emerged as a distinct language as a result of interaction between the Austric, the Dravidian and the Indo-Aryan people for centuries.

Historical accounts reveal that the contact situation between the two systems has not been reciprocated equally because of various socio-economic reasons. Normally, in a contact situation, one group becomes super-ordinate imposing its language on the other group, which become sub-ordinate. It also needs to be mentioned here that sub-ordinate migrants appear to be more rapidly assimilated than the super- ordinate indigenous population (Liberson, 1977: 53). In fact, it is our contention that the contact of tribes with non-tribes is a matter of interaction between an active culture and a culture which is more simple and passive in nature (Rajora,1987: 39). When the indigenous population communicates in the language of economically and politically dominant groups, a pidgin and, subsequently, a creole may emerge which becomes instrumental in fostering language shift.

The tribal culture of India appears to be either fully or partially incorporated into the non-tribal culture. Those groups which have been fully incorporated have also registered the non-tribal languages as their own mother tongue. On the other hand, those who have been partially assimilated have become bilinguals or multilinguals. There are also people living in relative isolation, who have remained monolingual and have registered their traditional/ancestral languages as their mother tongue. Fishman suggests that one of the important factors affecting language shift is the social setting. In his opinion, in every geographical area there are people of different linguistic affiliations and they may pick up the local language without giving up their own. But, assimilation of smaller linguistic groups, which have a loose social setting, is natural. Consequently a complete shift of a language cannot be denied. The presence of various linguistic groups in a geographical area in which inter-cultural contact developed was found to be correlated with linguistic shift (Roy, 1962: 160).

As far as language contact is concerned, it was found that those tribes living in urban and industrial settings have greater tendency towards language shift. On the other hand, tribes living in rural areas and with low language contact with the outsiders, have continued to communicate in their own traditional language.

Colonization

The process of colonization is an important mechanism of language shift. The super-ordinate group of people with their superior weapons and skills have colonized many parts of the world. In this process, large populations migrated from their native place to alien lands. They carried their cultural traits to the new areas and imposed them on the colonized people. The conqueror's superior culture dominated in all spheres of life of the conquered people forcing them to be assimilated into it. Those who did not accept the alien culture and showed resistance to it were pushed into the dense forests and highlands where they have lived in isolation till today, preserving their traditional cultural identity. Since the language of the alien group was patronised by the administration, it became the prestigious language and gradually replaced the less prestigious indigenous language (Fishman, 1976 : 321 and Southworth, 1974 : 221). Such a shift from native to the non-native language is commonly found in multilingual countries in which economic necessity and the need for lingua-franca could re-inforce the prestige factor. For instance, Europeans who have colonized Latin America, Africa and parts of Asia imposed their languages, such as English, Portuguese, Spanish, French, etc. on the colonized people. These languages served the needs of education, economy and administration as the local languages-associated with the non-elite masses-were considered less prestigious. Missionary activities, an aim of colonization, were undertaken with the support of the administration and brought a large section of the tribal population under the Christian fold. The change in their traditional religion somehow necessitated a shift in their language.

The Indian sub-continent, though protected by natural boundaries, has been invaded by outsiders from time immemorial. The Aryans, the Pathans, the Mughals and the Europeans came in sequence. It is believed that before the Aryans, probably, the sub-continent was occupied by the people of Australoid origin who spoke various forms of Austric language. The Aryans invaded the country and pushed the aboriginals into the forest and hills of the central India. Subsequently, Sanskrit received royal patronage and became the medium of Brahminical education and during the Sultanate period, Persian became the official language. It remained the language of the elite and was used only for official and literary purposes. Although it never became popular among the masses, its presence brought about drastic changes on the linguistic plane of India. One of them was the emergence of Urdu which is spoken by more than 35 million people in India, (about 5.4 per cent of the total population). English was declared the official language during the British rule in India. It is needless to say how much we depend on English especially in the areas of science and technology. Though the British have already left India, the roots of English are strong in Indian soil. This may be illustrated by the fact that about 2.5 lakh persons declared it as their mother tongue and about 25 per cent of the total bilingual population of India registered English as their subsidiary language (Khubchandani, 1972).

Cultural Change

Cultural change leads to language shift. Since language is a strong element of culture, any change in linguistic identity may indicate cultural change. There are a number of observations which suggest that the periods of change in culture are roughly coincident with the shift in linguistic structure (Hoijer, 1948 : 339). The transformation of traditional societies into modern political systems has been accompanied by linguistic modernization and shift (Dasgupta, 1970 : 17). The process of detribalisation and the assimilation of the tribal population into the cultures of their neighbouring people are taking place and as a result, the tribal languages are dying out (Burdhan, 1973 : 80). In the absence of frequent contact with the neighbouring people, the degree of acculturation among the tribals was insignificant before the British period. But wherever the tribes lived in proximity and in prolonged contact with their neighbours, they were gradually assimilated into the majority culture and switched over to the neighbour's languages. The development of communication facilities, the spread of schools, hospitals and banking facilities, etc. in the tribal areas accelerated the process of modernization. The gradual transformation of tribal areas since independence has, by and large, exposed the tribal societies to a series of social, economic and cultural changes. Both planned and unplanned interventions in the process of regional development or in search of agricultural land, mineral and forest resources resulted in overall social and economic transformation in the tribal areas. Such a transformation was accompanied by linguistic shift of varying degrees among the tribal population.

The traditional economic activities of the tribals, such as food gathering and primitive forms of agriculture (shifting or sedentary) have undergone a series of changes during this period. This has led to the structural changes in the tribal economy and society. With the establishment of industrial plants based on the mineral and forest resources in the tribal areas, a new demand for land acquisition began. Thus, the tribal land and forest areas were encroached by outsiders. This has reduced the tribal areas-which, therefore, could not sustain the population pressure. Consequently, tribals moved out to their surrounding areas and to urban centres where they were absorbed in low paid jobs. Those who could not move out lived on the scarce land and forest resources in the interior. Those who moved out to the urban centres had a greater chance of interaction with the non-tribal population, leading them to adopt the non-tribal languages.

The growth of literacy brings about a systematic linguistic shift. Barring a few exceptions, the regional language is the medium of instruction. These languages, invariably, are the non-tribal languages. Thus, the growth of literacy alienated the tribals from their own mother tongues and caused a language shift.

The process of social mobility has also been considered a powerful cause of linguistic shift. Some major tribal communities such as the Bhils, the Gonds, the Mundas, etc., have shown a strong tendency to get themselves assimilated into the dominant regional cultures by declaring the regional languages as their mother tongue. Evidently, it shows an inner urge to rehabilitate themselves and attain a viable social status within the dominant culture groups of their neighbourhood. Such a shift may also occur as a result of the compulsions of the existing social reality. Studies reveal that the majority of the tribals in central India have embraced Hinduism or Christianity as their religion (Volchok, 1964: 108). Those who were assimilated into the majority culture, have by and large, also lost their linguistic identity. On the other hand, those who are trying to preserve their cultural identity, have maintained their linguistic identity. Doshi (1972) believes that the central Indian tribal society, by and large, is an assimilationist society in which Hindustani or regional language has become the means of communication. Chatterji in his study (1969) referred to this process as "Sanskritization" of the tribal population.

2.4 Overview of Literature

The study of language revealed that the process of language shift is universal and continuous. Minority or folk languages are being absorbed by and assimilated into the more developed and advanced languages. For instance, the Sumerians gradually shifted to the great Babylonian speech while the ancient Egyptians to Arabic. The Amerindian people of the Americas shifted to English, Spanish or Portuguese. However, the old native speeches of the Americas are slowly on the way to extinction. Most of the Celtic-speaking Gauls shifted to French in France and to English in Britons in England (Chatterji, 1969:15).

Language shift, in most cases, occurred at a sub-conscious level as suggested by Scotton (1983), although shifts can also come about consciously, when motivated by social and political objectives. Chumaceiro (1983) while supporting the theory of social significance, has pointed out that the Sephardic community of Jerusalem shifted to Hebrew. This shift was not because of political or economic compulsions-rather, it was welcomed for its social significance. Dorian (1982) examined language shift from both a pragmatic and a cultural stance while the study of Fierman (1982) emphasized language shift only from the pragmatic stance.

Language shift is an evolutionary process; it begins slowly and accelerates in succeeding generations (Mazumdar, 1970). As suggested by Johnson (1976), this process may span centuries or two demographic generations. Peng (1979) while rejecting Johnson's view on language shift, opined that language shift need not cross generation boundaries. Rather, it is a continuum of constant change. Labov's major theoretical work on language change (1972) is diachronic in nature. He strongly asserted that the shift occurs only when system changes and may be observed both in real and apparent times. Hoijer (1948) held technological advancement in society responsible for changes in the language system. Contrary to this, Gal (1979) believed that it is a symbolic change and is correlated with the change of the value-system in society. Bonvillain (1978) observed that cultural contact played a major role in language shift among the Mohawk of Canada. Russell (1916), Ghurye (1963), Gopal (1966), Grierson (1967), Sachchidananda (1972) Dasgupta (1970), Doshi (1972 and 1985), have also agreed that language shift among the Indian tribes occurred as a result of cultural assimilation.

Chatterji in his study (1969) pointed out that in the process of Aryanisation, the pre-Aryans shifted to the Aryan languages. Roy (1962) traced the history of language shift in India from Sanskrit to Prakrit and then to Pali. While dealing with the census figures for several decades, Marten (1911), Hutton (1933) and Royburman (1972) concluded that language shift among the tribal population in India does not present a real situation. It more or less depends on the decadal variations among the speakers of a language. Dalton in his work (1872) observed that a change in religion was followed by the shift in language in many Oraon villages of the Chotanagpur region. Bose (1969), Mitra (1974) and Kachru (1977) observed that the political factor was an important clue to understanding language shift. Thus, the shift is quite flexible and depends on the changing political scenario of the country.

Joseph (1983) while studying the factors, pointed out that both external and internal factors are equally responsible in bringing about language shift. Pandey in his study (1977) laid greater emphasis on the external forces. In order to understand the mechanism, Weinreich, Labov and Herzog (1968) are of the opinion that language shift is a function of situation and is caused by variation in the socio-cultural milieu. Blount and Sanches (1977) tried to determine the socio-cultural dimensions of linguistic shift. Fishman (1976) suggested that urban dwellers are more inclined to language shift than rural. Mackinnon (1977) while ignoring the rural-urban differences, pointed out that language shift may be pronounced both in prestigious professionals and the groups of lower prestige. Liberson in his study (1970) examined the patterns of language shift and ethnic relations. The study also helps to establish the relationship between language shift and various demographic and ecological variables. Milroy and Milroy (1985) found that language shift is likely to be rapid in a society with social instability and also in a population with weak social ties. Liberson and McCabe (1978) tried to show that there exists a relationship between language usage in various domains and language shift. Apte (1962) and Ishtiaq (1982) also tried to find out the relationship between the degree of language shift and a set of socio-economic variables.

It is quite evident from the above paragraphs that the study on language shift in India, specially on the tribal population, is not only insufficient but also scanty. No research-either full or partial-has been taken up as yet to explain the nature of its regional variation, or to understand the mechanism/processes of such shifts. The present study is a maiden attempt in this direction. No doubt, some passing references are available on language shift among the tribal population but these do not deal with spatial parameters. The study of language under the disciplines of anthropology, linguistics and sociology may also be used for geographical analysis. Besides, some references of language shift may also be derived from the census reports. The works of Apte, Chatterji, Pandit, Khubchandani, Kachru, Nigam, and others, though linguistic in nature, provide a strong base to the social scientists for further studies and researches on language situation in India. It is necessary to mention here that the Deccan College Research Institute, Pune, the Central Institute of Indian Languages, Mysore, and the Language Division of the Census Office are also taking up such studies in India. Besides, the National Association of Geographers, India (NAGI) "Commission on Linguistic Geography" provides a platform for geographers and scholars from related disciplines to make combined efforts for the development of linguistic geography.

Chapter 3

TRIBAL LANGUAGES OF INDIA

3.1 Introduction

It is difficult to define a tribal language. It may simply be defined as the traditional language of the tribe. The classification on the basis of social groups, i.e., tribal languages and non-tribal languages does not have any linguistic relevance. A language may be tribal in one time and non-tribal in another. Further, a language which is unimportant in terms of functional values in one region may occupy a dominant position in another. In a nutshell, every language has a potential for further enrichment according to changing circumstances (Nigam, 1971). These, basically, depend on the socio-political conditions which vary temporally as well as spatially, making a particular language the standard/ prestigious one.

Similarly, the standard tribal language, in due course of time, may gain socio-political advantages and after the development of a suitable script, may not be classified as a tribal language. But, for explanatory purposes, tribal languages may be defined as folk languages having no literary tradition of their own and spoken by the people belonging to ethnic groups who preferred to live in relative isolation. In other words, tribal languages are simply the traditional languages of the tribal communities. However, the tribal languages of India though complex but are valuable relics of India's past which have been preserved orally in the form of songs, legends and other tales" (Chatterji, 1973 : 64).

Altogether about 20.5 million people, accounting for about 3.1 per cent of the total population of India, may be classified under tribal languages. Out of these, the Austric and Sino-Tibetan languages together accounted for about 11 million speakers. The remaining 4 million people speak the Dravidian languages (i.e., Gondi, Kui, Khond, Kurukh, etc.) and another 5.5 million people speak the Indo-Aryan languages (i.e., Bhili, Khandeshi and Halbi, etc.).

The number of tribal languages varied from time to time. Before 1960, the number of tribal languages was restricted to 56. This rose to slightly above 100 during the 1961 census (Appendix -II). All these tribal languages included 367 mother tongues. A total of 37 mother tongues could not be classified into any of the four linguistic families and have been grouped under a separate list known as 'Unclassified' tribal languages. It is also worth mentioning here that many tribal language such as Kol, Koraku, Malto, Birjia, Birhor, Chiru, Chote, Kom, Pochury and many others are missing from the list of the tribal language in 1971 and 1981 while some language like Limbu, Khandeshi, Kui, Mopna, Mogh, Sangtom, Zou, etc., which were not considered as tribal language in Linguistic Survey of India, 1961, have been included in the successive census reports. This leads us to conclude that the number of tribal language is much higher than the number listed in the census (Mamoria, 1957).

Unlike the non-tribal language, the tribal language have been confined to and concentrated in the forested and inaccessible parts of the country. A few of them are distributed over a large geographical terrioty and are spoken by millions of people but most of them are confined to one or two districts only. Santali, an Austric language, for example, is spoken by about 4.3 million persons distributed over 36 districts of eastern India (Fig. 2). On the other hand, Juang, another Austric dialect has been declared by a smaller number (about 18.5 thousand persons) who are confined to the two districts of Orissa (Dhenkanal and Keonjhar).

3.2 **Distribution of Austric Languages**

The Austric language of India are, by and large, decleared by the tribal population and thus all these languages have been grouped in the list of the tribal language. These languages belong to the mono-syllabic isolating type which are of great importance to the scholars of linguistics and anthropology. Much information about these languages is available in the commendable works of the Christion missionaries among these people. For some of these language, a written script was evolved only in the 19th century by the missionaries. Besides, some Indian scholar are also engaged in the synchronic and the diachronic studies of these languages in order to determine their relationship with the other languages of India. It is believed that there exists an Austric substratum in the present-day Aryan languages (Chatterji, 1973 :67). As a result of interaction and assimilation, these languages have been greatly influenced by the Indo-Aryan and the Dravidian languages. Thus the speakers of Austric were forced to switch over to the cultivated languages of their neighbours (i.e., Indo-Aryan or Dravidian). This has led to the gradual disappearance of the Austric languages on the periphery of the tribal homelands. This may be delayed in the areas of relative isolation and also in those areas where the tribals are more conscious about their linguistic identity.

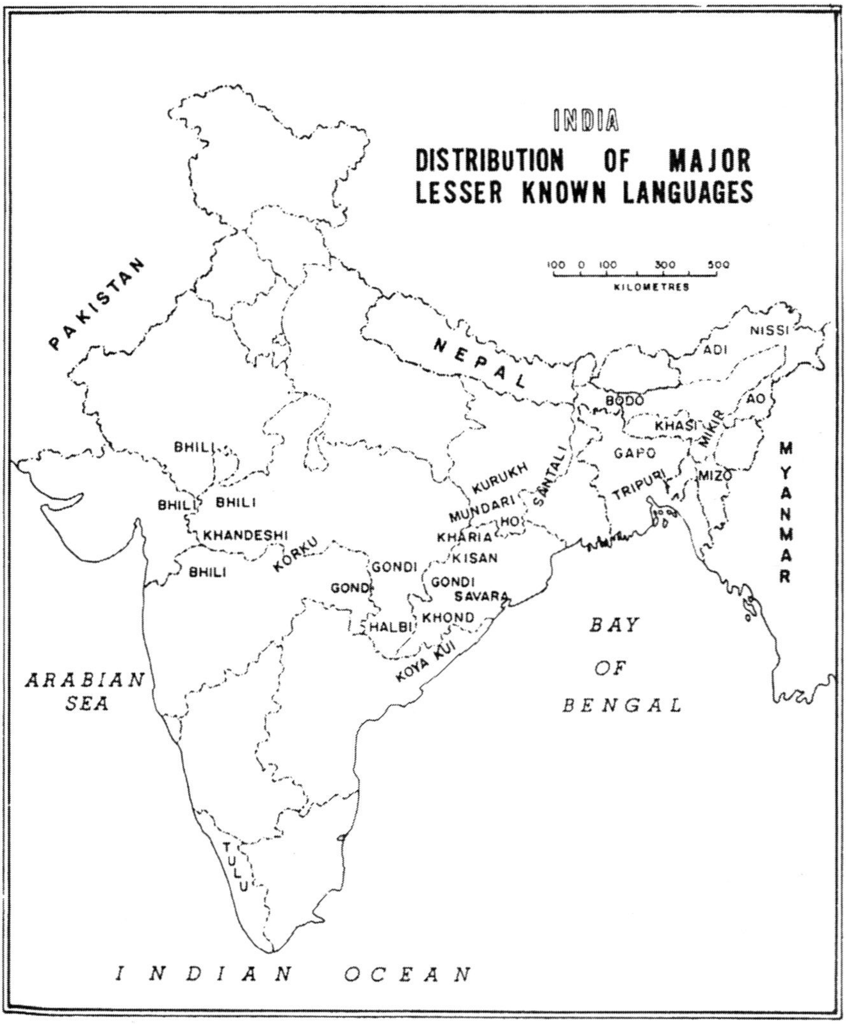
INDIA
DISTRIBUTION OF MAJOR LESSER KNOWN LANGUAGES
100 0 100 300 500
KILOMETRES
PAKISTAN
NEPAL
MYANMAR
NISSI
ADI
AO
BODO
KHASI
MIKIR
GARO
TRIPURI
MIZO
SANTALI
KURUKH
MUNDARI
HO
KHARIA
KISAN
GONDI
SAVARA
KHOND
HALBI
KOYA
KUI
GOND
KORKU
BHILI
KHANDESHI
TULU
ARABIAN SEA
BAY OF BENGAL
INDIAN OCEAN

Fig. 2

The Austric family of languages may broadly be classified into two sub-families : Austronesian and Austro-Asiatic. The Austronesian group of languages is spoken in Malaysia, Indonesia, Vietnam and the Hawaii and Malagasy Islands. Two branches of the Austro-Asiatic sub-family (Munda and Mon-Khmer) are confined to India.

The languages belonging to the Austro-Asiatic family are scattered over a vast geographical region extending from the Aravalli hills in the west to the Chotanagpur plateau in the east, continuing through West Bengal to the north-eastern states of India. Altogether, they are spread over 67 districts and 3 Union Territories as recorded in the 1961 census. Excluding the Andaman and Nicobar Islands where the Austric speech is confined only to the Car Nicobars, the mainland districts form a contiguous chain of the districts of these languages. It is important to note that the Austric region coincides with central India which has the highest concentration of the tribal population of India-with a little more than one-third belonging to the Austrics.

There were 65 mother tongues classified in the 1961 census as belonging to Austric languages (Appendix - III). Of which, 7 mother tongues belonged to the Mon-Khmer branch and 58 to the Munda branch {Census of India- 1961, Language Table, Pt. II-C (ii) Annexure IV}. The dominant linguistic communities are Santali, Mundari, Ho, Korku, Kharia, Savara and Khasi accounting for more than one lakh persons each (together constituting for about 97 per cent of the total Austric speaking population of the country) spread over a large geographical region (Table- 2). On the other hand, Asuri, Birjia, Birhor, Muwasi, etc., are highly compact and confined only to one or two districts. Broadly speaking, the western part of the Austric region is dominated by the Korku; the central by Mundari, Ho and Kharia; the eastern by Santali; the south-eastern by Savara and the north-eastern by Khasi languages (Roy, 1970 : 12).

Table-2 MAJOR AUSTRIC LANGUAGES OF INDIA

	Languages	Total Speakers
Munda Group		
	Bhumij	46,680
	Gadaba	27,567
	Ho	802,434
	Koda/Kora	21,983
	Kharia	197,840
	Korku	363,148
	Korwa	28,286
	Munda/Mundari	1,100,522
	Santali	4,208,304
	Savara	234,811
Mon-Khmer Group		
	Khasi	632,443
	Nicobarese	21,424

Source: Census of India, 1981 Sr. 1 INDIA, **Households and Household Population by Language Mainly Spoken in Household,** Table, HH- 16, Pt. B (i) pp. 436-505

3.3 **Distribution of Sino-Tibetan Languages**

The Sino-Tibetan languages are, by and large, registered by the Mongoloid people of India. According to Chatterji, these languages belong to the "isolating type in which there is no room for inflections. The relationship among words was indicated originally by means of root-words used in special contexts. In their modern form they have become mostly 'tone languages' in which the intonation or modulation of voice has a significant value" (Chatterji, 1973:67). Most of these languages are, numerically insignificant and do not have a literary tradition except Meithei/ Manipuri. For some of them, writing-in the Roman script-has only recently been introduced by the Christian missionaries. The vastness of the mountains and thick forest remained a great barrier in isolating them into smaller groups and keeping their languages unintelligible to others. Many languages have, undoubtedly, been affected by the Indo-Aryan languages (i.e., Assamese, Bengali, Nepali, Hindi) which are restricted to the valleys and in the urban centers only. On the other hand, many languages "have shown evidence of an inverted pride in exclusiveness and an anxiety to appear different" (Nigam, 1971)

With a total of 4 million persons (accounting for 0.62 per cent of the total population in India), these languages, by and large, are spoken by the tribal population distributed over a vast geographical territory extending from Ladakh in the north-west to the north-eastern region along the southern slope of the Himalayas. As many as 226 mother tongues were registered in the 1961 census. Except Meithei/Manipuri, all the remaining languages of the Sino-Tibetan family may be classified as tribal languages.

The Sino-Tibetan family of languages may be divided into two sub-families, namely Siamese-Chinese and Tibeto-Burman. The languages belonging to Siamese-Chinese are spoken outside the country except one-that is Khampti/Khamti. This means that the remaining 225 mother tongues have been classified under the Tibeto-Burman sub-family (Appendix- IV). The Tibeto-Burman sub-family has been divided into three distinct branches, namely Tibeto-Himalayan, North Assam, and Assam-Burmese. The Tibeto-Himalayan branch has been further sub-divided into two groups i.e. Tibetan or Bhotia group and Himalayan group. The Tibetan or Bhotia group of languages is spoken by more than 2.5 lakh persons mostly spread over the states of Jammu and Kashmir, Himachal Pradesh, Punjab, West Bengal, and Sikkim. Bhotia, Tibetan, Balti, Ladakhi and Lahuli, etc. are important languages belonging to this group. The Himalayan group of languages spoken by a total population of about 1.12 lakh persons are confined to Himachal Pradesh. Important languages of this group are Chamba, Limba, Kinauri, Lepcha, etc.

The languages included in the North-Assam branch cover approximately the geographical area now delineated Arunachal Pradesh. Important languages of this branch are Adi, Aka, Dafla, Miri, Mishmi, etc. The total number of speakers belonging to this branch is more than 2.8 lakh persons.

Numerically as well as culturally, the Assam-Burmese languages are the most important and are spoken by about 3 million people. This branch has been divided into five groups, viz., Bodo, Naga, Kachin, Kuki-Chin, and Burma. The majority of mother tongues are included under Bodo, Naga, and Kuki-Chin groups while Kachin and Burma groups fall outside India. Only six mother tongues (2 from Kachin and 4 from Burma groups) are spoken in India. Altogether these mother tongues are represented by about 17.5 thousand speakers. The Bodo group of languages is the most important and is spoken by about one million people. Important languages of this group are Bodo, Garo, Tripuri, Mikir, Koch, Rabha, Dimasa, etc. The Naga group of languages is spoken by about 0.84 million persons distributed mainly in Nagaland, Manipur and Arunachal Pradesh. Important languages of this group are Ao, Sema, Mao, Angami, Kabui, Lotha, Tangkhul, Konyak, etc. The Kuki-Chin group of languages has been represented by the largest number of mother tongues. The area inhabited by the speakers of these languages extends from the Naga hills to Cachar hills and along the Indo-Burma border. Altogether, this group is represented by about 1.5 million speakers. Manipuri, Lushai/Mizo, Lakher, Thado, Hmar, Halam, Kuki, Vaiphei, etc. are some of the important languages of this group (Table-3). Manipuri has been included in the VIIIth Schedule of the Indian Constitution only in 1992.

Table-3 MAJOR TIBETO-BURMAN LANGUAGES OF INDIA

Languages	Total Speakers	Languages	Total Speakers
Bhotia Group		Naga Group	
Balti	47,718	Kabui	53,142
Ladakhi	72,587	Mao	57,435
Tibetan	55,138	Tangkhul	79,058
Sherpa	12,607	Maring	11,532
Bhotia	30,545	Konyak	83,261
		Phom	24,265
Himalayan Group		Yimchungre	27,360
		Khiemnungam	17,044
Lahuli	20,110	Nocte	27,569
Kinauri	52,336	Wancho	32,169
Limbu	18,320	Tangsa	16,396
Lepcha	26,078	Naga	17,569
		Angami	78,398
North Assam Branch		Sema	93,869
		Rengma	15,036
Dafla	139,867	Khezha	15,908
Mishmi	24,059	Ao	105,610
		Lotha	57,913
Bodo Group		Chang	23,133
		Kacha Naga	16,033
Bodo	27,887	Zemi Naga	11,414
Garo	408,111		
Koch	16,682		
Rabha	19,270	Kuki-Chin Group	
Mikir	11,206	Thado	59,274
Tripuri	490,464	Paite	32,670
		Lakher	15,733
		Lushai/Mizo	384,747
		Halam	18,853
		Hmar	34,170
		Anal	10,780
		Vaiphei	16,311
		Kuki	46,271
		Manipuri/Meithie	178,728

Source: Census of India, 1981

3.4 Distribution of Dravidian Tribal Languages

The Dravidian languages of India are spoken by about 158 million people accounting for about 24 per cent of the total population of the country. There are 4 well known literary languages-Tamil, Telugu, Kannada and Malayalam-accounting for almost 96 per cent of the total speakers of this family. These four languages have been included in the VIIIth Schedule of the Indian Constitution. Two other languages, i.e., Tulu and Coorgi/ Kodagu may not to be counted among the tribal languages because these languages have , practically, been merged into Kannada. The remaining 147 mother tongues have been included in the list of the tribal languages. Important among them are Kui, Kolami, Gondi, Parji, Koya, Khond/Khondh, Konda, Kurukh/Oraon, Malto, etc. (Table-4). Although the Dravidian languages belong to the agglutinative type, very little is known about the tribal languages of this family.

Table-4 MAJOR DRAVIDIAN TRIBAL LANGUAGES OF INDIA

Languages	Total Speakers
Southern Group	
Coorgi/Kodagu	93,116
Tulu	1,376,306
Central Group	
Kui	507,639
Kolami	78,500
Gondi	1,954,693
Parji	33,091
Koya	242,534
Khond/Khondh	204,501
Konda	11,065
North Group	
Kurukh/Oraon	1,264,590
Malto	94,614

Source: Census of India, 1981

Geographically, the distribution of the Dravidian languages may be divided into three groups: Southern, Central and Northern. The languages belonging to the central and the northern groups are distributed over the central and eastern regions of India. The important tribal languages of the central group are Gondi, Khond, Kisan, Kui, Koya, Kolami, Parji, and Konda while Kurukh and Malto are important languages of the northern group of Dravidian languages. The important southern Dravidian tribal languages are Tulu, Coorgi, Toda, Kota and other minor tribal languages which are numerically insignificant but are of great importance to linguists. The majority of the tribal languages of the southern group have been abandoned in favour of the languages of the neighbouring people.

In the light of new classification of the Dravidian family of languages, it may not be profitable to discuss the mother tongue returns with reference to language groups as given in the Linguistic Survey of India scheme. It is also not advisable to take up the new geographical classification since this has not been yet quite established in its details. So we shall discuss the mother tongue data of the census with reference to the principal languages of the family and then with reference to the lesser-known languages. The principal languages are those which have been specified in the Eighth Schedule of the Indian Constitution viz. Tamil, Telugu, Kannada and Malayalam. Out of a total of 153 mother tongues of the family, it will be seen that 104 can be classified under the principal languages while only 49 mother tongues belong to the lesser-known ones (Appendix- V).

3.5 Distribution of Indo-Aryan Tribal Languages

The speakers of the Indo-Aryan family of languages are distributed over a vast geographical area with a total population of 491 million persons (accounting for about 74.24 per cent to the total population of the country). The central, northern, eastern and western parts of India are occupied by the people speaking the Indo-Aryan languages. As many as 574 mother tongues have been classified under this family. There are some well-known languages which have had great traditions of literary activities and on which there is no dearth of philological literature. However, there are three languages i.e., Bhili, Khandeshi and Halbi/ Halabi which have been classified as tribal languages. They are spread over 50 districts of Madhya Pradesh, Gujarat, Maharashtra and Rajasthan. The Bhili group of languages include 36 dialects spoken by a total of about 4.45 million persons. Boari, Barel, Bhilali, Chodhri, Dhodia, Gamti/Govit, Garasi, Kokna/Kokni/Kukna, Mawchi, Pardhi, Wagdi, etc., are some of the important mother tongues. While Khandeshi includes five mother tongues together spoken by a total population of about 1.2 million persons. Halbi/Halabi, another tribal language of the Indo-Aryan family was spoken by about 5.25 lakh persons in Madhya Pradesh and Maharashtra (Appendix-VI). Altogether, these three groups of tribal languages accounted for about 26 per cent of the total speakers of the tribal languages of India. The original language of the Bhils is thought to have an Austric origin. The Bhils have completely forgotten this language; they have now adopted the Indo-Aryan languages. Grierson considered Bhili to be a sort of bridge language between Gujarati and Rajasthani while Khandeshi is closely affiliated to Marathi. Linguistic analysis reveals that Bhili contains a number of non-Aryan words of either Mundari or Dravidian origin (Russell, 1916 : 293).

The territory in which these languages are found is rather extensive, but the Aravalli and the Vindhyan hills are regarded as their homes. For all practical purposes, the Bhils use non-tribal languages such as Gujarati, Hindi, Marathi, etc., and they appear to be completely assimilated into the non-tribal culture (Doshi, 1972:417).

To conclude, it may be added here that the tribal languages of India-spoken by only a little more than 3 per cent of the population-included more than 400 mother tongues. Such a long list of tribal mother tongue/ languages is, perhaps, due to the lack of a proper scheme of classification. This can be resolved only after a careful scrutiny. However, an attempt has been made to reclassify all these mother tongues in the 1981 census. A total of 83 group of tribal languages were identified. Out of these, 53 belong to Tibeto-Burman; 14 to Austro-Asiatic; 13 to Dravidian; and 3 to Indo-Aryan language families. The mother tongues, which have been tentatively classified, are posing more confusion. The real problem is faced in those cases where the tribals declared twin mother tongues such as Kisan-Bhumij or Jangali-Korwa, etc., though Kisan, Bhumij and Korwa are separate languages. Such cases ultimately affect the scheme of classification by multiplying the total number of the tribal languages. Consequently, the analysis of the study based on such data is also affected. Although efforts are made by the government for the preservation of the tribal languages, it appears to be difficult to hope to save these languages from further switching over to the stronger languages of their neighbours.

Chapter 4

AUSTRIC LANGUAGES : DISTRIBUTION AND PATTERNS OF LANGUAGE SHIFT

4.1 Introduction

The Austric languages of India are spoken by the people of the earliest races of the Indian sub-continent who are regarded as the descendants of the Proto-Australoids (Majumdar, 1958 : 46). Grierson (1967) and Chatterji (1963) opined that the oldest population of the Indian sub-continent must have spoken the Austric languages. Hunter (1877), Dalton (1872), Schmidt (1933) and Gait (1970) have also believed that the Austrics are one of the earliest peoples in India. Sir Herbert Risley, while accepting the above hypotheses, has claimed that the Mundas (who belong to the Proto-Australoids) are the earliest inhabitants on the Indian sub-continent and can be considered as the genuine autocthons (Risley, 1915 : 46). As opposed to this, Rai Bahadur S.C. Roy (1970) believed that the Proto-Australoids cannot be considered as the autocthons of this sub-continent because they came from outside India. Whatever the case, it is a fact that the tribal history of India be constructed from the origin of the Munda tribes (who speak the Austric languages). The Austric languages of India were first distinguished from the Dravidian languages by Max Muller who designated them the 'Munda Languages' while George Campbell called them 'Kolarian Languages'. Since both the Munda and the Kol are the two different tribal groups, it is appropriate to call these languages the 'Austro-Asiatic Languages'. Many anthropologists believe that both the Austrics and the Dravidians belong to the same social group though linguistically they are different from one another.

The distribution of the Austric languages is highly uneven which partly resulted from the uneven distribution of the tribal population itself and is partly due to the shift in their traditional languages. There are as many as 11 districts (including the Nicobar Islands) in which they constitute more than 80 per cent of the total tribal population who have declared Austric languages. The share of speakers of Austric languages varies from 50 to 80 per cent in 12 districts and 20 to 50 per cent in another 12 districts while in the remaining 32 districts less than 20 per cent population speak the Austric languages (Appendix - VII).

To understand the patterns of spatial distribution and the areas of their concentration, two methods have been used. First, the percentage of the speakers of a particular dialect to the total tribal population of a district is calculated to find out the patterns of the distribution. Second, the concentration index is calculated by dividing the total number of a particular dialect in a district by the total speakers of the same dialect in the country. To obtain the figure in percentage, the index values have been multiplied by 100. The above method of concentration index may also be represented by the following formula:

$$C = \frac{d}{n} \times 100$$

where C represents concentration index;

d represents the total number of speakers of the 'j' language in a district;

n represents the total number of speakers of 'j' language of the country.

Based on the above methods, tables for the spatial distribution and the index of concentration have been prepared for all the Austric languages to study the nature of their regional variations.

The tribal languages vary greatly in their numerical strength. Thus, they have been classified into 'the major' and 'the minor' linguistic groups. The only basis for this classification is, however, the numerical strength. A linguistic group with a total population of more than one lakh persons has been classified under the major group while the languages whose numerical strength is less than a lakh population have been included under the minor linguistic group. A brief description of some important tribal languages is given below:

4.2 Major Austric Languages

Santali

Santali has been registered by a total number of about 4.3 million persons accounting for 55.4 per cent of the total Austric speakers of India. Santali is considered to be the most important Austric language as well as a remarkably uniform one. It has reached a much higher stage of linguistic development than any other tribal language. It has two dialects and the difference between them mainly embodies certain regional differences. But these do not differ much from the standard form of language. The Santali spoken north of the River Damodar is regarded as the purer form while the southern Santali is the corrupt one (Kochar, 1970:24). Though it is the principal language of the Santals, 40 other tribal groups have also declared Santali as their mother tongue. These groups are distributed over 35 districts of Bihar (2.1 million), West Bengal (1.6 million), Orissa (0.52 million), Madhya Pradesh and Tripura. Though Santali is highly concentrated in Santal Parganas district (Bihar), there are as many as 17 districts in which more than 90 per cent Santals have registered Santali as their mother tongue, while it is declared by 60 to 90 per cent Santals in another 5 districts. The share of the Santali speaking population varies from 30 to 60 per cent in 7 districts whereas in another 7 districts, it is spoken by less than 30 per cent Santals (Table-5, Fig.3).

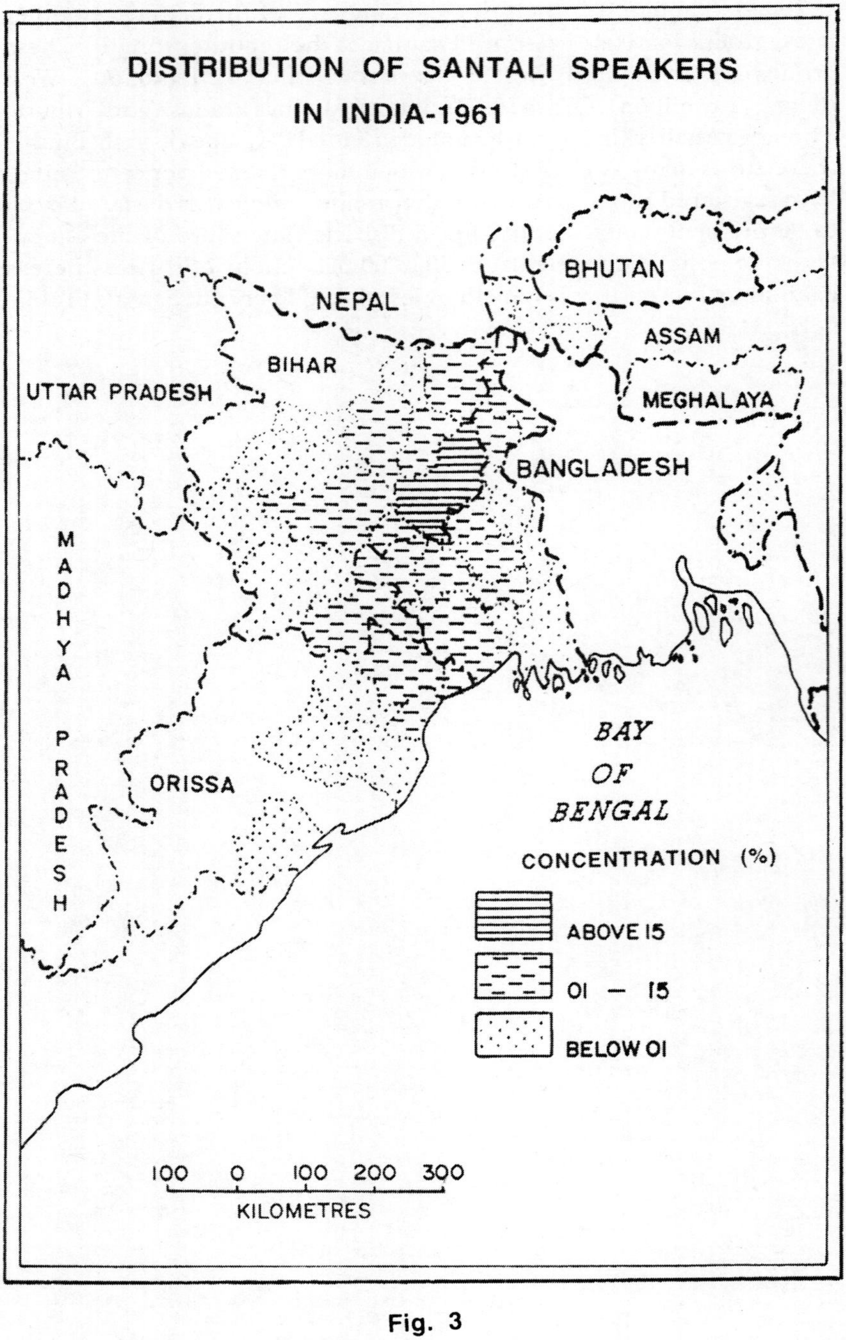
DISTRIBUTION OF SANTALI SPEAKERS
IN INDIA-1961
BHUTAN
NEPAL
ASSAM
BIHAR
UTTAR PRADESH
MEGHALAYA
BANGLADESH
MADHYA PRADESH
ORISSA
BAY OF BENGAL
CONCENTRATION (%)
ABOVE 15
01 — 15
BELOW 01
100 0 100 200 300
KILOMETRES

Fig. 3

Table-5 DISTRIBUTION OF SANTALI SPEAKERS

% group	% to total Santal pop. in a district	% to total Santali speakers in India
> 90	Monghyr,Dhanbad,Santal-Parganas, Hazaribagh, Bhagalpur, Purnea, Saharsa (Bihar); Birbhum, Murshidabad, Calcutta, Malda, West Dinajpur, Bankura, Midnapore, Purulia, Burdwan, Hooghly(W.Bengal)	-
75-90	Balasore(Orissa); Howrah, Nadia, 24- Parganas(W.Bengal)	-
60-75	Cuttuck(Orissa)	-
45-60	Mayurbhanj(Orissa); Patna (Bihar); Darjeeling,Cooch Behar(W.Bengal)	-
30-45	Gaya (Bihar); Jalpaiguri (W.Bengal); Tripura	-
15-30	Keonjhar(Orissa); Singhbhum (Bihar)	Santal Parganas (Bihar)
1 -15	Dhenkanal(Orissa)	West Dinajpur,Malda, Hooghly,Burdwan,Birbhum, Bankura, Midnapore, Purulia (W.Bengal); Bhagalpur, Purnea, Monghyr, Dhanbad, Singhbhum, Hazaribagh(Bihar); Mayur-bhanj, Balasore, (Orissa)
< 1	Ganjam(Orissa); Palamau, Ranchi(Bihar); Chhindwara (M.P.)	Darjeeling, Jalpaiguri, Cooch Behar, Murshidabad, Nadia, 24-Parganas, Calcutta, Howrah(W. Bengal); Patna, Saharsa, Ranchi (Bihar); Keonjhar, Cuttuck, Dhenkanal, (Orissa); Tripura

Munda/Mundari

It is, basically, a language of the Munda tribe and is spoken by more than 1.1 million tribals in the country, out of which 6.5 lakh persons reside in Bihar. The states of Orissa, with a total Mundari population of 3.6 lakh persons, and West Bengal with 0.7 lakh population occupied the second and the third places respectively. Apart from the Chotanagpur

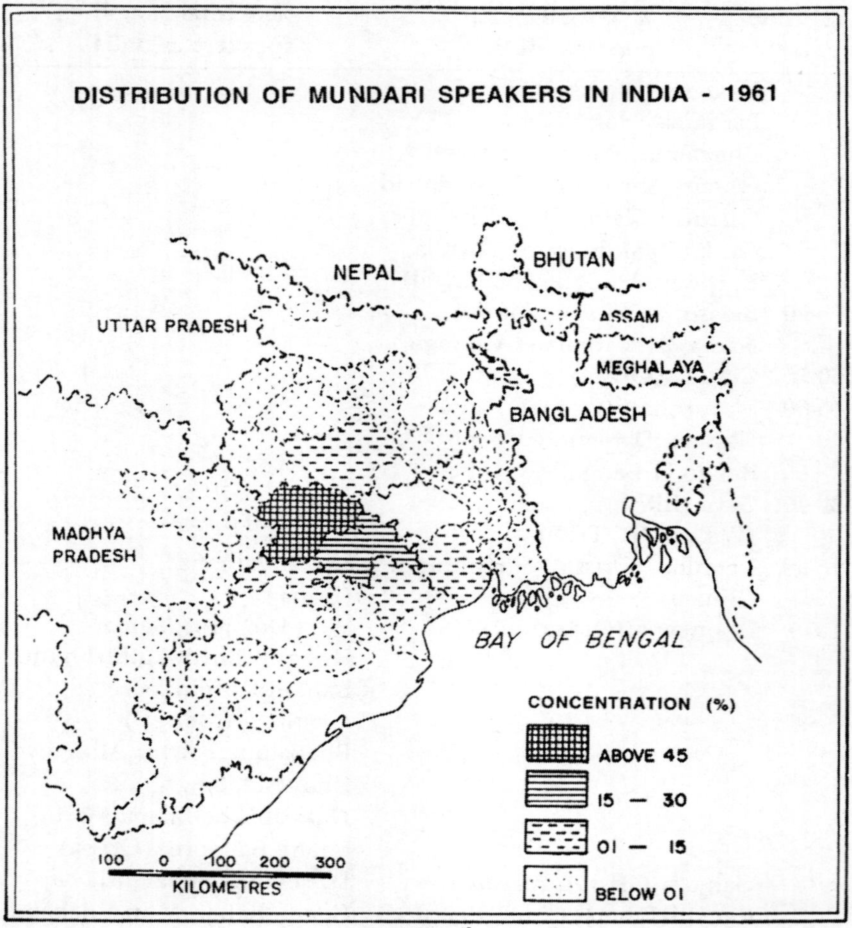
DISTRIBUTION OF MUNDARI SPEAKERS IN INDIA - 1961
NEPAL
BHUTAN
ASSAM
MEGHALAYA
UTTAR PRADESH
BANGLADESH
MADHYA PRADESH
BAY OF BENGAL
CONCENTRATION (%)
ABOVE 45
15 — 30
01 — 15
BELOW 01
100 0 100 200 300
KILOMETRES

Fig. 4

Plateau, the immigrants have also brought this language to Jalpaiguri, Dinajpur, Tripura and the Tea Gardens of Assam. Altogether, Mundari is distributed over 40 districts of Bihar, Orissa, West Bengal, and Madhya Pradesh. The speakers of this language accounted for 12 per cent of the total Austric tribes of India. It has been declared by 32 tribal groups other than the Mundas as their mother tongue. Mundari is spoken most idiomatically in Ranchi, which is regarded as its home (Grierson 1967; IV:79). Like Santali, Mundari is a uniform language and its purest form is spoken in Khunti and its adjacent areas located in the south east of Ranchi. The dialectal difference derives from the vocabulary borrowed from the Aryan languages. On the basis of such differences, Mundari may be classified into four types :

i. Tamari—spoken in and around the anchals of Tamar, Bundu, Sonahatu;
ii. Hansda—spoken in and around the anchals of Khunti and Murhu;
iii. Nagpuri—spoken in and around the anchals of Torpa, Gobindpur; and lastly,
iv. Kera—spoken in and around Ranchi town. The majority of the Oraon tribe declared Kera Mundari as their mother tongue.

There are only 4 districts : Gaya, Champaran, Ranchi and Shahabad in which more than 60 per cent of the Mundas have declared Mundari as their mother tongue. The percentage of its speakers varies from 15 to 45 per cent in 5 districts and from 5 to 15 per cent in another 11 districts. In the remaining 20 districts, Mundari has been registered by about 5 per cent of the Munda population.

The speakers of the Mundari language are highly concentrated in the districts of Bihar. More than 75 per cent of its speakers live in the districts of Ranchi and Singhbhum. There are altogether 27 districts in which Mundari has been registered by less than 15 per cent of the Munda population (Table-6, Fig.4).

Table-6 DISTRIBUTION OF MUNDARI SPEAKERS

% group	% to total Munda pop. in a district	% to total Mundari speakers in India
> 90	Shahabad (Bihar)	-
75-90	Champaran, Ranchi (Bihar)	-
60-75	Gaya (Bihar)	-
45-60	Sundargarh (Orissa)	Ranchi (Bihar)
30-45	Patna (Bihar)	-
15-30	Howrah, 24-Parganas (W.Bengal); Palamau (Bihar)	Singhbhum (Bihar)
1- 15	Nadia, Malda, W.Dinajpur, Midnapore, Cooch Behar, (W.Bengal); Raigarh, Raipur (M.P.); Dhanbad, Singhbhum (Bihar); Mayurbhanj, Balasore, Bolangir, Dhenkanal, Kalahandi (Orissa); Tripura	West Dinajpur, Midnapore (W.Bengal); Hazaribagh (Bihar); Mayurbhanj, Sundargarh (Orissa)
< 1	Birbhum, Murshidabad, Calcutta, Bankura, Purulia, Burdwan, Hooghly (W.Bengal); Surguja (M.P.); Monghyr, Santal Parganas (Bihar); Baudhkhondmals (Orissa)	Cooch Behar, Malda, Murshidabad, Nadia, Howrah, 24-Parganas, Hooghly, Burdwan, Birbhum, Bankura, Purulia (W.Bengal); Patna, Santal Parganas, Palamau, Dhanbad (Bihar); Raipur, Raigarh (M.P.); Keonjhar, Balasore, Bolangir, Dhenkanal, Kalahandi (Orissa)

Ho

It has been declared by a compact group of about 8.1 lakh persons spread over 18 districts of Bihar, Orissa and West Bengal. Ho accounted for about 10 per cent of the total Austric speakers of India. Although it is the principal language of the Ho tribe, it has also been registered by 16 other tribal groups as their mother tongue. Linguistically, it is closely related to Mundari. There is only one district (i.e., Singhbhum) in which more than 50 per cent of the Hos have declared their traditional language as mother tongue. The share of speakers of the Ho language varies from 15 to 45 per cent in Mayurbhanj, Keonjhar Dhenkanal and Patna districts and is less than 15 per cent in another 13 districts.

The nucleus of the Ho language is in Singhbhum district in which about 70 per cent of the country's total Ho speaking people are concentrated. About 28 per cent of the Ho speakers are concentrated in the district of Mayurbhanj, Keonjhar and Sundargarh (Table-7, Fig.5).

Table-7
DISTRIBUTION OF HO SPEAKERS

% group	% to total Ho pop. in a district	% to total Ho speakers in India
60-75	-	Singhbhum(Bihar)
45-60	Singhbhum (Bihar)	-
30-45	Keonjhar, Dhenkanal (Orissa)	-
15-30	Mayurbhanj (Orissa); Patna (Bihar)	Mayurbhanj (Orissa)
1 -15	Cuttuck, Balasore, Bolangir, Sundargarh, Sambalpur, Kalahandi (Orissa)	Keonjhar, Sundargarh (Orissa)
< 1	Ranchi, Hazaribagh (Bihar); Howrah, Calcutta, Bankura, Cooch Behar, Jalpaiguri(W.Bengal)	Jalpaiguri, Bankura, (W.Bengal) ; Patna, Hazaribagh, Ranchi, (Bihar); Cuttuck, Balasore, Bolangir, Dhenkanal, Sambalpur, Kalahandi (Orissa)

Khasi

It is the principal language of the Khasi tribe and is spoken by about 6.3 lakh tribals spread over the United Khasi and Jaintia hills and the United Mikir and Cachar hills of the state of Assam. The Khasi group of languages is the eastern most Austric language and belongs to the Mon-khmer branch. The speakers of the Khasi language accounted for about 8.1 per cent of the total Austric speaking population of the country. The Khasi speakers comprised 82 per cent of the total Austric speaking population in the United Khasi and Jaintia hills (now Meghalaya) and 75 per cent in the United Mikir and North Cachar hills. More than 98 per cent of the Khasi speakers of the country are concentrated in the united Khasi and Jaintia hills (Table-8, Fig.6).

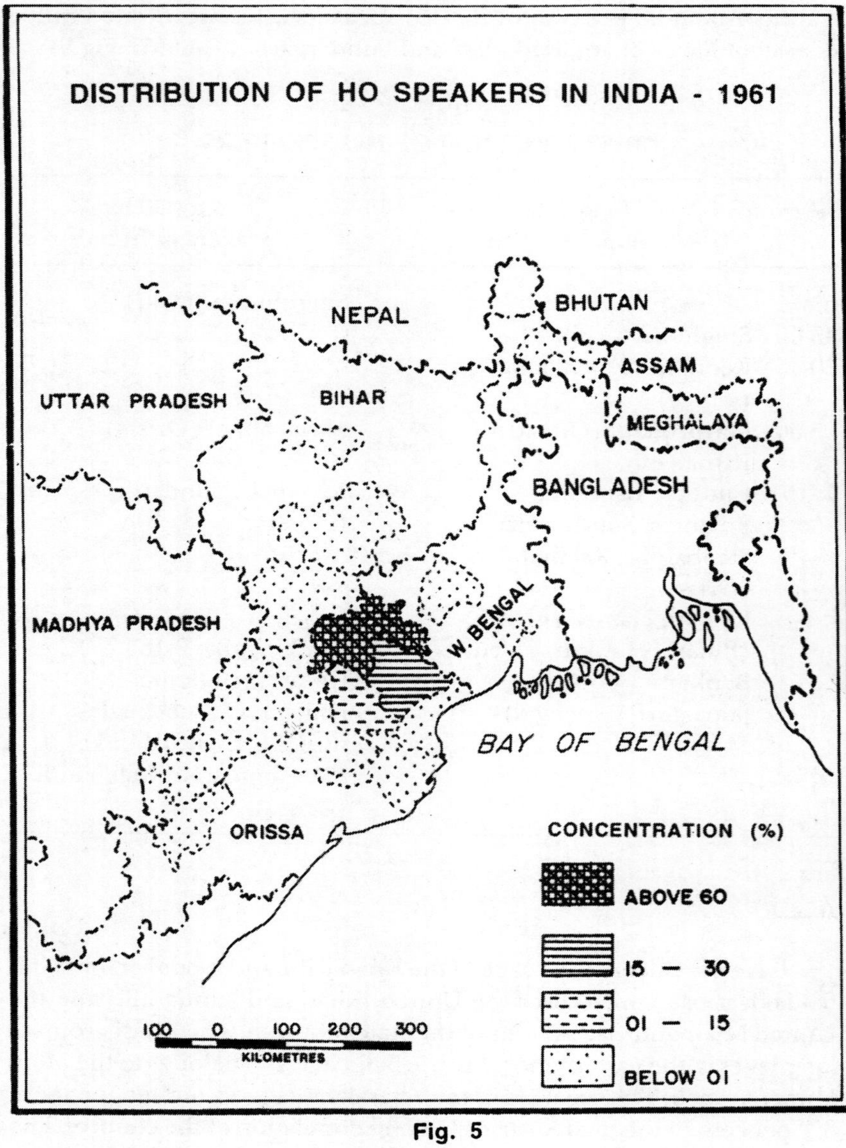
DISTRIBUTION OF HO SPEAKERS IN INDIA - 1961
NEPAL
BHUTAN
ASSAM
MEGHALAYA
UTTAR PRADESH
BIHAR
BANGLADESH
MADHYA PRADESH
W. BENGAL
BAY OF BENGAL
ORISSA
CONCENTRATION (%)
ABOVE 60
15 — 30
01 — 15
BELOW 01
100 0 100 200 300
KILOMETRES

Fig. 5

Table-8
DISTRIBUTION OF KHASI SPEAKERS

% group	% to total Khasi pop. in a district	% to total Khasi speakers in India
> 90	Mizoram, Garo Hills	United Khasi and Jaintia Hills(Meghalaya)
60-75	United Khasi and Jaintia Hills	-
30-45	Nagaland	-
1-15	Tripura	North Cachar Hills(Assam)
< 1	-	Nagaland,Mizoram,Tripura Garo Hills

Three dialects of Khasi have been reported. They include Lyngngam which is spoken in the south western corner of the hills bordering the Garo hills; the second is Synteng or Pnar which is spoken in the upper parts of the Jawai located in the east of Shillong; and the third is War which is spoken in the low valley extending towards the south and opening out to the plains of Sylhet. The purest form of the Khasi language is spoken in and around Cherrapunji.

Korku

Korku is the western most language of the Munda branch and accounts for about 4.5 per cent of the total Austric speakers of India. Though it is the principal language of the Korku tribe, it has also been registered by 5 other tribal groups as their mother tongue. Altogether it has been declared by over 3.6 lakh persons in 10 districts of Madhya Pradesh and Maharashtra. Madhya Pradesh alone accounted for more than 2.5 lakh speakers of this dialect. Amravati, Betul and East Nimar districts together accounted for more than 90 per cent of the total Korku speakers in India. About one-third of the total Korku speakers are confined to Amravati district of Maharashtra only (Table-9, Fig.7).

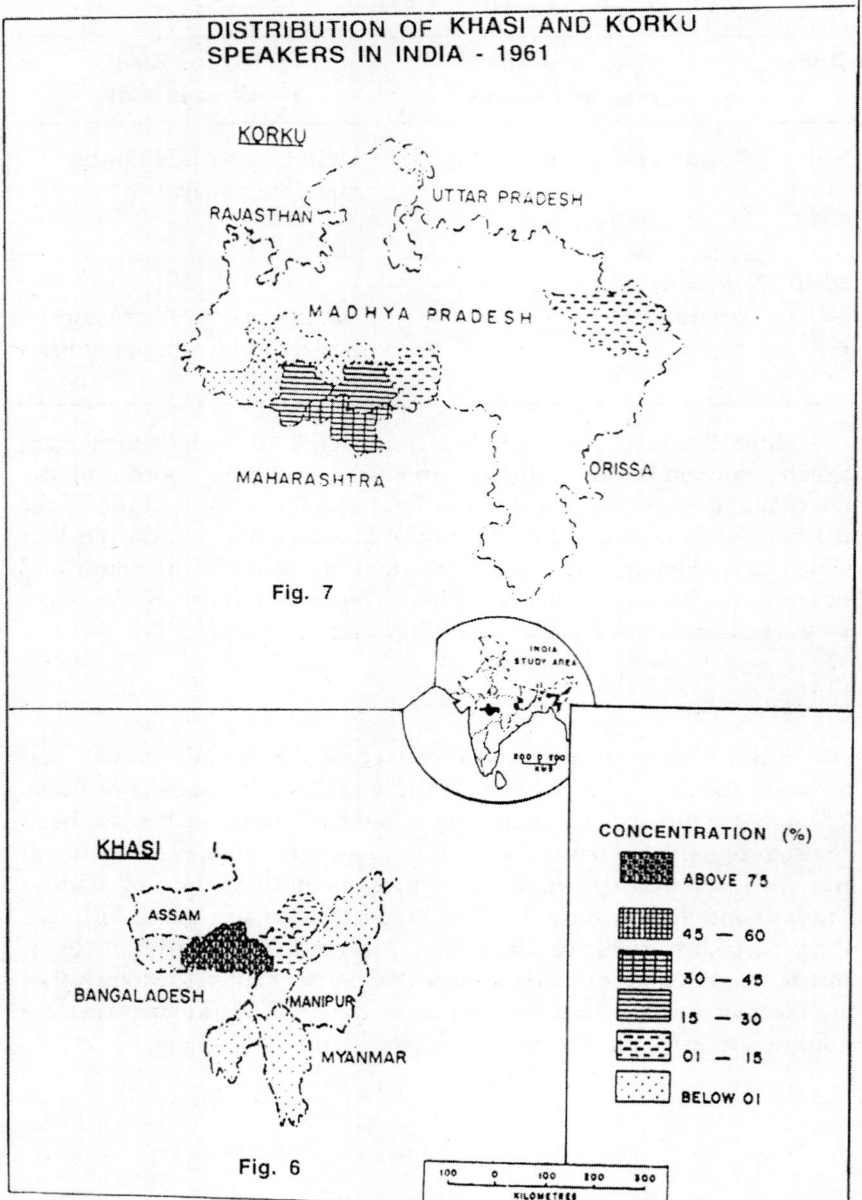
DISTRIBUTION OF KHASI AND KORKU
SPEAKERS IN INDIA - 1961
KORKU
UTTAR PRADESH
RAJASTHAN
MADHYA PRADESH
MAHARASHTRA
ORISSA
INDIA
STUDY AREA
KHASI
ASSAM
BANGALADESH
MANIPUR
MYANMAR
CONCENTRATION (%)
ABOVE 75
45 — 60
30 — 45
15 — 30
01 — 15
BELOW 01
100 0 100 200 300
KILOMETRES

Fig. 7

Fig. 6

Table - 9
DISTRIBUTION OF KORKU SPEAKERS

% group	% to total Korku pop. in a district	% to total Korku speakers in India
> 90	Amravati(Maharashtra) Hoshangabad, Dewas, East Nimar, Betul(M.P.)	-
75-90	Surguja (M.P.)	-
30-45	-	Amravati (Maharashtra)
15-30	West Nimar(M.P.)	Betul, East Nimar (M.P.)
1-15	-	Chhindwara, Surguja (M.P.)
< 1	-	Dewas, Hoshangabad, West Nimar (M.P.)

The home of the Korku language is in the hills of Satpura, Mahadeo and Maikal. Linguistically Korku is also a remarkable uniform Austric language. Muwasi, spoken in Chhindwara, is the only dialect of Korku which does not differ much from ordinary Korku (Grierson, 1967; IV: 167). Nearly 90 per cent of the Korkus have clung to their traditional language. Though Korku does not have a literary tradition, many old songs have been preserved orally and passed on from one generation to another. Linguistically, it is closely related to Kharia and Juang but it has not, however, been influenced by the Aryan languages to the extent the Juang and the Kharia dialects have been.

Kharia

Kharia is basically a dialect of agriculturist tribal groups of the Chotanagpur region (Grierson, 1967; IV: 190). It is spoken by about 2 lakh tribals distributed over 21 districts of Bihar, Madhya Pradesh, Orissa and West Bengal. Its speakers accounted for about 2.7 per cent of the total Austric speakers of the country. Kharia has been declared as mother tongue by more than 14 tribal groups. A little more than half of the country's Kharia speakers are concentrated in Ranchi district and around one-fifth in Sundargarh district. More than 90 per cent of the Kharias in Bilaspur district and 60 to 75 per cent in Raigarh and Raipur districts have declared it as their mother tongue. In another 4 districts the share of its speakers varies from 15 to 45 per cent while in the remaining 14 districts it has been registered by less than 15 per cent of the Kharia tribe (Table-10, Fig.8).

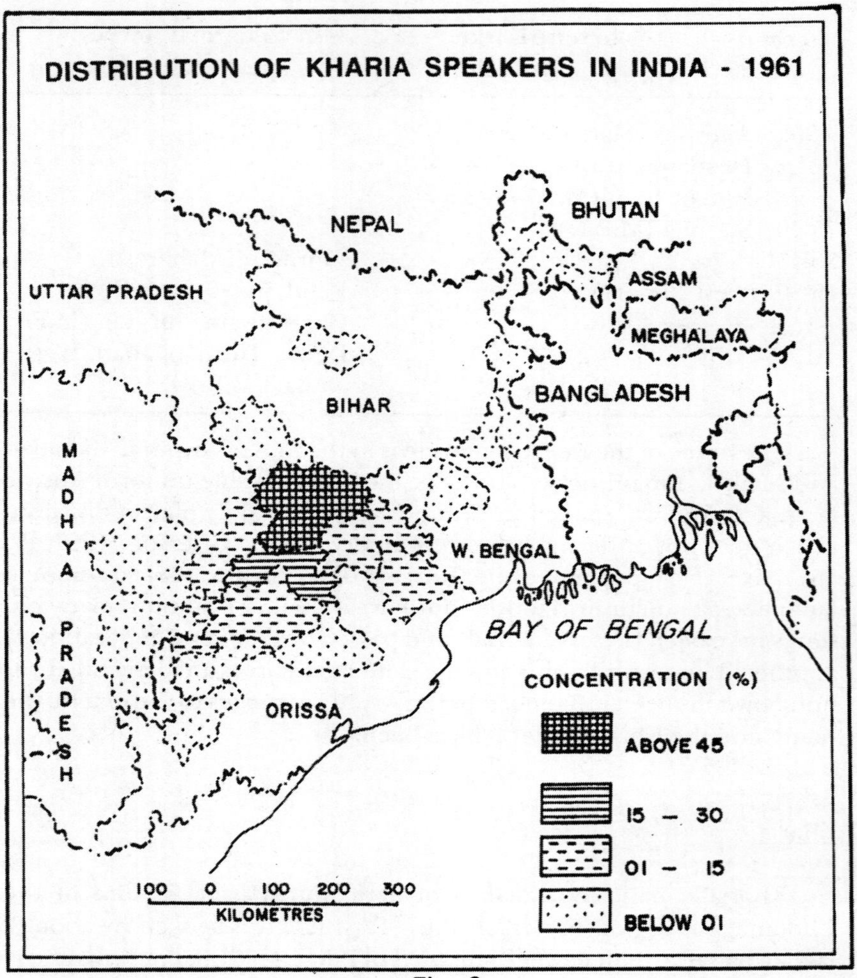
DISTRIBUTION OF KHARIA SPEAKERS IN INDIA - 1961
NEPAL
BHUTAN
ASSAM
MEGHALAYA
UTTAR PRADESH
BIHAR
BANGLADESH
MADHYA PRADESH
W. BENGAL
BAY OF BENGAL
ORISSA
CONCENTRATION (%)
ABOVE 45
15 - 30
01 - 15
BELOW 01
100 0 100 200 300
KILOMETRES

Fig. 8

Kharia does not remain a pure language because its vocabulary as well as its grammatical structure have been Aryanised. Therefore, the present form of Kharia is no longer a typical Munda language (Grierson, 1967; IV: 190).

Table-10
DISTRIBUTION OF KHARIA SPEAKERS

% group	% to total Kharia pop. in a district	% to total Kharia speakers in India
> 90	Bilaspur(M.P.)	-
60-75	Raigarh(M.P.)	-
45-60	Raipur(M.P.)	Ranchi(Bihar)
30-45	Sundargarh, Sambalpur (Orissa)	-
15-30	Ranchi(Bihar); Cooch Behar(W.Bengal)	Sundargarh(Orissa)
1 -15	Mayurbhanj,Kalahandi (Orissa); Patna(Bihar); Darjeeling(W.Bengal)	Singhbhum(Bihar); Mayurbhanj,Sambalpur (Orissa);Raigarh(M.P.)
< 1	Bolangir,Dhenkanal(Orissa); Palamau,Singhbhum(Bihar); Murshidabad,Nadia,Bankura, Malda,Burdwan,Jalpaiguri (W.Bengal)	Darjeeling, Jalpaiguri, Cooch Behar,Malda, Murshidabad,Burdwan, Bankura (W.Bengal);Palamau (Bihar);Bilaspur,Raipur (M.P.);Bolangir,Kalahandi, Dhenkanal(Orissa)

Savara

Savara is the southern most language of the Munda branch. It has been declared by about 2.3 lakh tribals as their mother tongue. Though it is basically a language of the Savaras, 13 other tribal groups have also registered it as their mother tongue. The language is spread over a wide tract of Orissa, Andhra Pradesh, West Bengal and Tripura. Its speakers accounted for about 2.7 per cent of the total Austric speakers of the country. More than 90 per cent of the Savaras in the districts of Puri, Ganjam, Baudhkhondmals and Visakhapatnam have declared it as their mother tongue while 60 to 90 per cent have done so in Srikakulam and in Koraput districts. In the remaining districts, it is spoken only by 15 per cent of people. More than 98 per cent of the Savara speakers are concentrated in Baudhkhondmals, Koraput, Ganjam and Srikakulam districts. About 60 per cent Savara speakers of the country live in the districts of Orissa (Table-11, Fig.9).

Table-11 DISTRIBUTION OF SAVARA SPEAKERS

% group	% to total Savara pop. in a district	% to total Savara speakers in India
> 90	Puri,Ganjam,Baudhkhondmals (Orissa); Visakhapatnam (A.P.)	-
75-90	Srikakulam(A.P.)	-
60-75	Koraput(Orissa)	-
30-45	-	Ganjam(Orissa)
15-30	-	Srikakulam(Andhra); Koraput,Baudhkhondmals (Orissa)
1 -15	Darjeeling(W.Bengal)	-
< 1	Dhenkanal, Kalahandi (Orissa);West Dinajpur, Burdwan, Jalpaiguri (W.Bengal); Tripura.	Dhenkanal,Puri,Kalahandi (Orissa);Darjeeling, West Dinajpur, Jalpaiguri, Burdwan(W.Bengal); Visakhapatnam(Andhra); Tripura

Most of the Savara tribes have now embraced Hinduism and speak Aryan languages, mostly Oriya and Telugu. At present, the language is exclusively spoken in the hilly tracts of Ganjam and Visakhapatnam districts only. Linguistically, it is closely related to the Kharia and Juang languages.

4.3 **Minor Austric Languages**

Bhumij

It is the traditional language of the Bhumij tribe and has also been registered by 6 other tribal groups as mother tongue. Linguistically, it is almost identical with Mundari. Its numerical strength has been reduced from 1.3 lakh persons in 1961 to about 47 thousand in 1981. As per the former census, the Bhumij language accounted for 2 per cent of the total Austric speakers of India while its share came down to 0.64 per cent in 1981. It is spoken in over 33 districts of Bihar, West Bengal and Orissa. More than 26 per cent of the Bhumij population in Cuttuck district have

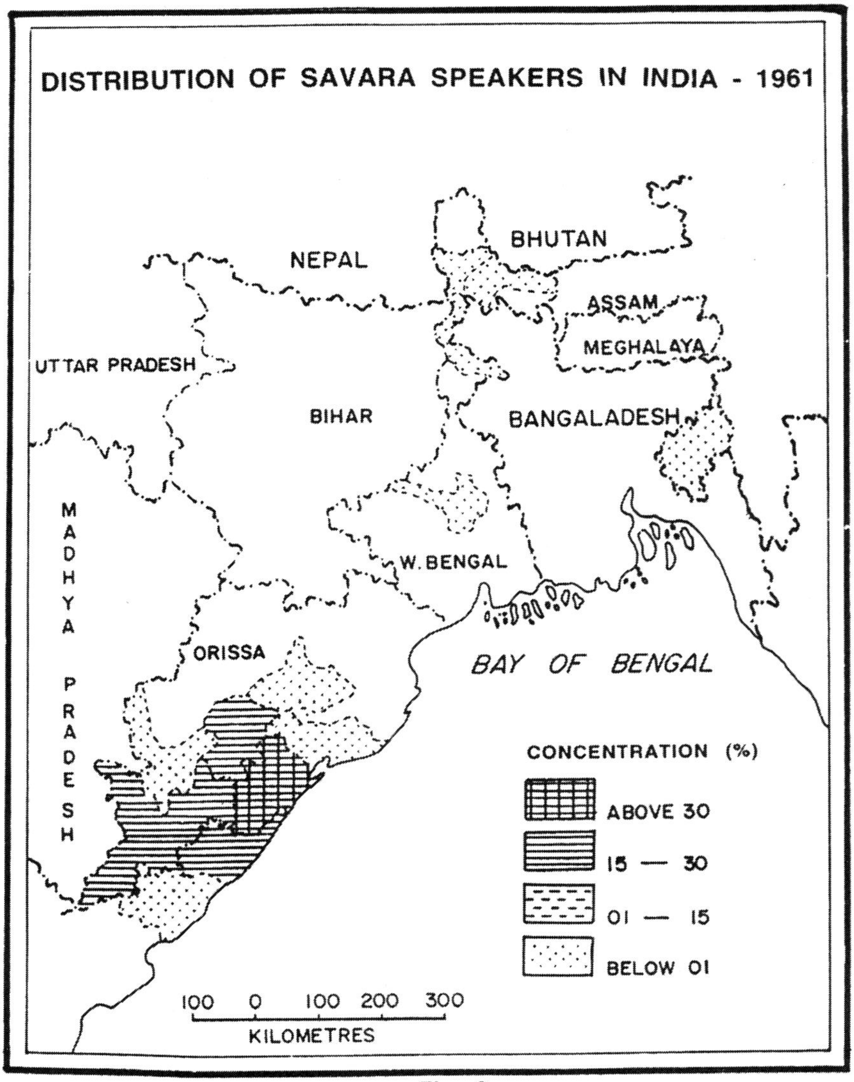
DISTRIBUTION OF SAVARA SPEAKERS IN INDIA - 1961
NEPAL
BHUTAN
ASSAM
MEGHALAYA
UTTAR PRADESH
BIHAR
BANGALADESH
MADHYA PRADESH
W. BENGAL
ORISSA
BAY OF BENGAL
CONCENTRATION (%)
ABOVE 30
15 — 30
01 — 15
BELOW 01
100 0 100 200 300
KILOMETRES

Fig. 9

declared it as their traditional language although their numerical strength is very low in the district. On the other hand, it accounted for less than 15 per cent of the population in Mayurbhanj and Singhbhum districts, while these two districts together accounted for almost 90 per cent of the country's Bhumij speakers (Table-12, Fig.10).

Table-12 DISTRIBUTION OF BHUMIJ SPEAKERS

% group	% to total Bhumij pop. in a district	% to total Bhumij speakers in India
30-45	-	Mayurbhanj (Orissa)
15-30	Cuttuck (Orissa)	Singhbhum (Bihar)
1-15	Mayurbhanj, Sundargarh (Orissa); Singhbhum (Bihar)	Cuttuck, Sundargarh (Orissa)
< 1	Midnapore, Jalpaiguri (W.Bengal); Sambalpur (Orissa)	Sambalpur (Orissa); Midnapore, Jalpaiguri (W.Bengal)

Korwa

Though it has been registered as mother tongue by eight tribal groups , it is the principal language of the Korwa tribe. Altogether Korwa is spoken by about 28 thousand persons. According to the 1961 census, it accounted for about 0.3 per cent of the total Austric speaking population of the country. The share of its speakers varies from 30 to 45 per cent in Palamau and Surguja; from 15 to 30 per cent in Raigarh and in Santal Parganas it has been registered by less than 15 per cent of the population. It is highly concentrated in Surguja and Palamau districts where it is spoken in its purer form (Table-13, Fig.11).

Table-13 DISTRIBUTION OF KORWA SPEAKERS

% group	% to total Korwa pop. in a district	% to total Korwa speakers in India
30-45	Palamau (Bihar); Surguja (M.P.)	Surguja, Raigarh (M.P.)
15-30	Raigarh (M.P.)	Palamau (Bihar)
1 -15	Bilaspur (M.P.)	-
< 1	Santal Parganas (Bihar)	Santal Parganas (Bihar); Bilaspur (M.P.)

Gadaba

It is one of the southern most languages of the Munda branch. It was declared by 40 thousand persons in 1961 as mother tongue. The strength of this language has been reduced to 28 thousand persons distributed over 4 districts, namely Koraput, Srikakulam, Visakhapatnam and East Godavari. More than 80 per cent of its speakers are concentrated in Koraput district only. Besides the Gadaba tribe, four other tribal groups have also declared it as their mother tongue. Linguistically, it is not a uniform language (Table-14, Fig.12).

Table-14
DISTRIBUTION OF GADABA SPEAKERS

% group	% to total Gadaba pop. in a district	% to total Gadaba speakers in India
> 90	East Godavari (Andhra)	-
45-60	Koraput (Orissa)	Koraput (Orissa)
1 -15	Srikakulam (Andhra)	Srikakulam, Visakhapatnam (Andhra)
< 1	Visakhapatnam	East Godavari

Koda/Kora

About 22 thousand persons have declared Koda/Kora as their mother tongue. Its speakers are distributed in 20 districts of West Bengal, Orissa, Bihar and Madhya Pradesh. Except Raipur district, the remaining districts have a lower proportion of speakers of this language. About two-thirds of its speakers are concentrated in the districts of West Bengal (Table-15, Fig.13). Besides the Koda/Kora tribe, sixteen other tribal groups have also registered it as their mother tongue. According to the 1961 census, it accounted for about 0.2 per cent of the total Austric speakers of India.

Grierson believed that it is a language of the tribe primarily engaged in tank digging, road making and earthworks whose native place, according to legend, was in Dalbhum, Manbhum (now Hazaribagh and Dhanbad) and nearby localities. Linguistically, the language is uniform but in its periphery, specially in the south of Santal Parganas, it is almost identical to Mundari.

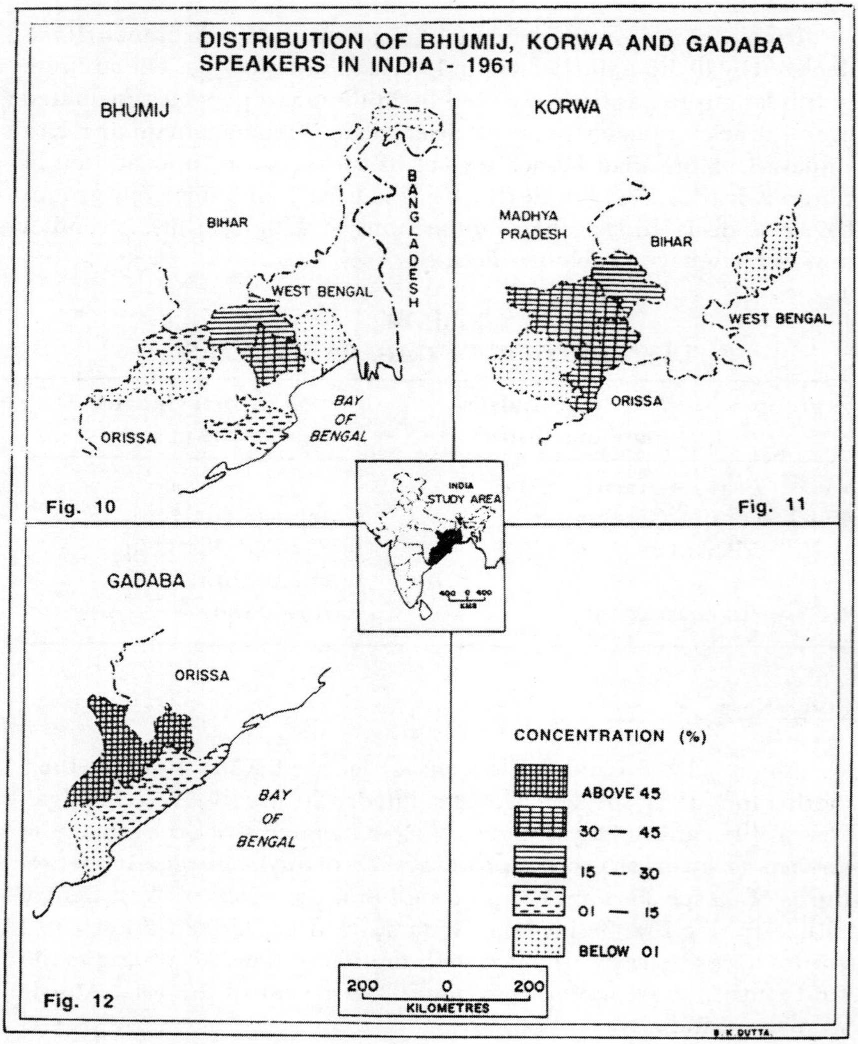
DISTRIBUTION OF BHUMIJ, KORWA AND GADABA SPEAKERS IN INDIA - 1961
BHUMIJ
BIHAR
BANGLADESH
WEST BENGAL
ORISSA
BAY OF BENGAL
Fig. 10
KORWA
MADHYA PRADESH
BIHAR
WEST BENGAL
ORISSA
Fig. 11
INDIA
STUDY AREA
GADABA
ORISSA
BAY OF BENGAL
Fig. 12
CONCENTRATION (%)
ABOVE 45
30 — 45
15 — 30
01 — 15
BELOW 01
200 0 200
KILOMETRES
S. K. DUTTA

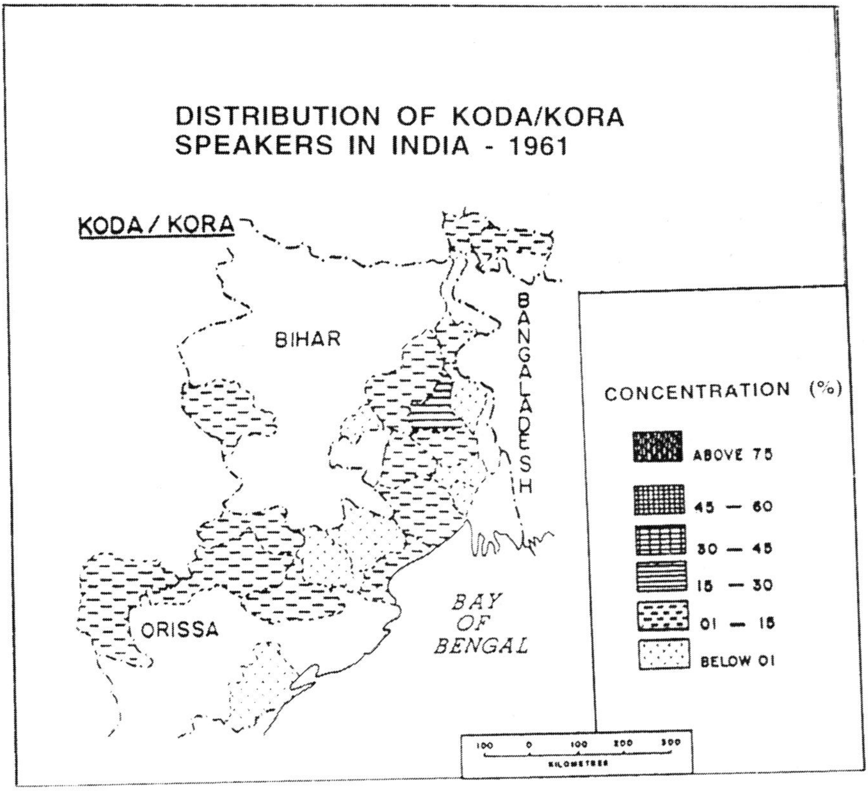
DISTRIBUTION OF KODA/KORA
SPEAKERS IN INDIA - 1961
KODA / KORA
BIHAR
BANGLADESH
ORISSA
BAY OF BENGAL
CONCENTRATION (%)
ABOVE 75
45 — 60
30 — 45
15 — 30
01 — 15
BELOW 01
100 0 100 200 300
KILOMETRES

Fig. 13

Table-15
DISTRIBUTION OF KODA/KORA SPEAKERS

% group	% to total Koda/Kora pop. in a district	% to total Koda/Kora speakers in India
15-30	Raipur(M.P.)	Burdwan(W.Bengal)
1 -15	Dhenkanal,Sambalpur (Orissa); Palamau(Bihar); Birbhum,Darjeeling, Burdwan(W.Bengal)	Darjeeling, Jalpaiguri, Malda,Hooghly,Birbhum, Bankura,Midnapore (W.Bengal);Santal Parganas,Palamau(Bihar); Raipur(M.P.);Balasore, Dhenkanal,Sundargah, Sambalpur(Orissa)
< 1	Mayurbhanj, Balasore, Ganjam,Sundargarh (Orissa);Santal Parganas (Bihar); Howrah,Murshidabad,Malda,Bankura, Midnapore,Hooghly, Jalpaiguri(W.Bengal)	Murshidabad,Howrah, (W.Bengal);Dhanbad (Bihar);Mayurbhanj, Ganjam,Keonjhar (Orissa)

Nicobarese

It is a language belonging to the Mon-Khmer branch of the Austric family and is confined only to the Car Nicobar Islands. It has been registered by about 21.5 thousand persons accounting for about 0.26 per cent of the total Austric population of the country.

Juang

It is the principal language of the Juang tribe which is concentrated in Dhenkanal and Keonjhar districts of Orissa. Besides the Juang tribe, six other tribal groups have also declared it as their mother tongue. Altogether it is spoken by 18.5 thousand persons.

Besides the above mentioned languages, 19 other languages were also classified in the Linguistic Survey of India (LSI) and were also registered in the 1961 census. It is to be noted that some of these have not been registered in the 1981 census. The obvious reasons are that these minor dialects do not differ much from the major ones. Thus, they might have been classified under the major languages and secondly, the speakers might have abandoned their traditional language and switched over to the non-tribal languages. The following table-16 shows the distribution of these languages:

Table-16
LESSER-KNOWN AUSTRIC LANGUAGES

Languages	Reporting Areas
Agariya	Surguja
Asuri	Ranchi, Palamau, Raigarh
Birhor	Singhbhum, Hazaribagh, Raigarh
Birjia	Palamau, Sundargarh, Jalpaiguri, Darjeeling
Karmali	Purulia, Singhbhum, Ranchi, Keonjhar
Khaira	Jalpaiguri
Kherwari	Surguja, Purulia, Midnapore, Darjeeling
Kol	Keonjhar, Santal Parganas, Ganjam, Sundargarh Sambalpur
Koraku	Raipur, Bastar
Kurmi	Jalpaiguri, Burdwan, Birbhum
Mahali	Midnapore, Singhbhum, Mayurbhanj
Manjhi	Birbhum, Jalpaiguri
Muwasi	Chhindwara
Nihali	W. Nimar, E. Nimar, Betul
Paharia	Malda, W. Dinajpur
Pnar/Synteng	United Khasi and Jaintia Hills and Nagaland
Thar	Singhbhum, Midnapore
Turi	Sundargarh, Sambalpur
War	United Khasi and Jaintia Hills and Nagaland

4.4 Changing Linguistic Identity

As has already been pointed out, the tribes of India have been changing their linguistic identity for a number of reasons . This change is multi-dimensional including shifts towards the tribal languages as well as towards the languages of the non-tribes. Similarly, the Austric tribes of India registered a number of languages, besides their traditional ones, as their mother tongue. All these may be classified under the following groups:

a) declaring their traditional mother tongue;
b) declaring the languages of other tribal group;
c) declaring the regional languages; and,
d) declaring non-regional non-tribal languages.

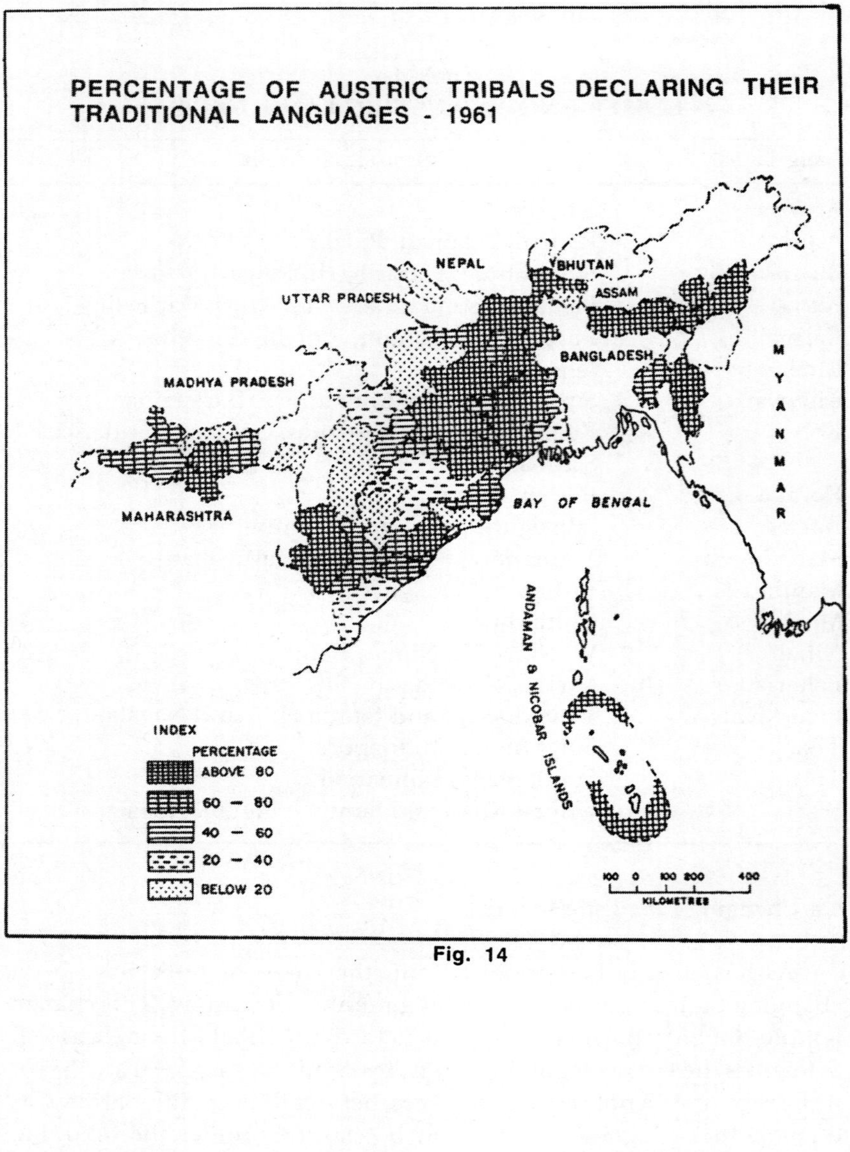
PERCENTAGE OF AUSTRIC TRIBALS DECLARING THEIR TRADITIONAL LANGUAGES - 1961
NEPAL
BHUTAN
ASSAM
UTTAR PRADESH
BANGLADESH
MADHYA PRADESH
MYANMAR
MAHARASHTRA
BAY OF BENGAL
ANDAMAN & NICOBAR ISLANDS
INDEX
PERCENTAGE
ABOVE 80
60 — 80
40 — 60
20 — 40
BELOW 20
100 0 100 200 400
KILOMETRES

Fig. 14

Declaring Their Traditional Mother Tongue

The earlier census data reveals that about 53 lakh Austric speaking tribals of the country continued to retain their linguistic identity and declared their traditional languages as their mother tongue. They constituted a little over 77 per cent of the total Austric speaking tribal population of the region. This share varies from 34 per cent in Madhya Pradesh to more then 90 per cent in Assam and Nagaland while it is 100 per cent in the Nicobar Islands. In the states of Bihar, Orissa, Andhra Pradesh, West Bengal and Tripura, the share is between 60 and 70 per cent. It is necessary to mention here that the picture which emerged out of the state level study is too generalised to draw any meaningful conclusion. In order to get a better result as well as to demarcate the areas of language shift and continuity, one has to come down to the lower unit. The data are such as to restrict the study to the district level. The study at the district level shows more variations in the degree of language shift and continuity. This is evident from the fact that the percentage of language maintenance varies from 1 to 100 per cent. There are 24 districts/ Union Territories in which more than 80 per cent Austric speaking tribes declared their traditional dialects as their mother tongue. These districts are mainly situated in the eastern and the north-eastern regions of the country. The percentage of language maintenance varies from 60 to 80 in 16 districts while in another 8 districts it ranges between 20 and 60 per cent. Less than 20 per cent of the Austric tribes in another 17 districts have registered their traditional language an mother tongue (Table - 17, Fig. 14).

Table-17
AUSTRIC TRIBES DECLARING THEIR OWN MOTHER TONGUES-1961

% Category	No.	Districts/ Union Territories
> 80	24	Garo Hills, Mizo Hills, United Khasi & Jaintia Hills, United Mikir & North Cachar Hills, (Assam); Monghyr, Saharsa, Purnea, Santal Parganas, Hazaribagh, Dhanbad, Singhbhum (Bihar); Ganjam, Mayurbhanj (Orissa); West Dinajpur, Malda, Murshidabad, Hooghly, Burdwan, Birbhum, Bankura, Midnapore (W. Bengal); Amravati (Maharashtra); Nagaland; Nicobar Islands
60-80	16	Srikakulam (Andhra); Patna, Bhagalpur, Ranchi (Bihar); East Nimar, Betul, Chhindwara (M.P.); Koraput, Sundargarh, Keonjhar, Cuttuck, Balasore (Orissa); Darjeeling, Jalpaiguri, Purulia (W.Bengal); Tripura
40-60	3	Nadia, Calcutta, Howrah (W.Bengal)
20-40	5	Visakhapatnam, East Godavari (Andhra); Surguja, Raigarh (M.P.); Dhenkanal (Orissa)
< 20	17	Bilaspur, Raipur, Bastar (M.P.); Kalahandi, Sambalpur, Bolangir, Baudhkhondmals (Orissa); Cooch Behar, 24-Parganas (W.Bengal)

Declaring Languages of Other Tribal Groups

Some 2 lakh Austric speaking tribes of India have adopted the languages of other tribal groups. These tribes accounted for about 3.3 per cent of the total Austric speakers. These other tribal languages mainly belong to the Dravidian and the Tibeto-Burman language families. More than 20 such languages are registered by them as their mother tongue in West Bengal alone. The share of the other tribal languages varies from 2 per cent in Tripura to 6.8 per cent in Madhya Pradesh. Besides Nagaland and Tripura, there are 50 districts in which the Austric speaking tribes declared languages of other tribal groups as their own mother tongue. But in most of these districts less than 5 per cent of their speakers adopted other tribal languages. With the exception of Bastar district in which more than 80 per cent of the Austric tribes declared languages of other tribal groups, in the other 4 districts, namely West

Nimar, Betul, Baudhkhondmals and Jalpaiguri the proportion varies between 20 and 60 per cent. The share varies from 5 to 20 per cent in another 12 districts. In the remaining districts/UT, its share was even less than 5 per cent (Table-18, Fig. 15).

Table-18
AUSTRIC TRIBES DECLARING LANGUAGES OF OTHER TRIBAL GROUPS-1961

% Category	No.	Districts/ Union Territories
> 80	1	Bastar(M.P.)
40-60	1	West Nimar(M.P.)
20-40	3	Betul(M.P.); Baudhkhondmals(Orissa); Jalpaiguri(W.Bengal)
10-20	4	Garo Hills(Assam); Ranchi(Bihar); Raigarh(M.P.); Kalahandi(Orissa)
5-10	8	United Mikir & North Cachar Hills(Assam); Patna,Shahabad(Bihar); Sambalpur, Dhenkanal, Keonjhar(Orissa); Darjeeling(W.Bengal)
1-5	15	United Khasi & Jaintia Hills (Assam); Palamau,Dhanbad(Bihar); Dewas(M.P.); Koraput,Bolangir,Ganjam,Balasore(Orissa); Cooch Behar,Nadia,24-Parganas,Howrah, Birbhum(W.Bengal); Tripura; Nagaland.
< 1	20	Hazaribagh,Singhbhum(Bihar); East Nimar, Hoshangabad,Chhindwara,Surguja,Bilaspur, Raipur(M.P.); Amravati(Maharashtra); Sundargarh,Puri(Orissa); West Dinajpur, Malda, Murshidabad, Hooghly, Bankura, Midnapore (W.Bengal)

Declaring Regional Languages

Some 12.5 lakh Austric tribes adopted regional languages as their mother tongue. They accounted for about 18.2 per cent of the total Austric speaking tribals of the country. Hindi has been widely accepted by them over parts of Bihar and Madhya Pradesh while they adopted Bengali and Oriya in West Bengal and Orissa respectively. The share of the Austric tribes declaring regional languages varies from 9 per cent in Bihar to 50 per cent in Madhya Pradesh. In Assam, this share was almost nil. There are 12 districts of Bihar, Madhya Pradesh and Orissa in which more than 80 per cent of the Austric tribes have declared regional

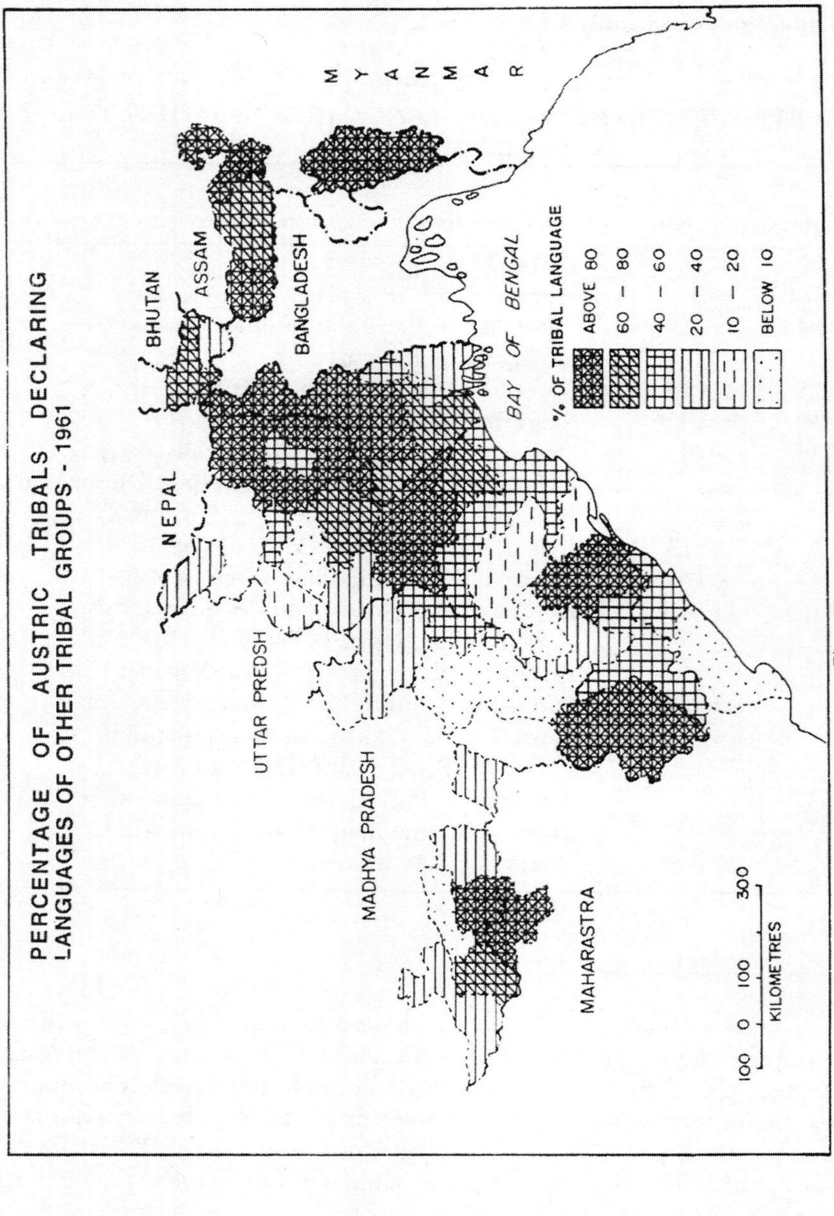
PERCENTAGE OF AUSTRIC TRIBALS DECLARING LANGUAGES OF OTHER TRIBAL GROUPS - 1961
BHUTAN
ASSAM
NEPAL
BANGLADESH
M Y A N M A R
UTTAR PREDSH
MADHYA PRADESH
MAHARASTRA
BAY OF BENGAL
% OF TRIBAL LANGUAGE
ABOVE 80
60 — 80
40 — 60
20 — 40
10 — 20
BELOW 10
100 0 100 300
KILOMETRES

Fig. 15

languages as their mother tongue. The share varies from 40 to 80 per cent in 10 districts and 20 to 40 per cent in 13 districts. There are altogether 26 districts/UT in which their share was less than 20 per cent (Table-19, Fig.16).

Table-19
AUSTRIC TRIBES DECLARING REGIONAL LANGUAGES-1961

% Category	No.	Districts/ Union Territories
> 80	12	Gaya, Shahabad, Champaran, Palamau (Bihar); Dewas, Sidhi, Hoshangabad, Balaghat, Bilaspur, (M.P.); Kalahandi, Bolangir, Puri(Orissa)
60-80	7	Visakhapatnam, East Godavari(Andhra); Surguja(M.P.); Sambalpur, Baudhkhondmals, Dhenkanal(Orissa); 24-Parganas (W.Bengal)
40-60	3	West Nimar, Raigarh(M.P.); Nadia (W. Bengal)
20-40	13	Srikakulam (Andhra); Patna, Bhagalpur (Bihar); East Nimar, Chhindwara(M.P.); Koraput, Sundargarh, Cuttuck, Balasore(Orissa); Cooch Behar, Calcutta, Howrah, Purulia (W. Bengal)
< 20	26	Monghyr, Saharsa, Purnea, Santal Parganas, Hazaribagh, Ranchi, Dhanbad, Singhbhum (Bihar); Betul, Raipur, Bastar(M.P.); Amravati (Maharashtra); Ganjam, Keonjhar, Mayurbhanj (Orissa); Darjeeling, Jalpaiguri, West Dinajpur, Malda, Murshidabad, Hooghly, Burdwan, Birbhum, Bankura, Midnapore (W.Bengal); Tripura

Declaring Non-regional Non-tribal Languages

A little more than one lakh Austric tribes declared non-regional non-tribal languages as their mother tongue. They accounted for about 1.5 per cent of the total Austric speaking tribal population of the country. In West Bengal more than 10 such languages are spoken by them. The speakers of non-regional non-tribal languages, however, did not occupy a significant share in any state/UT. The share varies from less than 1 per cent in Orissa to almost 90 per cent in Madhya Pradesh. Besides Tripura, there are 43 districts in which the Austric tribals have registered non-regional non-tribal languages as their mother tongue. There are 25 districts in which less than 1 per cent of the Austric tribes declared non-regional non-tribal languages as their mother tongue. The share ranges

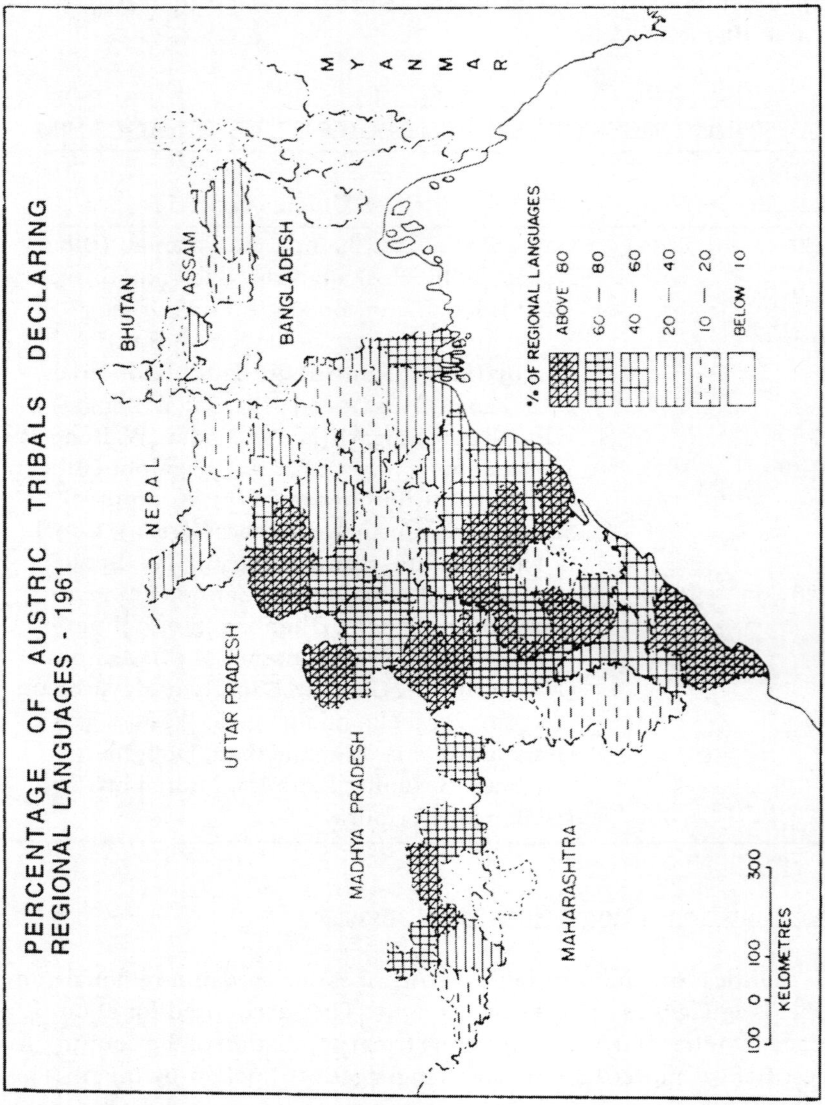
PERCENTAGE OF AUSTRIC TRIBALS DECLARING REGIONAL LANGUAGES - 1961
NEPAL
BHUTAN
ASSAM
BANGLADESH
MYANMAR
UTTAR PRADESH
MADHYA PRADESH
MAHARASHTRA
% OF REGIONAL LANGUAGES
ABOVE 80
60 — 80
40 — 60
20 — 40
10 — 20
BELOW 10
100 0 100 300
KILOMETRES

Fig. 16

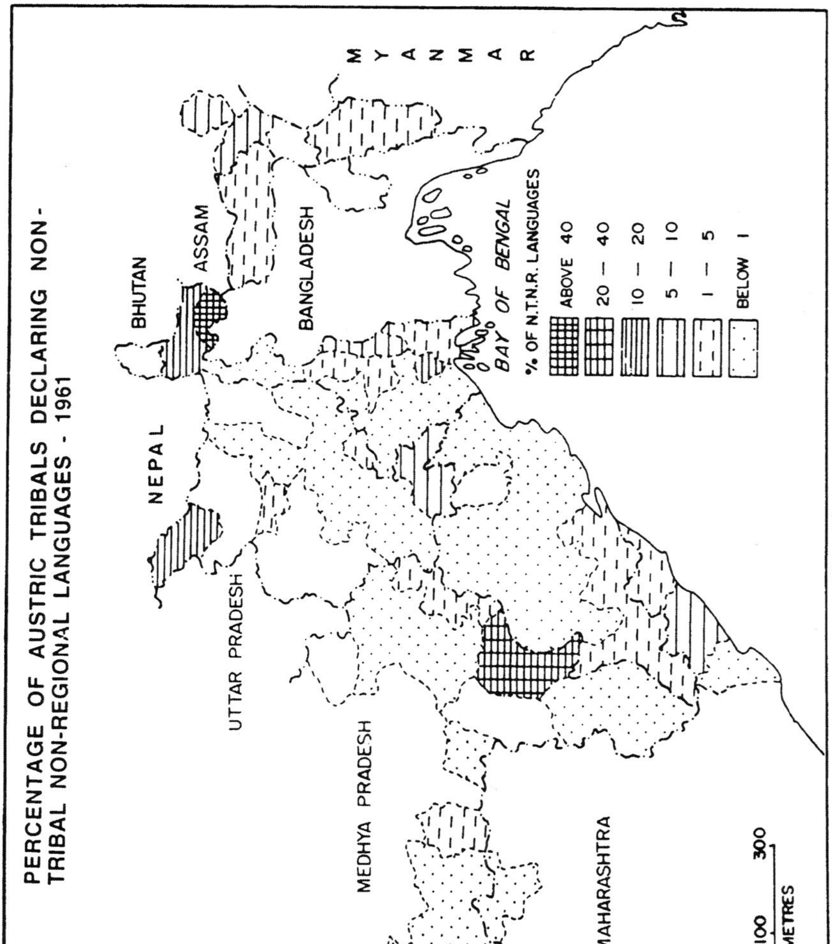
PERCENTAGE OF AUSTRIC TRIBALS DECLARING NON-TRIBAL NON-REGIONAL LANGUAGES - 1961
BHUTAN
ASSAM
M Y A N M A R
BANGLADESH
NEPAL
UTTAR PRADESH
MEDHYA PRADESH
MAHARASHTRA
BAY OF BENGAL
% OF N.T.N.R. LANGUAGES
ABOVE 40
20 — 40
10 — 20
5 — 10
1 — 5
BELOW 1
100 0 100 300
KILOMETRES

Fig. 17

between 1 to 10 per cent in 11 districts and about 10 to 20 per cent in 5 districts. There are only 2 districts, namely Raipur and Cooch Behar in which more than 20 per cent of the Austric tribes have declared non-tribal non-regional languages as their mother tongue (Table-20, Fig.17).

Table-20
AUSTRIC TRIBES DECLARING NON-REGIONAL NON-TRIBAL LANGUAGES-1961

% Category	No.	Districts/ Union Territories
20-40	2	Raipur(M.P.); Cooch Behar (W.Bengal)
10-20	5	Raigarh,(M.P.); Darjeeling, Calcutta, Howrah (W.Bengal); Tripura
1-10	11	Srikakulam, Visakhapatnam(Andhra); Dhanbad, Singhbhum(Bihar); Chhindwara,Bilaspur(M.P.); Koraput, Ganjam(Orissa); Jalpaiguri, Nadia, 24-Parganas(W.Bengal)
< 1	25	Patna, Bhagalpur, Saharsa, Santal Parganas, Hazaribagh, Ranchi (Bihar); Betul, Surguja, Bastar (M.P.); Amravati (Maharashtra); Malda, Murshidabad, Burdwan, Birbhum, Bankura, Midnapore, Purulia, West Dinajpur (W.Bengal); Kalahandi, Bolangir, Sundargarh, Dhenkanal, Puri, Cuttuck, Balasore (Orissa)

The chapter may be concluded by stating that the number of the Austric languages has been reduced to 14 in 1981 from 65 in 1961. It seems that the people belonging to minor dialectal groups have been assimilated into the major tribal linguistic groups or into the regional languages of the non-tribals. It is to be noted that the figure for the Mundari language in this chapter includes both Mundari and Munda languages. Since Munda is a tribe whose principal language is Mundari, there is no justification for classifying Munda and Mundari languages separately. It is also necessary to mention here that the patterns of distribution at the district level are based on the census data of 1961 because data are not available for the successive censes at the district level. But the total number of speakers given for all the major and minor dialects in this chapter has been derived from the census of 1981.

Chapter 5

TYPOLOGY OF LANGUAGE SHIFT AND MAINTENANCE

5.1 Decadal Variations and Language Shift

The decadal variations in the number of speakers of a language also indicate the nature of language shift and maintenance. Unlike the well-known languages, the lesser-known ones, as evident from the census records, show a very high degree of fluctuation in the number of people speaking them (Itagi,et al,1986). If such a variation occurs in accordance with the pattern of population growth, it seems natural. But when it does not keep pace with the growth of population, it becomes a matter of serious concern to every one (Hoijer,1964 and Doshi,1972).

The decadal variation either in the number of speakers of a language or in the size of the population of a group is not a recent, rather a historical phenomenon. Natural calamities such as earthquakes, floods, droughts, famines, epidemics, etc. are important in bringing about changes in population sizes while colonisation, conversion to new religious beliefs, exposure of isolated regions to a new world order, etc. may lead to decadal variation in a language. Some important reasons for un-natural growth (a growth which does not follow the natural growth of a population) in the number of speakers of a language are migration, industrialisation, urbanisation, literacy, employment, etc. These are all external forces. All these factors are also considered to be cogent in bringing about linguistic shift. It is, therefore, argued that the higher the degree of decadal variation, the higher would be the degree of language shift and vice versa.

The tribal groups which are still occupying the remote and isolated patches of the hills and forests and have limited interaction with outsiders, have retained their own cultural heritage, including their traditional language. In such groups, the degree of decadal variation may be less than in those tribal groups whose interaction with the outside world is more, indicating a higher degree of language maintenance.

The decadal variation in a language may also be consciously used to manipulate social and political situations in order to fulfill some vested interests (Scotton,1983). In this process, a traditional language is glorified and all those who had adopted non-traditional language earlier, are forced to return to their traditional language. Such a revival of the traditional language in a tribal group may increase the decadal variation. The language of those groups which are politically less conscious may exhibit less decadal variation. For explicatory purposes, it may be assumed that the traditional languages of politically conscious tribal groups, may show less decadal variation and high language maintenance.

Methodological Procedure

In the absence of the up-to-date data, my study is based on 1961, 1971 and 1981 data. Since there are hundreds of lesser-known languages, the number of whose speakers may range from a few to more than four million, I have decided to select only those languages which have more than one lakh speakers each.

The 1981 census has recorded 23 languages which were spoken by more than one lakh persons. The number of such languages was 22 in 1971 and 18 in 1961. But this study includes all those languages which have attained the above mentioned criterion at any point of time. The following formula has been used to calculate the growth of languages and the size of population :

$$\frac{\text{Population of succeeding year - population of preceding year}}{\text{Population of preceding year}} \times 100$$

In other words, the growth rate of population between 1961 and 1971 may be calculated as follow :

$$\frac{\text{Population of 1971 - population of 1961}}{\text{Population of 1961}} \times 100$$

To find out the relationship between the decadal variation in languages and socio-economic variables, a computer programme of multiple correlation has been applied to obtain the correlation matrix.

The decadal variation in the number of speakers of the tribal languages is not uniform over the years: rather, it varies from negative to positive growth and vice versa. The degree of variation in the major lesser-known tribal languages has been discussed in the following paragraphs.

1. **Adi** : It belongs to the North-Assam branch of languages and was spoken in Arunachal Pradesh by about 99.2 Thousand persons in 1971

and by about 1.2 lakh persons in 1981. Numerically, the language had an insignificant position during 1961, when only 705 speakers reported Adi as their mother tongue. Therefore, the growth was very high (13975%) during 1961-71 and was reduced to 21 per cent during 1971-81.

2. **Ao** : It belongs to the Naga group of languages. Concentrated in Nagaland, Ao was declared by about 56 thousand persons in 1961, by 75.4 thousand persons in 1971 while in 1981 it was registered by more than one lakh speakers. The growth of the language between 1961-1971 was 33.69 per cent while between 1971-1981 it increased to 40 per cent.

3. **Bhili** : It is the most important tribal language belonging to the Indo-Aryan family. It is spoken in more than 50 districts of Rajasthan, Maharashtra, Gujarat, Madhya Pradesh and Karnataka. The speakers of Bhili are highly concentrated in the districts of Bhilwara, Udaipur, Banswara, and Dungarpur.

According to the 1961 census, Bhili was registered by about 8.29 lakh persons. The number of Bhili speakers rose to 34 lakh in 1971 and 44.5 lakh in 1981. Although the number of speakers kept on increasing, the growth rate has decreased from 310.25 per cent between 1961-71 to 30.93 per cent between 1971-81.

4. **Bodo** : It is spoken mainly in 5 districts-Jalpaiguri, CoochBehar, Hooghly and Burdwan in West Bengal and the Garo hills of Assam. The speakers of Bodo are highly concentrated in Jalpaiguri and the Garo hill districts.

Bodo was registered by about 2.86 lakh persons in 1961, by about 5.57 lakh persons in 1971, and by only 27.9 thousand in 1981. The growth rate between 1961-1971 was 94.38 per cent while between 1971-1981 the number of speakers has shown a sharp decline of -94.98 per cent.

5. **Garo** : It is another language belonging to the Bodo group. Its speakers are distributed over 11 districts in Nagaland, Assam, Tripura and West Bengal and highly concentrated in Meghalaya.

Garo was registered by about 3.1 lakh persons in 1961, by 4.11 lakh persons in 1971, and by about 4.08 lakh persons in 1981 with decadal growth rates of 34.1 per cent and -0.08 per cent respectively.

6. **Gondi** : It belongs to the Central Dravidian group of languages and is spoken in more than 35 districts in Madhya Pradesh, Maharashtra, West Bengal, Bihar, and Karnataka. The speakers of Gondi are highly concentrated in 8 districts of Maharashtra and Madhya Pradesh.

More than 13.8 lakh persons in 1961, more than 16.8 lakh persons in 1971, and more than 19.5 lakh persons in 1981 declared Gondi to be their mother tongue. Though the number of speakers is growing, the growth rate decreased from 21.96 per cent over 1961-71 to 15.78 per cent over 1971-81.

7. **Halbi/Halabi** : It is an Indo-Aryan language spoken over 5 districts-Nagpur and Chanda (Maharashtra), Koraput (Orissa), Raipur and Bastar (Madhya Pradesh). Bastar alone accounted for more than 90 per cent of the total Halbi speakers of the country.

Halbi was registered by about 3 lakh persons in 1961, by more than 3.46 lakh persons in 1971, and by about 5.24 lakh persons in 1981. The growth of Halbi was 15.55 during 1961-71 and 51.45 per cent during 1971-81.

8. **Ho** : It belongs to the Munda group of languages and accounted for about 11 per cent of the total Austric speaking population in the country. The speakers of Ho are distributed over 20 districts in Bihar, Orissa and West Bengal.

Ho was registered by 16 tribal groups. The number of its speakers is continuously increasing from 6.48 lakhs in 1961 to 7.51 lakhs in 1971, and to more than 8 lakh in 1981, with decadal growth rates of 15.9 per cent and 6.79 per cent respectively.

9. **Khandeshi** : It is the second most important tribal language of the Indo-Aryan family. Its speakers live in central India, including parts of Madhya pradesh, Maharashtra and Gujarat. It was registered as mother tongue by 3692 persons in 1961 which jumped to 2.52 lakh persons in 1971, and more than 11.87 lakh persons in 1981 with decadal growth rates of 7623 per cent and 371 per cent respectively.

10. **Kharia** : Belonging to the Munda group of languages, Kharia is the mother tongue of 14 tribal groups. It is spoken in 21 districts in Bihar, Madhya Pradesh, Orissa and West Bengal. Kharia accounted for about 2.7 per cent of the total Austric speakers. A little more than half of the country's Kharia speakers are concentrated in Ranchi district and one-fourth in Sundargarh district.

Kharia was registered by 1.7 lakh persons in 1961, by about 1.91 lakh persons in 1971, and by about 1.98 lakhs in 1981. The language recorded a positive growth of 11.77 per cent during 1961-71 and of 3.35 per cent during 1971-1981.

11. **Khasi** : It is the most important and uniform language of the Mon-khmer branch of the Austro-Asiatic family. Most of the speakers are concentrated in Meghalaya.

Khasi was registered by about 2.89 lakh persons during 1961 which increased to 4.79 lakh persons in 1971 and to 6.32 lakh persons in 1981 registering decadal growth rates of 65 per cent and 32.03 per cent respectively.

12. **Khond/Kondh** : It belongs to the Central Dravidian family of languages. It was registered by speakers in 12 districts in Orissa, Andhra Pradesh and West Bengal. About 67 per cent of its speakers are concentrated in the district of Koraput.

Khond was registered by 1.68 lakh persons in 1961 which increased to 1.96 lakh in 1971 and 2.05 lakh speakers in 1981. The growth rate was 16.84 per cent during 1961-71 which decreased to 4.17 per cent during 1971-81.

13. **Kisan** : Belonging to the Central Dravidian languages, Kisan was registered in 8 districts in Bihar and Orissa. Its speakers are highly concentrated in the districts of Sundargarh and Sambalpur.

The number of Kisan speakers was 50 thousand in 1961, 73.8 thousand in 1971 and jumped to 15.5 lakhs in 1981. The language showed a growth rate of 46.56 per cent during 1961-71 and a very high growth rate of 110.28 per cent during 1971-81.

14. **Korku** : It is the western most language of the Munda group, registered by speakers from 10 districts in Maharashtra and Madhya Pradesh. More than 90 per cent of its speakers are concentrated in the districts of Amravati, Betul, and East Nimar.

It was registered by 6 tribal groups with a total population of 2.08 lakh persons in 1961, by 3.07 lakh persons in 1971, and by 3.63 lakh persons in 1981. The language has experienced a continuous growth rate of 47.68 per cent during 1961-71 and 18.12 per cent during 1971-81.

15. **Koya** : It belongs to the Central Dravidian family of languages. Its speakers are highly concentrated in Koraput district of Orissa.

Koya was registered by 1.4 lakh persons in 1961 and by 2.11 lakh persons in 1971 and by about 2.42 lakhs in 1981. The growth recorded was 50.5 per cent and 14.47 per cent respectively.

16. **Kui** : It is a Central Dravidian language which was spoken by 5.1 lakh persons in 1961, by 3.51 persons in 1971 and by 5.07 lakhs in 1981, showing a negative growth of -31.3 per cent during 1961-71 and a positive growth of 83.58 per cent during 1971-81. The speakers of Kui are highly concentrated in the districts of Orissa and Andhra Pradesh.

17. **Kurukh/Oraon** : It belongs to the Northern Dravidian group of languages and was registered by the speakers in 15 districts of Bihar and West Bengal. The speakers of this language are highly concentrated in Ranchi district.

The 1961 census recorded 11.3 lakh speakers of Kurukh/Oraon while the number rose to 12.35 lakhs in 1971 and 12.64 lakhs in 1981. The language had experienced a continuous growth of 9.07 per cent and 2.34 per cent respectively.

18. **Lushai/Mizo** : It belongs to the Kuki-Chin group of the Assam-Burmese Branch. It is spoken mainly in the districts of Assam, Nagaland, Mizoram, and Tripura. Its speakers are highly concentrated in Mizoram.

Mizo was registered by 2.2 lakh persons in 1961, by 2.72 lakh persons in 1971 and by about 3.85 lakh persons in 1981 with decadal growth rates of 22.32 per cent and 41.68 per cent respectively.

19. **Mikir** : It belongs to the Bodo group of languages. It was registered by about 1.55 lakh persons in 1961 and by about 2 lakh persons in 1971 which decreased to 11 thousand during 1981. Thus it showed a positive growth of 28.64 per cent during 1961-71 and a negative growth of 94.37 per cent during 1971-81. The speakers of Mikir are distributed in Meghalaya and Assam.

20. **Munda/Mundari** : It is the second most important language of the Munda group, spoken in more than 40 districts in Bihar, West Bengal, Orissa, and Madhya Pradesh. Mundari accounted for about 13 per cent of the Austric speakers of the country. There were more than 30 tribal groups who declared Mundari as their mother tongue. The districts Ranchi and Singhbhum together accounted for more than 75 per cent of the country's Mundari speakers.

Mundari was registered by 9 lakh speakers in 1961, by more than 10.8 lakh persons in 1971 and by about 11.02 lakh speakers in 1981. The language has shown a continuous increasing trend with a growth rate of 19.6 per cent during 1961-71 and of 1.94 per cent during 1971-81.

21. **Nissi/Dafla** : It belongs to the NEFA group of languages whose speakers are highly concentrated in Arunachal Pradesh. It was registered by about 1.15 lakh persons in 1971 and by about 1.39 lakh speakers in 1981 with a growth rate of 21.96 per cent. Numerically, the language was insignificant during 1961 as the total number of its speakers was even less than 2 thousand.

22. **Santali** : It is the most important language of the Munda group and is an uniform one. It accounted for about 52.5 per cent of the Austric speakers. Santali is spoken in 35 districts of Bihar, Orissa, Madhya Pradesh, West Bengal, and Tripura. More than 88 per cent of its speakers are confined to Bihar and West Bengal. The district Santal Parganas accounted for about one-third of the country's Santali speaking population.

Santali was registered by about 31.3 lakh speakers in 1961, by 37.86 lakh persons in 1971 and by about 42.08 lakh persons in 1981 with growth rates of 20.96 per cent and 11.13 per cent respectively.

23. **Savara** : It is the southern most language of the Munda group. It is spoken in 13 districts in Orissa, Andhra Pradesh, West Bengal and Tripura. More than 98 per cent of its speakers are concentrated in the districts of Srikakulam, Baudhkhondmals, Koraput and Ganjam.

Savara was registered by about 2.65 lakh persons in 1961, by about 2.22 lakh persons in 1971, and by 2.3 lakh persons in 1981. A negative growth (16.45 %) was recorded during 1961-71 while a positive growth of 5.76 per cent was recorded during 1971-81.

24. **Tripuri** : Belonging to the Bodo group of languages, Tripuri was registered by 2.15 lakh persons in 1961, by 3.72 lakh persons in 1971 and by more than 4.9 lakhs in 1981. The language recorded a growth rate of 72.79 per cent during 1961-71 while during 1971-81, it had come down to 31.64 per cent. The speakers of Tripuri are highly concentrated in Tripura.

25. **Tulu** : It belongs to the South Dravidian group of languages. Its speakers are distributed over the states of Karnataka, Kerala and Maharashtra. Almost 96 per cent of the Tulu speakers are confined to Kerala.

Tulu was registered by about 9.35 lakh persons in 1961, by 11.58 lakh persons in 1971, and by 13.76 lakhs in 1981 with decadal growth rates of 23.92 per cent and 18.8 per cent respectively (Fig.18).

Decadal Variation and its Correlates

The decadal variation in the number of speakers of a language depends on a number of factors. All factors may be classified into two broad groups: internal and external. Among the internal, the natural growth of population may be considered to be the most important, while urbanisation, migration, literacy, diversion of work-force from primary to non-primary activities, conversion to a new value system, etc. may be

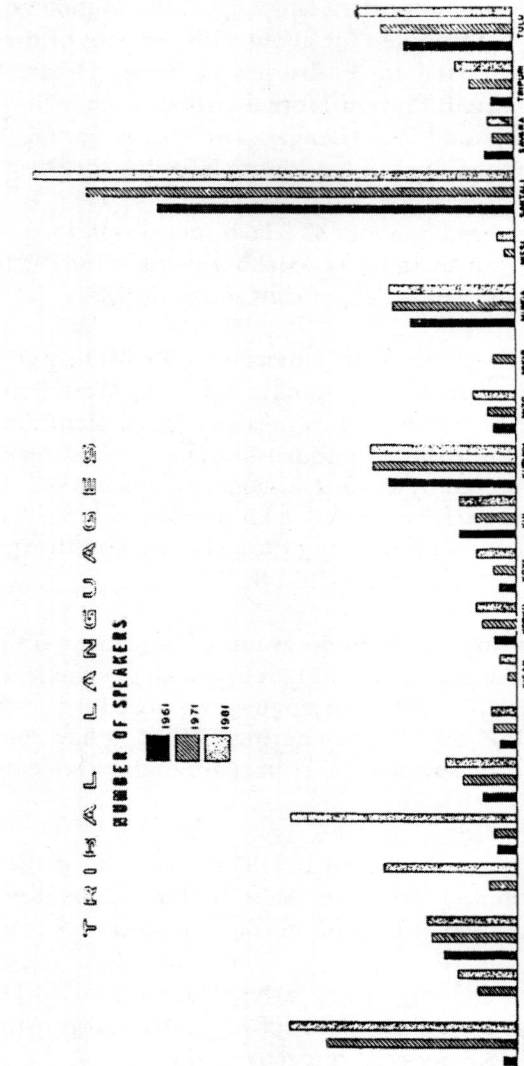
TRIBAL LANGUAGES
NUMBER OF SPEAKERS
1961
1971
1981
SPEAKERS IN LAKHS
0
5
10
15
20
25
30
35
40
ADI
AO
BHILI
BODO
GARO
GONDI
HALABI
HO
KHASI
KHOND
KISAN
KORKU
KOTA
KUI
KURUKH
MIZO
MUNDA
SANTALI
SAVARA
TRIPURI
TULU

Fig. 18

classified as 'external forces' which may bring about a significant variation in the number of speakers of a language, especially among the tribal languages. In the following paragraph, an attempt has been made to determine the relationship between decadal variation and the natural growth of population on the one hand and with the external variables on the other. The former has also been shown cartographically.

Relationship with population growth

The growth of the population of a tribal group and of its parental language have been superimposed in figure-19 for the period between 1961-71. Out of a total of 18 tribal languages (the remaining 7 languages have been excluded from this exercise as their corresponding population figures are not available), as many as 17 showed a positive growth while only Savara had shown a negative growth (-16.45%). The range of positive growth varies from 9.07 per cent in the case of Kurukh to 310 per cent in Bhili. Such large variations in growth (in the number of speakers) may be classified into 4 categories :

i. Very High Growth, with 100 per cent and above;
ii. High Growth, with 50-100 per cent;
iii. Medium Growth, with 25 -50 per cent; and,
iv. Low Growth, with less than 25 per cent.

The study of table-21 reveals that Bhili had a very high growth while a high growth occurred in 4 languages i.e. Bodo (94.38 %), Khasi (65.38%), Koya (50.50%), and Tripuri(72.79%). Medium growth occurred in Garo (34.10 %), Kisan (46.56%), and Korku (47.68 %). Nine tribal languages-Gondi (21.96%), Kurukh (9.07 %), Khond (16.84%), Santali (20.96 %), Mizo (22.32 %), Mundari (19.57%) Kharia (11.77%), Halbi (15.55%), and Ho (15.94 %), showed a low rate of growth.

The study of table - 22 reveals that barring the Garos, who showed a negative growth (-6.14%) , the remaining 17 tribal groups had shown a positive growth in the size of their population during 1961-71. But majority of them had experienced either low or medium growth although the Savaras had shown a very high (198%) positive growth. The Bodo, the Korku, and the Tripuri with growth rates of 76.13, 71.55 and 73.83 percentages may be classified in the medium growth category.

The study of the growth of speakers of languages during 1971-81 shows that out of 18 languages (the remaining 7 languages have been left out as the population figures for them are not available) as many as 17 languages had shown a positive growth in the number of their speakers.

Table-21
GROWTH OF MAJOR TRIBAL LANGUAGES

Tribal Languages	Speakers			Growth Rate	
	1961	1971	1981	1961-71	1971-81
1. Adi	705	99229	119833	13974.89	20.76
2. Ao	56385	75381	105610	33.69	40.11
3. Bhili/Bhilodi	828583	3399285	4450771	310.25	30.93
4. Bodo	286339	556576	27887	94.38	-94.98
5. Garo	307026	411731	408111	34.10	-00.08
6. Gondi	1384321	1688284	1954693	21.96	15.78
7. Halabi/Halbi	299660	346259	524758	15.55	51.55
8. Ho	648066	751389	802434	15.94	6.79
9. Khandeshi	3692	251896	1186921	7622.75	371.19
10. Kharia	171269	191421	197840	11.77	3.35
11. Khasi	289650	479028	632443	65.38	32.03
12. Khond	168027	196316	204501	16.84	4.17
13. Kisan	50378	73847	155283	46.56	110.28
14. Korku	208165	307434	363148	47.68	18.12
15. Koya	140776	211877	242534	50.50	14.47
16. Kui	510907	351017	507639	-31.30	83.58
17. Kurukh/Oraon	1132931	1235665	1264590	9.07	2.34
18. Lushai/Mizo	221985	271554	384747	22.32	41.68
19. Mikir	154786	199121	11206	28.64	-94.37
20. Munda/Mundari	903683	1080546	1101522	19.57	1.94
21. Nissi/Dafla	1175	114678	139867	9658.82	21.96
22. Santali	3130829	3786899	4208304	20.96	11.13
23. Savara	265721	222018	234811	-16.45	5.76
24. Tripuri	215624	372579	490464	72.79	31.64
25. Tulu	934849	1158419	1376306	32.92	18.80

Soures: Census of India, 1961, Language Tables, pt. II c (ii)
Census of India, 1971, Socio-cultural Tables, pt. II c (i)
Census of India, 1981, Households and household Population by Language mainly spoken in the Household.

Table-22
POPULATION GROWTH OF MAJOR TRIBAL GROUPS

Tribal Languages	Population			Growth Rate	
	1961	1971	1981	1961-71	1971-81
1. Adi	N.A.	N.A.	24206	—	—
2. Ao	N.A.	65630	104578	—	59.35
3. Bhil	3738025	4952126	7392152	32.48	49.27
4. Bodo	343381	604781	N.A.	76.13	—
5. Garo	261564	245494	412747	-6.14	68.13
6. Gond	3891416	5146322	7442148	32.25	44.61
7. Halabi	126794	176008	479194	38.81	172.26
8. Ho	481621	515760	581019	7.08	12.65
9. Khandeshi	N.A.	N.A.	N.A.	—	—
10. Kharia	259693	310132	304254	19.42	-1.89
11. Khasi	338516	407218	628104	22.29	54.25
12. Khond	840132	868406	989342	3.37	13.93
13. Kisan	136567	188893	256782	38.32	35.94
14. Korku	160101	274650	182754	71.55	-33.45
15. Koya	274526	339706	474867	23.74	39.79
16. Kui	N.A.	N.A.	N.A.	—	—
17. Kurukh/Oraon	1389930	1624480	1860777	16.93	14.55
18. Lushai/Mizo	160852	218782	357466	36.01	63.40
19. Mikir	N.A.	N.A.	17727	—	—
20. Munda/Mundari	970851	1085001	1447498	11.75	33.40
21. Nissi/Dafla	N.A.	N.A.	N.A.	—	—
22. Santal	3115147	3577177	4258115	14.83	19.03
23. Savara	163221	486314	556496	197.95	14.45
24. Tripuri	186261	323781	330872	73.83	2.19
25. Tulu	N.A.	N.A.	N.A.	—	—

Soures: Census of India, 1961, 1971, 1981

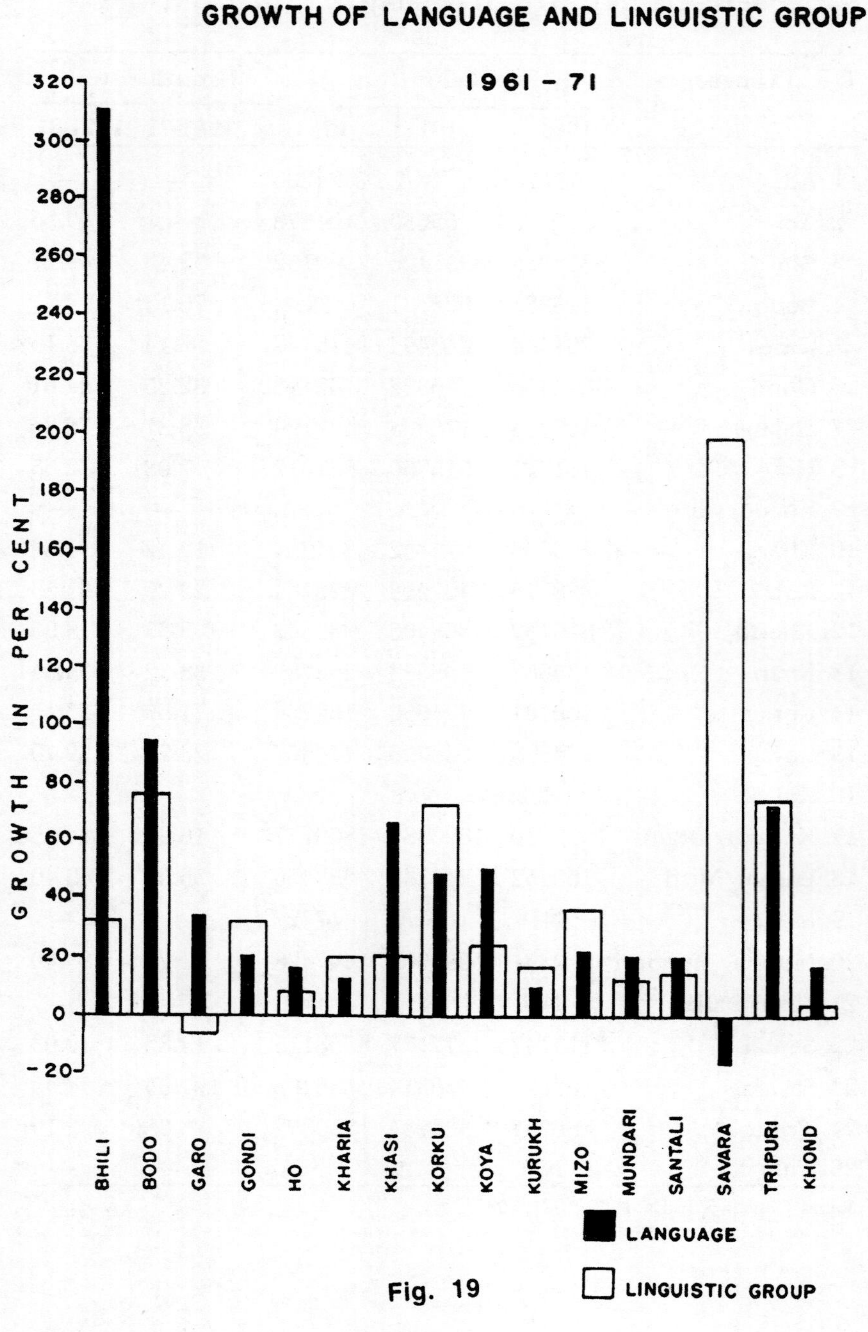
GROWTH OF LANGUAGE AND LINGUISTIC GROUP
1961 - 71
GROWTH IN PER CENT
320
300
280
260
240
220
200
180
160
140
120
100
80
60
40
20
0
-20
BHILI
BODO
GARO
GONDI
HO
KHARIA
KHASI
KORKU
KOYA
KURUKH
MIZO
MUNDARI
SANTALI
SAVARA
TRIPURI
KHOND
LANGUAGE
LINGUISTIC GROUP

Fig. 19

Garo was the only tribal language which registered a negative growth (-0.08). It is interesting to note that most of these languages have shown medium or low rates of growth. Kisan with 110 per cent and Halbi with 51.55 per cent growth were classified under the higher categories of growth.

The study of the growth of population between 1971-81 reveals that the Kharias and the Korkus had experienced a negative growth of 1.89 per cent and by 33 per cent respectively. The remaining 16 tribal groups showed a positive growth ranging from 2.19 per cent in the case of Tripuri to 172.26 per cent among the Halbi. It is interesting to note that as many as 11 of them had either low or medium levels of growth. A total of 4 tribal groups including Ao (59.35%), Garo (68.13%), Khasi (54.25%) and Mizo (63.40%) have been classified under high levels of population growth (Fig.20).

From the above paragraphs, we may conclude that although the growth of population size and the number of speakers shows a positive trend (leaving aside some exceptions), the growth in the number of speakers was much higher, in 1961-71, than in the size of population while the situation was different during 1971-81. In other words, it may be said that the contribution made by the natural growth of population to the growth of a language is obvious but other factors must also have contributed significantly.

Relationship with External Factors

The correlation matrix in table-23 reveals that there exists a positive relationship between decadal variation in a language and the percentage of language maintenance, the percentage of urban population, the percentage of literate population, the percentage of Christians, the percentage of workers engaged in non-primary sectors, the percentage of males in the population and the percentage of natural growth of population. A negative correlation was found with the percentage of the population under 45 years of age.

The values of correlation coefficients do not show a strong relationship as the values are not close to +1 or -1. Two variables, i.e. percentage of urban population and percentage of natural growth of population are found to be more important than others, with coefficient values of 0.352 and 0.388 respectively. In the case of other variables with positive correlations, the values of the coefficients are found to be less than 0.2. Even the negative factor is weak as its correlation coefficient is -0.092.

The values of coefficients of correlation for both urbanisation and natural growth are weak. But they are significant at 5 per cent level of confidence. It is interesting to note that the contribution made by urbanisation is 13 per cent more than that made by the natural growth

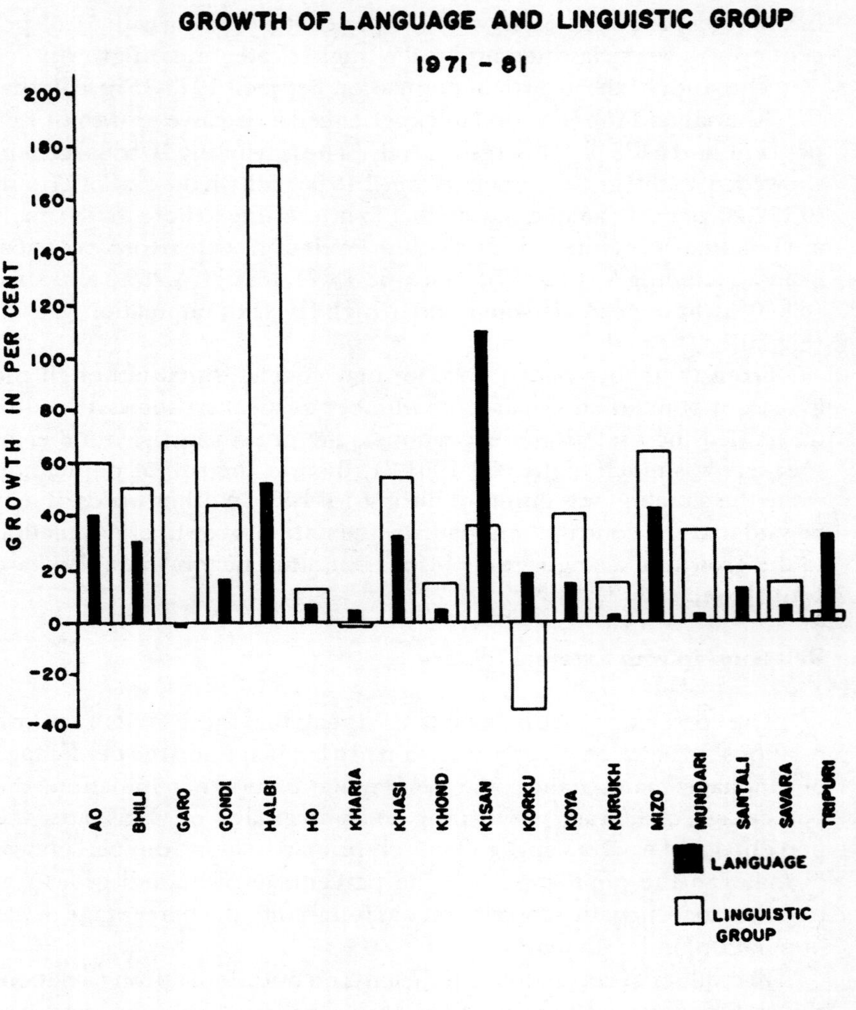
GROWTH OF LANGUAGE AND LINGUISTIC GROUP
1971 - 81
GROWTH IN PER CENT
200
180
160
140
120
100
80
60
40
20
0
-20
-40
AO
BHILI
GARO
GONDI
HALBI
HO
KHARIA
KHASI
KHOND
KISAN
KORKU
KOYA
KURUKH
MIZO
MUNDARI
SANTALI
SAVARA
TRIPURI
LANGUAGE
LINGUISTIC GROUP

Fig. 20

Table-23
CORRELATION MATRIX

	% Growth in Lang. I	% Lang. maint. II	% Urban POP. III	% Litrate IV	% Christian V	% NP Workers VI	% Male POP. VII	% POP <45 yr. VIII	% Growth in POP. IX
I	1.00								
II	0.027	1.00							
III	0.352*	0.275	1.00						
IV	0.043	0.232	0.660	1.00					
V	0.107	0.264	0.618	0.002	1.00				
VI	0.144	0.353	0.491	0.825	0.027	1.00			
VII	0.155	0.436	0.403	0.596	-0.023	0.396	1.00		
VIII	-0.092	-0.174	-0.373	-0.508	-0.291	-0.439	-0.130	1.00	
IX	0.388*	-0.224	0.595	0.468	0.056	0.111	0.298	-0.210	1.00

* Significant at 5 % level of confidence

of population in bringing about variations in the number of speakers of a language. This means that urbanisation emerges as the most important correlate, followed by the natural growth of population. The exceptional decadal variations in the case of Adi, Khandeshi, Bodo, Mikir, and Kisan may be related to the degree of political and cultural consciousness which have emerged among these people during the last two to three decades (Khubchandani, 1992,43).

5.2 **Patterns of Language Shift and Maintenance: Case Studies**

Since language shift varies not only according to region but also according to tribe, I have decided to focus on some tribal groups to investigate the degree of language shift and maintenance among them. Thus, the chapter highlights the distributional patterns to demarcate the areas of language shift and maintenance among some of the dominant linguistic communities of the Munda Branch (i.e., the Korkus, the Santals and the Mundas) and the Bhils of the Indo-Aryan language family. Geographically, these tribal groups are distributed over the western, central and the eastern regions of the country. The Aravalli hills are believed to be the principal homes for the Bhils, as are the Satpura hills for the Korkus and the Rajmahal hills and the Chotanagpur Plateau for the Santals and Mundas.

5.2.1 **The Bhils**

1. <u>Declared Traditional Language</u>

Out of a total of 53 districts, there are only 20 in which the Bhils have declared Bhili and its dialects as their mother tongue. 99.6 per cent Bhils in Dungarpur and 81.9 per cent in Jhabua districts have declared Bhili. In another 3 districts, the share of Bhili speakers ranges from 60 to 80 per cent. In the remaining 15 districts, this share is insignificant. Most of these districts are classified in a group in which this share is less than 20 per cent (Table-24).

2. <u>Declared Other Tribal Languages</u>

There are 23 districts in which the Bhils have registered other tribal languages as their mother tongue. Out of these, there are 15 districts in which less than 10 per cent Bhils have registered other tribal languages. This share ranges from 10 to 20 per cent in 3 districts and from 20 to 60 per cent in another 7 districts. In Jaipur, this share is 72 per cent. Among these languages Malvi, Dangi, Bard, Ahirni, Harauti, etc. are important.

3. Declared Regional Languages

There are 48 districts in which the Bhils have declared regional languages as their mother tongue. Out of these, there are 23 districts where more than 90 per cent Bhils have shifted from their traditional language to regional languages. There are as many as 5 districts in which cent per cent Bhils have declared regional languages. This share varies between 40 and 80 per cent in another 10 districts; it ranges from 20 to 40 in 5 districts and in another 3 districts from 10 to 20 per cent. Hindi and its dialects are considered the regional language in Madhya Pradesh and Rajasthan while Gujarati and Marathi are considered the regional languages in the the states of Gujarat and Maharashtra respectively.

4. Declared Non-tribal Non-regional Languages

There are 40 districts in which the Bhils have declared non-tribal non-regional languages as their mother tongue. Except for 6 districts in which the share of speakers varies from 10 to 60 per cent, the share is less than 10 per cent in the remaining 34 districts. The languages under this group include Hindi, Gujarati, Telugu, Kannada in Maharashtra; Hindi, Marathi, Telugu and Kannada in Gujarat and Gujarati, Marathi, Telugu in Madhya Pradesh and Rajasthan.

Table-24
LANGUAGE SHIFT AND MAINTENANCE AMONG THE BHILS

% category	Traditional language	Other tribal languages	Regional languages	NT.NR languages
> 80	2	-	30	-
60-80	3	1	7	-
40-60	1	2	3	2
20-40	4	2	5	2
10-20	3	3	2	2
< 10	7	15	1	34
Total	20	23	48	40

5.2.2 **The Korkus**

1. Declared Traditional Language

Out of a total of 10 districts, there are as many as 8 districts in which the Korkus have declared Korku, their traditional language, as their mother tongue. In Amravati, almost cent per cent Korkus have declared it as their mother tongue while in Sarguja, Chhindwara, Betul and East Nimar the share of the speakers of Korku varies from 77 to 82 per cent. In the remaining 3 districts, namely Hoshangabad, West Nimar and Dewas this share is 11.7, 3.0 and 0.3 per cent respectively.

2. Declared Other Tribal Languages

Except for the Korkus in East Nimar and Bhind districts, those in the remaining 8 districts have registered the languages of other tribal groups. But the share does not exceed 5 per cent in any of these districts except in Betul district in which about 22 per cent Korkus have been grouped under this category. Gondi and Malvi are the two main languages in this group.

3. Declared Regional Languages

Korkus in all the 10 districts have declared regional languages as their mother tongue. The change was almost cent per cent in Bhind district followed by Dewas (99%), West Nimar (92%), Indore (93%) and Hoshangabad (88%). There are 2 districts, East Nimar and Chhindwara in which about 21 per cent Korkus have declared regional language while the share was less than one per cent in Amravati and Betul districts. Hindi and its regional dialects are considered the regional languages in Madhya Pradesh and Marathi is considered the regional language in Amravati district.

4. Declared Non-tribal Non-regional Languages

There are only 4 districts in which the Korkus have declared non-tribal non-regional languages as their mother tongue. In all these districts the share of these languages among the speakers is less than 7 per cent. The district of Chhindwara with the highest percentage of 6 is followed by Indore and West Nimar with less than 3 per cent, and Amravati with only 0.2 per cent. Hindi and its regional dialects are considered the non-tribal non-regional languages in Amravati while Marathi and Telugu have a similar status in Madhya Pradesh (Table-25).

Table-25
LANGUAGE SHIFT AND MAINTENANCE AMONG THE KORKUS

% category	Traditional language	Other tribal languages	Regional languages	NT.NR languages
> 80	2	-	5	-
60-80	3	-	-	-
40-60	-	-	-	-
20-40	-	1	2	-
10-20	1	-	1	-
< 10	2	7	2	4
Total	8	8	10	4

5.2.3 The Mundas

1. Declared Traditional Language

Out of a total of 41 districts, there are 30 districts in which the Mundas have declared Mundari as their mother tongue. Among these districts there are only 2 (i.e., Patna and Singhbhum) in which more than 80 per cent Mundas have declared Mundari. On the other hand, there are 8 districts in which the share of Mundari speakers varies from 0 to 10 per cent. In another 13 districts, this share ranges from 10 to 40 per cent. The share was between 60 and 80 per cent in 4 districts and between 40 and 60 per cent in 3 districts.

2. Declared Other Tribal Languages

There are 37 districts in which the Mundas have declared other tribal languages as their mother tongue. Out of these, there are altogether 15 districts where the share of the speakers of these languages is confined to only 10 per cent. In another 11 districts their share ranges from 10 to 40 per cent whereas it varies between 40 and 80 per cent in another 9 districts. There are only 2 districts (i.e., Jalpaiguri and Balasore) in which more than 80 per cent Mundas have declared other tribal languages as their mother tongue. Kurukh, Santali, Sadari, Kharia, etc. are some of the important languages which may be classified under this group.

3. Declared Regional Languages

There are 41 districts in which the Mundas have declared regional languages as their mother tongue. Out of these, there are 9 districts in which more than 80 per cent Mundas have declared regional languages. The percentage share ranges between 20 and 40 in 12 districts. There are 3 districts in which the share varies from 10 to 20 per cent. There are only 6 districts in which the share is restricted to 10 per cent. On the other hand, the share varies between 60 and 80 per cent in another 5 districts and between 40 and 60 per cent in 6 districts. Hindi and its regional dialects are considered the regional language for the Mundas living in Bihar while Oriya in Orissa and Bengali in West Bengal have a similar status.

4. Declared Non-tribal Non-regional Languages

There are 29 districts in which the Mundas have declared non-tribal non-regional languages as their mother tongue. Out of these, 22 districts have less than 10 per cent share of speakers while in the remaining 7 districts, the share varies from 15 to 46 per cent (Table-26).

Table- 26
LANGUAGE SHIFT AND MAINTENANCE AMONG THE MUNDAS

% category	Traditional language	Other tribal languages	Regional languages	NT.NR languages
> 80	2	2	9	-
60-80	4	6	5	2
40-60	3	3	6	1
20-40	8	3	12	2
10-20	5	8	3	2
< 10	8	15	6	22
Total	30	37	41	29

5.2.4 **The Santals**

1. Declared Traditional Language

Out of a total of 37 districts, there are 35 districts (including Tripura) in which the Santals have reported Santali as their mother tongue. Out of these, there are 21 districts in which more than 80 per cent Santals have declared Santali. In 18 districts the share of Santali speakers exceeds 90 per cent. This share varies from 40 to 80 per cent in 9 districts. There are only 3 districts in which this share is less than 10 per cent. In another 2 districts this share varies between 20 and 40 per cent (Table-27).

2. Declared Other Tribal Languages

There are altogether 26 districts including Tripura in which the Santals have declared languages of other tribes as their mother tongue. The share of the speakers of these languages is not more than 24 per cent in any case. There are as many as 21 districts in which the share ranges from 0 to 10 per cent. The share varies from 10 to 20 per cent in 3 districts and from 20 to 40 per cent in another 2 districts. Mundari, Kurukh, Korwa and Sadari are important among these languages.

3. Declared Regional Languages

In 36 districts, the Santals have registered the regional language as their mother tongue. There are only 5 districts in which the share of the speakers of regional languages exceeds 80 per cent. On the other hand, in 21 districts this share is less than 10 per cent. The share ranges from 10 to 20 per cent in 3 districts and between 20 and 40 per cent in another 4 districts. In the remaining 3 districts the share varies from 46 to 61 per cent. Hindi and its regional dialects are considered the regional languages for the Santals of Bihar whereas Oriya in Orissa and Bengali in West Bengal have a similar status.

4. Declared Non-tribal Non-regional Languages

There are only 21 districts in which non-tribal non-regional languages have been declared by the Santals. In each of these districts, the share of the speakers of these languages remained under 13 per cent. Fifteen of these districts are in West Bengal, one is in Orissa, 4 districts are in Bihar and the remaining one is Tripura. The highest share of the speakers of these languages is 12.1 per cent in Tripura followed by Calcutta, 24-Parganas and Darjeeling districts. Bengali and Oriya are considered non-tribal non-regional languages in Bihar while Hindi and Bengali in Orissa and Hindi and Oriya in West Bengal have a similar status.

Table-27
LANGUAGE SHIFT AND MAINTENANCE AMONG THE SANTALS

% category	Traditional language	Other tribal languages	Regional languages	NT.NR languages
> 80	21	-	5	-
60-80	6	-	2	-
40-60	3	-	1	-
20-40	2	2	4	-
10-20	-	3	3	-
< 10	3	21	21	21
Total	35	26	36	21

5.3 The Empirical Evidence

The pattern which emerges out of the study at the district level does not give us a true picture of the real situation that exists at the household level. In order to overcome such anomalies, an extensive household survey was conducted among the Bhils, the Korkus, the Mundas and the Santals.

The analysis of the study at the household level reveals that the Korkus of Punasa, Richhi and Udaipur villages (Khandwa Tehsil) have already been switched over to the regional language. On the other hand, the Korkus of Mirpur, Kalamkala, Kutbi and Sunderdeo villages (Hersud Tehsil) have registered Korku, their traditional language, as their mother tongue. The Mundas and the Santals of eastern India present a different picture. It has been found that cent per cent Santals of Dumka town and Suraj Beda village have declared Santali as their mother tongue. On the other hand, about 92 per cent Mundas of Ranchi town have shifted from their traditional language to Sadari which they declared as their mother tongue. The remaining 8 per cent retained Mundari, their traditional language. The situation is different in rural areas where the majority of the Mundas reside, retaining their traditional mother tongue. The Mundas of Kula Buru and Litingdih villages (Bundu Block) and Bande village (Murhu Block) in Ranchi district have retained their traditional tongue. Out of 8 households headed by high school teachers (belong to Munda tribe) at Murhu, it was found that Hindi is used as mother tongue in 5 households whereas in the remaining 3 households Mundari has been registered as mother tongue.

The foregoing study on the nature of linguistic shift among the tribal communities in India revealed that the Mundas in Ranchi and the

Korkus in East Nimar are more inclined towards language shift than the Santals of Santal Parganas and the Bhils of Banswara district. Besides, there is a regional variation in the degree of language shift and maintenance. For example, the Korkus of Khalwa Development Block (Hersud Tehsil) have more affiliation with their traditional language whereas the Korkus of Punasa Development Block (Khandwa Tehsil) have adopted the regional language. The majority of the Mundas living in Ranchi town have displayed a shifting tendency whereas the Mundas residing in rural areas have a tendency to maintain their old tongue. As far as the Bhils and the Santals are concerned, there is no rural-urban differential as regards of language shift. Cent per cent Santals of Dumka town and Littipara Block and the Bhils of Banswara town and Bagidora Tehsil have retained their traditional language as their mother tongue.

5.4 Typology of Language Shift and Maintenance

The degree of language shift and maintenance among the selected tribal groups varies from less than one per cent in some districts to almost cent per cent in others. Such a large variation in the data has to be classified into different categories to arrive at some meaningful conclusion. To overcome this problem, an exercise has been attempted in this section to identify the typology of language shift and maintenance in order to demarcate the areas with very high, high, medium, and low degrees of language shift and maintenance.

Methodological Procedure

The percentages of language shift and maintenance have been calculated separately for all the districts and for each tribal group. On the basis of the range of variation, they have been divided into four groups of :

a) very high (with percentages above 75);
b) high (with percentages from 50 to 75);
c) medium (with percentages between 25 and 50); and,
d) low (with percentages below 25).

It is to be noted here that less than 0.5 per cent has been considered as zero while more than 99.5 per cent has been rounded off to 100 per cent.

In order to determine the typology, the above identified groups of maintenance and shift have been shown on the maps for each tribal group. The maps of shift and maintenance have been superimposed to demarcate the areas of mixed degree of the shift and maintenance. Theoretically, 16 types are possible but in the case of the above mentioned tribes, the number of types ranged from three in the case of the Korkus to four for the remaining tribal groups. These types, which emerged out of the superimposition of the maps, have been listed as follows :

a) Areas of very high maintenance with low shift (Vl);
b) Areas with high maintenance with medium shift (Hm);
c) Areas of medium maintenance with high shift (Mh); and
d) Areas of low maintenance with very high shift (Lv).

In order to determine the patterns of regional variation, the value of the coefficient of variance has been calculated by using the following formula :

$$CV = \frac{SD}{\bar{x}} \times 100$$

where CV = Coefficient of variation;
SD = standard deviation;
$\bar{x}$ = mean value.

1. *Linguistic Typology among the Bhils*

Out of a total of 53 districts, there are only 21 districts in which the Bhils have registered Bhili as their mother tongue. Among these, the magnitude of variation of language maintenance ranges from 1.33 per cent to 81.84 per cent except in the district of Dungarpur (Rajasthan) in which almost cent per cent Bhils have declared Bhili as their mother tongue. Both Banswara and Jhabua districts (with percentages of 76.53 and 81.84 respectively) have been classified under the areas of 'very high degree of language maintenance' whereas Ratlam and Dhulia districts have been considered as the districts with 'high degree of language maintenance'. A medium degree of language maintenance has been found in 4 districts-Dhar, West Nimar, East Nimar and Bhir in which the percentage of language maintenance varies from 25 to 50. The degree of language maintenance is of a low order in 12 districts in which less than 25 per cent of Bhils have declared Bhili as their mother tongue.

There are altogether 32 districts in which cent per cent Bhils have declared non-traditional languages as their mother tongue. In the remaining 20 districts, the magnitude of language shift varies from 18.16 to 98.67 per cent. Among these, there are 12 districts which have been classified as the areas of 'very high degree of language shift'. A high degree of language shift has been found in 4 districts while medium and low grades of shift has been reported from only 4 districts (Table-28).

Table-28
TYPOLOGY OF LANGUAGE SHIFT AND MAINTENANCE AMONG THE BHILS

% category	Type	No. of Dist.	Name of District
> 75	(Vl)	2	Banswara, Jhabua
50-75	(Hm)	2	Ratlam, Dhulia
25-50	(Mh)	4	Dhar, West Nimar, East Nimar, Bhir
<25	(Lv)	12	Bharoach, Surat, Udaipur, Chittorgarh, Sehore, Jalgaon, Ahmadnagar, Sholapur, Aurangabad, Nanded, Osmanabad, Parbhani

100 % **shift** in Kutch, Banaskantha, Sabarkantha, Mehsana, Kaira, Ahmadabad, Panchmahal, Baroda, Dangs (Gujarat); Bharatpur, Sawai Madhopur, Jaipur, Ajmer, Tonk, Jaisalmer, Jodhpur, Nagaur, Pali, Barmer, Jalore, Sirohi, Bundi, Kota, Jhalawar (Rajasthan); Panna, Satna, Raisan (M.P.); Greater Bombay, Nasik, Poona, Thana (Maharashtra).

100 % **Maintenance** in Dungarpur (Rajasthan)

The value of the coefficient of variance is 88.44 for language maintenance indicating a higher regional variation whereas it is 34.43 for the language shift representing a lower regional variation for language shift among the Bhils.

Types of Language Shift and Maintenance

Areas of Vl Type

There is only one pocket comprising two districts, namely Banswara and Jhabua, in which a very high degree of language maintenance is associated with a low grade of language shift. The pocket is located along the Rajasthan and Madhya Pradesh border and is almost in the centre of the Bhili region of the country.

Areas of Hm Type

There are two districts, namely Ratlam and Dhulia, in which a high grade of language maintenance is associated with a medium degree of shift. It is located in Dhulia district, adjacent to the south of the Vl type while the other district (Ratlam) is at the north-east border of the Vl type.

Areas of Mh Type

The districts falling under the areas of a medium grade of language maintenance and a high degree of shift are located in two pockets. The districts of Dhar, West Nimar and East Nimar form a large pocket and are adjacent to the southern border of the Vl type. Bhir district forming, another pocket of this type, is located in central Maharashtra.

Areas of Lv Type

The areas of low maintenance with a high degree of language shift consist of four pockets which are located on the periphery of the Bhil region in the country. Altogether there are 12 districts in which low maintenance is associated with a very high degree of language shift (Fig. 21).

2. *Linguistic Typology among the Korkus*

Out of a total of 10 districts, there are 7 districts in which the Korkus have maintained their traditional language as their mother tongue and in the remaining 3 districts they have shifted to other languages of the region. The magnitude of variation in the case of language maintenance varies from 3.21 to 99.42 per cent. There are 4 districts namely, East Nimar, Betul, Sarguja, and Amravati in which more than 75 per cent of the Korkus have registered the Korku language as their mother tongue. These districts have been classified under 'very high degree of language maintenance'. The district of Chhindwara has been classified under 'high degree of language maintenance' whereas West Nimar and Hoshangabad districts are grouped under 'low degree of language maintenance'.

Besides 3 districts in which cent per cent Korkus have registered non-traditional languages as their mother tongue, there are 7 districts in which the magnitude of variation of language shift varies from 0.58 to 96.79 per cent. There are two districts, namely West Nimar and Hoshangabad, in which more than 75 per cent shift has been found and thus, these may be classified under 'very high degree of shift'. The district Chhindwara has been classified under 'medium degree of shift' whereas a low degree of shift prevails in East Nimar, Betul, Surguja and Amravati districts (Table- 29).

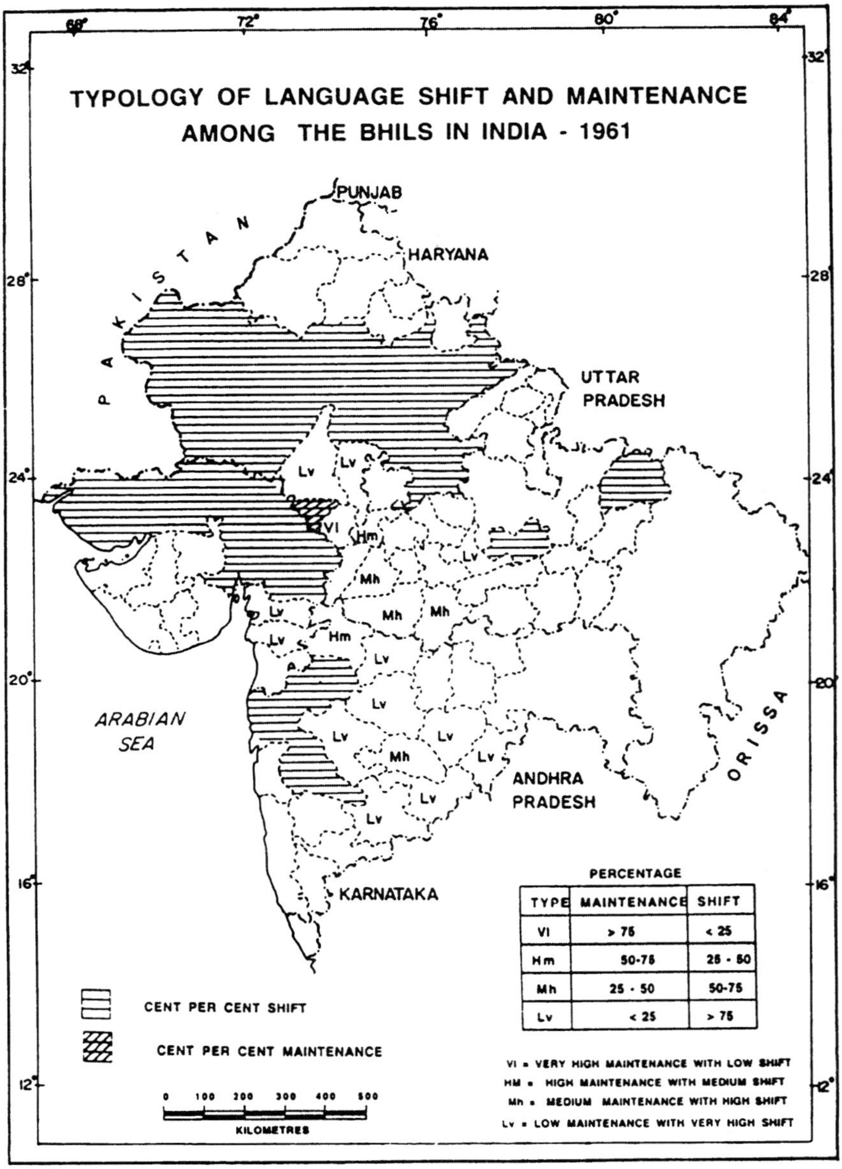

PERCENTAGE

TYPE	MAINTENANCE	SHIFT
Vl	> 75	< 25
Hm	50-75	25 - 50
Mh	25 - 50	50-75
Lv	< 25	> 75

Fig. 21

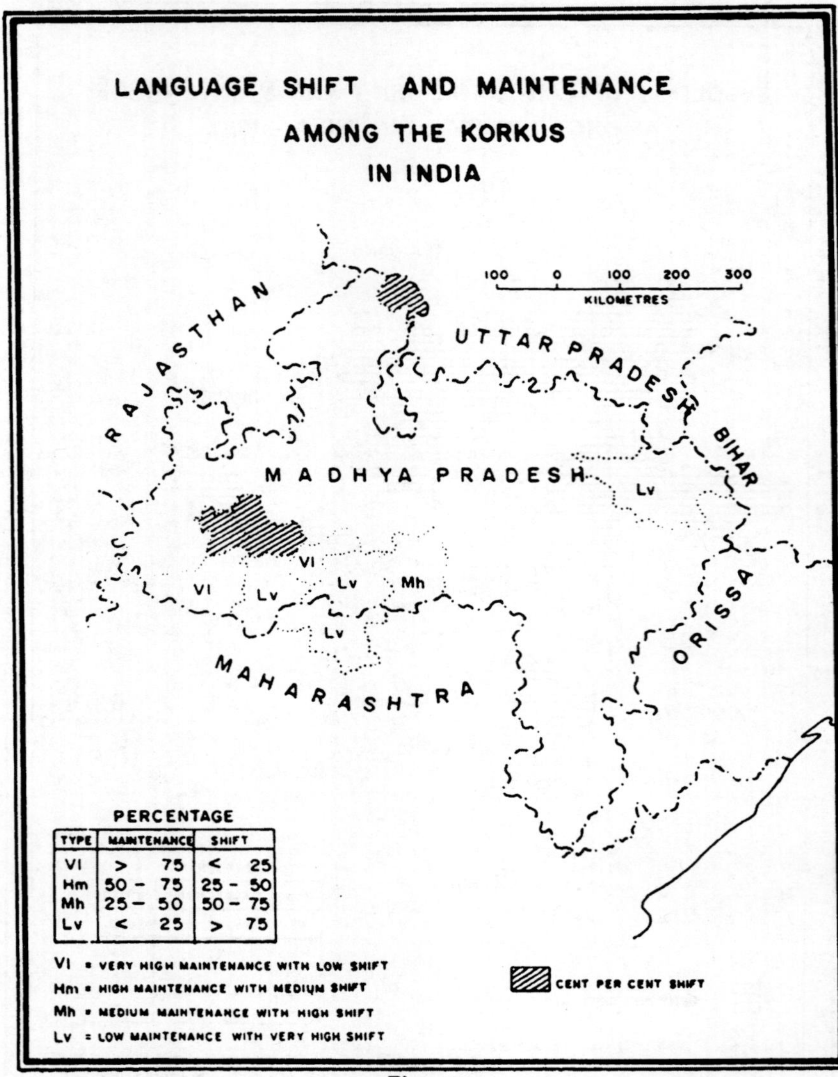
LANGUAGE SHIFT AND MAINTENANCE
AMONG THE KORKUS
IN INDIA
100 0 100 200 300
KILOMETRES
RAJASTHAN
UTTAR PRADESH
BIHAR
MADHYA PRADESH
ORISSA
MAHARASHTRA
Lv
Vl
Vl
Lv
Lv
Mh
Lv
PERCENTAGE
TYPE | MAINTENANCE | SHIFT
Vl | > 75 | < 25
Hm | 50 - 75 | 25 - 50
Mh | 25 - 50 | 50 - 75
Lv | < 25 | > 75
Vl = VERY HIGH MAINTENANCE WITH LOW SHIFT
Hm = HIGH MAINTENANCE WITH MEDIUM SHIFT
Mh = MEDIUM MAINTENANCE WITH HIGH SHIFT
Lv = LOW MAINTENANCE WITH VERY HIGH SHIFT
CENT PER CENT SHIFT

Fig. 22

Table-29
TYPOLOGY OF LANGUAGE SHIFT AND MAINTENANCE AMONG THE KORKUS

% Category	Type	No. of Dist.	Name of District
> 75	(Vl)	4	East Nimar, Betul, Sarguja (M.P.) Amravati (Maharashtra)
50-75	(Hm)	1	Chhindwara (M.P.)
25-50	(Mh)	-	-
< 25	(Lv)	2	West Nimar, Hoshangabad (M.P.)

100 % **Shift** in Bhind, Indore, Dewas (M.P.)

The value of the coefficient of variance is 57.06 for language maintenance indicating moderate regional variation whereas the value for the shift is 89.30 indicating high regional variation among the Korku tribal population.

Types of Language Shift and Maintenance

Areas of Vl Type

The areas with very high maintenance and low degree of language shift consist of two pockets. One is comprised of 3 districts, namely East Nimar, Betul and Amravati in central India whereas the other pocket is in Sarguja district of Madhya Pradesh located along the Bihar - Madhya Pradesh border.

Areas of Hm Type

There is only one district belonging to this type in which 'high degree of maintenance' is associated with 'medium degree of language shift'. It is the district of Chhindwara of Madhya Pradesh located to the east of Vl type in central India.

Areas of Lv Type

The districts of West Nimar and Hoshangabad have been classified under this type in which 'low maintenance' is associated with 'very high degree of language shift'. Hoshangabad is located to the north of the Vl type whereas West Nimar is towards the west (Fig. 22).

3. *Linguistic Typology among the Mundas*

Out of a total of 41 districts, there are 28 districts in which the Mundas have retained their traditional language as their mother tongue. Among these districts, the magnitude of variation ranges from 1.30 to 93.46 per cent. The percentage is more than 75 in the districts of Patna, Ranchi, and Singhbhum which have been considered as the areas of 'very high degree of maintenance' whereas 'high degree of maintenance' has been found in another 4 districts. A medium degree of maintenance is found in 7 districts whereas in another 14 districts, low percentages of maintenance of Mundari have been registered.

There are 13 districts in which almost cent per cent language shift among the Mundas has occurred. In the remaining 28 districts, the magnitude of the shift ranges from 6.54 to 98.70 per cent. Among these, there are 14 districts which have been classified as the areas of 'very high degree of language shift'. 7 districts have been grouped under high, 4 districts under medium and the remaining 3 districts as the areas with a low grade of language shift. (Table-30)

Table-30
TYPOLOGY OF LANGUAGE SHIFT AND MAINTENANCE AMONG THE MUNDAS

% Category	Type	No. of Dist.	Name of District
> 75	(Vl)	3	Patna, Ranchi, Singhbhum
50 - 75	(Hm)	4	West Dinajpur, Malda, Midnapore, Sundargarh
25 - 50	(Mh)	7	Palamau, Hazaribagh, Dhanbad, Murshidabad, Howrah, Burdwan, Bankura
< 25	(Lv)	14	Shahabad,Santal Parganas, Raigarh, Raipur, Nadia, 24- Parganas, Calcutta,Hooghly,Purulia, Cooch Behar, Baudhkhondmals, Mayurbhanj, Dhenkanal; Tripura.
100 % **shift** in			Bhagalpur, Purnea, Surguja, Darjeeling, Jalpaiguri, Ganjam, Balasore, Cuttuck, Keonjhar, Bolangir, Sambalpur, Kalahandi, Koraput

The value of the co-efficient of variance is 82.42 for language maintenance and 40.65 for language shift indicating a high degree of regional variation for maintenance and a low degree of regional variation for language shift among the Mundas.

Types of Language Shift and Maintenance

Areas of Vl Type

The areas of 'very high maintenance' with 'low degree of language shift' consist of 3 districts and are divided into two pockets. The districts of Ranchi and Singhbhum are on the Chotanagpur plateau and form a larger pocket than the second pocket which is located in Patna district.

Areas of Hm Type

There are 4 districts with a high degree of language maintenance and medium grade of shift. These are divided into 3 pockets. Except Sundargarh district which is in Orissa, the other two pockets are in West Bengal located in the northern and southern parts of the state.

Areas of Mh Type

The areas of 'medium grade of maintenance' associated with 'high degree of language shift' comprise 7 districts and form 3 pockets. To the north of the Vl type, there is a pocket consisting of 3 districts-Hazaribagh, Palamau and Dhanbad in Bihar. The second pocket contains the districts of Bankura, Burdwan and Murshidabad while the third pocket has only one district of Howrah in West Bengal.

Areas of Lv Type

There are 14 districts falling under the areas of a low grade of maintenance and very high degree of language shift among the Mundas. The area under this type is fragmented into 8 pockets. All these districts are located on the periphery of the Munda homelands except for Purulia district which is on the Chotanagpur plateau (Fig.23).

4. *Linguistic Typology among the Santals*

Out of a total of 35 districts, there are 4 districts in which cent per cent Santals have retained Santali as their mother tongue. In the remaining 31 districts, the magnitude of variation ranges from 0.71 to

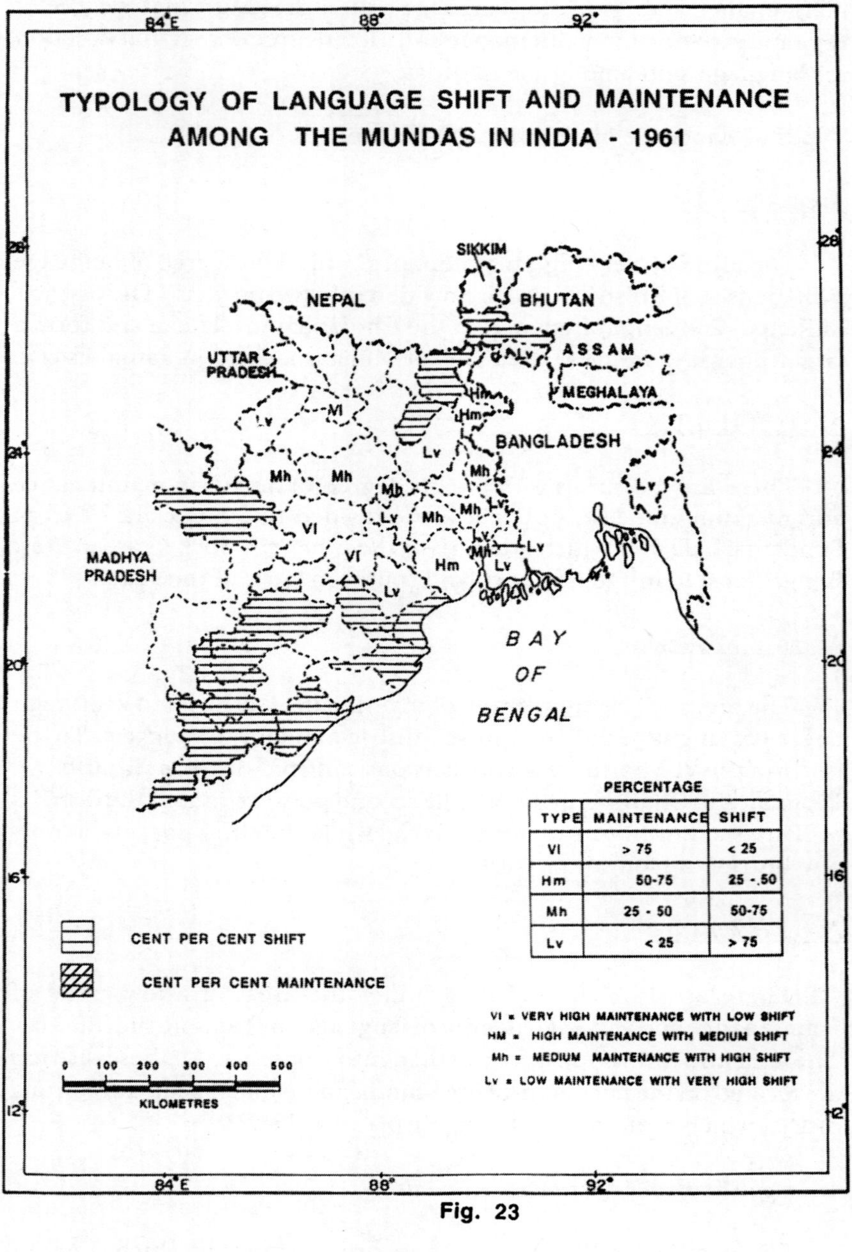
TYPOLOGY OF LANGUAGE SHIFT AND MAINTENANCE AMONG THE MUNDAS IN INDIA - 1961
84°E
88°
92°
SIKKIM
NEPAL
BHUTAN
ASSAM
MEGHALAYA
UTTAR PRADESH
BANGLADESH
MADHYA PRADESH
BAY OF BENGAL
PERCENTAGE
TYPE MAINTENANCE SHIFT
Vl > 75 < 25
Hm 50-75 25 -.50
Mh 25 - 50 50-75
Lv < 25 > 75
CENT PER CENT SHIFT
CENT PER CENT MAINTENANCE
Vl = VERY HIGH MAINTENANCE WITH LOW SHIFT
HM = HIGH MAINTENANCE WITH MEDIUM SHIFT
Mh = MEDIUM MAINTENANCE WITH HIGH SHIFT
Lv = LOW MAINTENANCE WITH VERY HIGH SHIFT
0 100 200 300 400 500
KILOMETRES

Fig. 23

99.28 per cent. Among these districts, 19 have been classified as the areas of 'very high degree of maintenance' and 7 as the areas of 'high degree of maintenance'. Of the remaining 5 districts,'medium degree of language maintenance' has been found in 2 whereas 3 may be classified under 'low degree of maintenance'.

There are 31 districts in which the magnitude of language shift varies from less than 1 to more than 99 per cent barring the districts of Puri and Sundargarh in which almost cent per cent Santals have shifted from their traditional language to the non-Santali languages. There are 19 districts which may be classified under the areas with 'low degree of language shift'. There are 7 districts with a medium degree of shift; 2 districts with high, and another 3 districts with very high degree of language shift (Table-31)

Table-31
TYPOLOGY OF LANGUAGE SHIFT AND MAINTENANCE AMONG THE SANTALS

% Category	Type	No. of Dist.	Name of District
> 75	(Vl)	19	Monghyr, Singhbhum, Darjeeling, West Dinajpur, Murshidabad, Nadia, Hooghly, Burdwan, Birbhum, Bankura, Midnapore, Balasore, Mayurbhanj, Tripura, Bhagalpur, Santal Parganas, Hazaribagh, Ranchi, Dhanbad,
50-75	(Hm)	7	Jalpaiguri, Calcutta, Howrah, Purulia, Ganjam, Keonjhar, Dhenkanal,
25-50	(Mh)	2	Cooch Behar, 24- Parganas
< 25	(Lv)	3	Gaya, Palamau, Koraput

100 % **Maintenance** in Saharsa, Purnea, Malda, Cuttuck.
100 % **shift** in Puri, Sundargarh.

The value of the coefficient of variance is 39.57 indicating lower regional variation in language maintenance while the value for the shift is 109 indicating very high degree of regional variation for the language shift among the Santals.

Types of Language Shift and Maintenance

Areas of Vl Type

There are three pockets consisting of 19 districts falling under this type. The largest pocket comprised 16 districts in the Chotanagpur

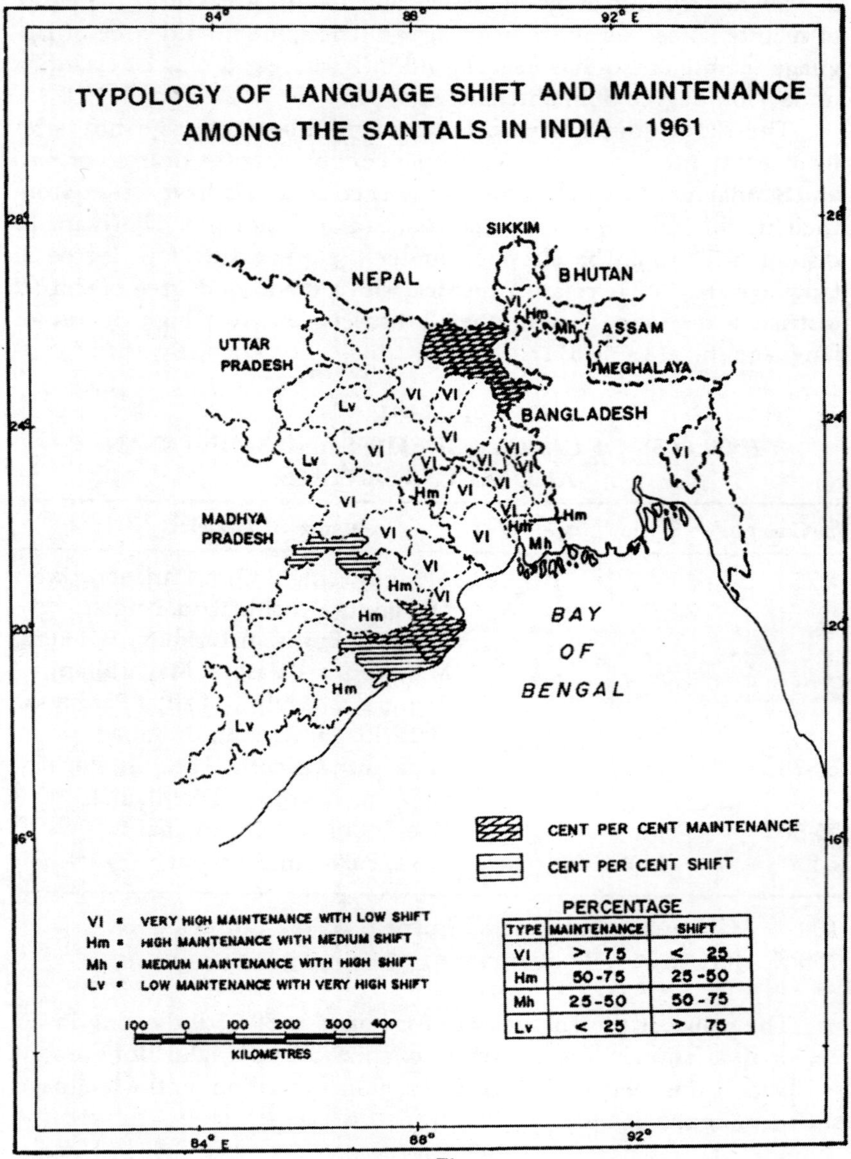
TYPOLOGY OF LANGUAGE SHIFT AND MAINTENANCE
AMONG THE SANTALS IN INDIA - 1961
SIKKIM
NEPAL
BHUTAN
ASSAM
MEGHALAYA
UTTAR PRADESH
BANGLADESH
MADHYA PRADESH
BAY OF BENGAL
CENT PER CENT MAINTENANCE
CENT PER CENT SHIFT
VI = VERY HIGH MAINTENANCE WITH LOW SHIFT
Hm = HIGH MAINTENANCE WITH MEDIUM SHIFT
Mh = MEDIUM MAINTENANCE WITH HIGH SHIFT
Lv = LOW MAINTENANCE WITH VERY HIGH SHIFT
PERCENTAGE
TYPE MAINTENANCE SHIFT
VI > 75 < 25
Hm 50-75 25-50
Mh 25-50 50-75
Lv < 25 > 75
100 0 100 200 300 400
KILOMETRES

Fig. 24

region. This pocket extends to the north and east of the Chotanagpur region. Another pocket is located in Darjeeling district in the northern part of West Bengal. Tripura, forming the third pocket, is located away from the mainland.

Areas of Hm Type

There are 5 small pockets with 'high degree of language maintenance' with 'low degree of shift' among the Santals. Except for Purulia district which is in the midst of the Vl type in the Chotanagpur region, the other two pockets are south of the Vl type located in Orissa. The remaining two pockets of this type are located in West Bengal comprising Calcutta and Howrah districts in the south and Jalpaiguri district in the northern part of the state.

Areas of Mh Type

There are only two districts namely, Cooch Behar and 24-Parganas of West Bengal which have been classified under the areas of 'medium degree of language maintenance' with 'high degree of language shift' among the Santals.

Areas of Lv Type

There are two pockets consisting of 3 districts in which 'low degree of maintenance' is associated with 'very high degree of language shift'. One consists of the districts of Gaya and Palamau in Bihar and the other pocket is in Koraput district in Orissa. (Fig.24).

The study of the typology of language shift and maintenance reveals that the areas of 'very high language maintenance' with 'low degree of shift' (Vl) type are located in the core areas of the tribal heartland whereas the areas of the 'low grades of language maintenance' with 'very high degree of shift' (Lv) type are on the periphery of the tribal homelands. The areas of 'high degree of maintenance with medium shift' (Hm) type and the medium grade of maintenance with high shift (Mh) types are located in between the Vl and Lv types. Some irregularities in the patterns of distribution of these types may also be noticed. These are mainly, due to the establishment of industrial plants and the development of urban centres in the tribal regions of the country.

The values of the coefficient of variance for language maintenance revealed that regional variation is least among the Santals followed by the Korkus, the Mundas and the Bhils while the values for language shift indicate lowest regional variation among the Bhils followed by the

Mundas, the Korkus and the Santals. The Santals, in comparison with the other tribals, have shown the highest degree of regional variation in the magnitude of language shift. On the other hand , the Bhils have shown the lowest degree of regional variation in the magnitude of language maintenance.

Chapter 6

DETERMINANTS AND CORRELATES OF LANGUAGE SHIFT

6.1 **Introduction**

As has already been pointed out in the earlier chapter, the processes of language shift do not operate with equal intensity everywhere. There exist regional as well as social variations in the degree of the shift. The magnitude of these variations may be determined by a number of linguistic and extra linguistic parameters such as linguistic diversity, linguistic exposure, bilingualism, change of religion and work-force and migration,etc. The first section of this chapter deals with some linguistic parameters to understand their effects on the process of language shift while in the second, an attempt has been made to establish the relationship between a set of socio-economic variables and language shift among the tribal people in India. It is assumed that the higher the degree of linguistic exposure the more will be the degree of linguistic diversity leading to language shift. In other words, tribals with a high degree of linguistic exposure to non-tribal languages may have a greater opportunity to switch over from their traditional language to non-traditional ones. On the other hand, linguistically homogenous tribal groups may have a greater chance of retaining their old language.

Linguistic association also indicates the state of language shift among the tribal population in India. A close association with the parental or traditional language indicates resistance to language shift while a close association with the cultivated languages of other linguistic groups may lead to language shift. The Oraons, for example, have no association with their parental groups of languages of the Dravidian family-rather, they have been closely associated with the Indo-Aryan and the Austric languages of the Chotanagpur region. As a result, many of them have declared either the Indo-Aryan or the Austric languages as their mother tongue (Ishtiaq, 1985: 75).

Language dependence is another factor leading to language shift. If a tribal group, for all practical purposes (i.e., education, literature, vernacular and medium of instruction, etc.), depends on other linguistic groups, it is likely to have a high degree of language shift. The degree of maintenance would be more among those groups who have developed their own literature and depend mainly on their own language. The Santals and the Khasis may be cited as examples: they have been using their traditional language not only for day-to-day activities but also for educational purposes and have developed their own literature. The restricted use of the non-traditional languages among these tribal groups led to a high degree of retention of their traditional language.

6.2 Linguistic Diversity

Linguistic diversity commonly prevails in a multilingual society. It helps to identify the size of linguistic groups, their regional distribution and their socio-cultural conditions (Dasgupta, 1970). The tribal people of India, as a result of interaction with other linguistic groups, may reflect various levels of linguistic diversity. Linguistic diversity may vary from individual to society and also among societies. For example, the Mundas of Ranchi town, the Bhils of Banswara town and the Korkus of Punasa, Udaipur, Richhi and Pangra villages use different languages in different domains. They speak their traditional dialect at home and the regional language or Hindi outside their homes. The people of the above areas use more than 50 per cent words of subsidiary languages. Thus, these may be classified as the areas of high diversity. On the other hand, the Mundas of Litingdih, the Bhils of Wanerapara, Umedgarhi, Nai Abadi, Regania and the Santals of Dumka town may be classified under the medium category of linguistic diversity. In these areas the share of tribes using words of subsidiary languages varies from 25 to 50 per cent. A low degree of linguistic diversity has been noticed among the Korkus of Kalamkala and Kutbi and among the Mundas of Kula Buru and Bande villages. In these villages the percentage of users of words of subsidiary languages was less than 25 per cent.

The above classification of linguistic diversity is based on the investigations carried out during field-work. The knowledge of words of subsidiary languages among these tribes ranges from zero among the Korkus in Mirpur village to almost cent per cent among the Korkus of Punasa, Richhi, and Udaipur villages of Khandwa Tehsil and among the Mundas of Ranchi town and among the Bhils of Banswara town. The percentage variation has been classified into three categories : areas of high diversification, medium diversification and low diversification. Areas with more than 50 per cent of people using words of subsidiary languages along with their mother tongue have been classified as areas of high diversification while the areas with less than 25 per cent may be classified as the areas of low diversification. Areas where 25 to 50 per cent of people speak words of subsidiary languages may be considered as the areas of a medium degree of linguistic diversification (Table- 32).

Table-32
AREAS OF LINGUISTIC DIVERSITY

% Category	Type	Areas
> 75	High	*Town* : Ranchi, Banswara; *Village* : Punasa, Udaipur, Richhi, Pangra
25-75	Medium	*Town* : Dumka *Village* : Wanera Para, Umedgarhi, Nai Abadi, Regania, Litingdih
< 25	Low	*Village* : Kalamkala, Kutbi, Kula Buru, Bande

6.3 **Linguistic Exposure**

The purpose of this section is, basically, to measure the degree of linguistic exposure in order to understand the patterns of language shift among different tribal communities. The index values have also been used for a comparative analysis between a) the tribal groups and b) within members of the same tribe in different domains. Since the degree of exposure cannot be measured through percentages, a method has been developed to measure the degree of linguistic exposure. In this method, the index value varies from 0 to 1. Values close to 0 indicate a high degree of exposure while values close to 1 indicate minimum exposure(Green berg, 1956). The method may be expressed by the following formula :

$$E = 1 - \frac{\Sigma(m + f)^2}{n}$$

where E = exposure index;
m = exposure in unity for males;
f = exposure in unity for females;
n = number of age-sex groups in a village.

Note : To obtain unity, the average percentage is divided by 100.

Methodological Procedure

The data for this exercise have been generated from the household survey by giving a set of Hindi words to the tribal people of different age groups and different sexes. The number of words they knew has been converted into a percentage form for all age groups and sexes. An average of percentages for different age groups and sexes is calculated separately in different columns. These percentages have been divided by 100 to bring unity among the variables. These values have been squared, added and then divided by the number of age-groups. Finally, they have been subtracted from 1. The procedure of its calculation is illustrated below.

Table-33
ILLUSTRATION FOR CALCULATING EXPOSURE INDEX

Village	Age and Sex group							
Age Group	00-19		20-39		40-59		60 +	
Sex Group	M	F	M	F	M	F	M	F
Mean	62	54.5	76	41	82.8	51.5	39	25
Mean/100	.62	.55	.76	.41	.83	.52	.39	.25
Sq. root	.38	.30	.58	.17	.67	.27	.15	.06

Total of all age and sex groups = 2.50

Total/8 or 2.50/8 = 0.31

Index value = 1 - 0.31 = 0.69

The findings of this exercise revealed that there are 4 villages namely, Pangra, Punasa, Udaipur, and Richhi in which cent per cent Korkus are exposed to Hindi. On the other hand, the Korkus of Mirpur and Kutbi villages are least exposed. The exposure index of these two villages are 0.93 and 0.86 respectively. The Korkus of Kalamkala are fairly exposed, the exposure index being 0.65.

Almost cent per cent Bhils of Banswara town are exposed to Hindi whereas the Bhils in Regania, Nai Abadi and Wanera Para are fairly exposed to Hindi. These villages had index values of 0.62, 0.57 and 0.56 respectively. Umedgarhi village falls under the category 'more exposed' as its index value is 0.37.

The Mundas of Ranchi town are the most exposed with the exposure index value of 0.14 whereas the Mundas of Bande and Kula Buru are least exposed to Hindi. The index value for these two villages are 0.79 and 0.94 respectively. The index value for Litingdih village is 0.34. It has been classified as 'more exposed' to Hindi (Table- 34).

Table-34
EXPOSURE INDEX

Index value	Category		Village/Town
0.00	Cent per cent Exposed	*Town* *Village*	: Banswara : Punasa, Udaipur, Richhi, Pangra,
0.00-0.25	Most Exposed	*Town*	: Ranchi
0.25-0.50	More Exposed	*Village*	: Litingdih, Umedgarhi
0.50-0.75	Fair Exposed	*Town* *Village*	: Dumka : Regania, Nai Abadi, Wanera Para, Kalamkala
0.75-1.00	Least Exposed	*Village*	: Bande, Kula Buru, Mirpur, Kutbi

The Santals of Dumka town fall under the category 'fairly exposed' to Hindi as their index value is 0.64. The Santals of Surajbeda could not be classified because they were very hostile to outsiders, specially to the Government Officials, and did not provide any information which could be used for this exercise. The school teachers of Murhu Missionary School (at Murhu Block) have also not been included in this exercise because all of them are qualified graduates and have a sufficient knowledge of Hindi (Appendix-VIII).

6.4 **Bilingualism/Multilingualism**

Bilingualism is a world-wide phenomenon. Liberal political development compounded with scientific and technological advancement has brought the multilingual and multi national people of the world in close contact necessitating a bilingual situation. However, this was promoted at a higher speed after the Second World War, especially in the Afro-Asian countries. Weinreich (1953) views bilingualism as "the practice of alternately using two languages". Sharma (1977) looks upon it as a "dual linguistic competence - the potential of performing in two distinct languages". While explaining the ideal bilingual people, Haugen (1972) pointed out that they are "of course, two native speakers rolled inside one skin".

Sociolinguists regard necessity as the mother of bilingualism (which may be motivated by individual, social, cultural, economic or political factors). Jag Dev Singh's view (1977) on Indian bilingualism is similar to the socio-linguists'. In his opinion, "bilingualism is primarily a result of the necessity of establishing linguistic communication between two communities speaking different dialects". Srivastava (1977) believes that job contact, marriage contact, school contact, group living, migration, competitiveness, business and caste identity are some of the important factors leading to Indian bilingualism. Gill (1977) classified Indian bilingualism into two types : market type - marked by linguistic competents of an extremely low level; and secondly, school type - representing the teaching of the language of logic. Misra (1977) underlined the necessity of distinguishing between inter-lingual bilingualism which refers to the knowledge of two different languages (i.e. Tamil and Hindi) and intra-lingual bilingualism which refers to knowledge of a major language and its variant dialect (i.e. Hindi and Maithili). Srivastava (1977) counts the distinctive features of Indian bilingualism as follows :

i) Indian bilingualism at the level of the nation is the result of two distinct internal tendencies - nationism and nationalism;
ii) all major languages are lingua franca but Hindi and English are more functionally potent languages of wider communication;
iii) Indian bilingualism is not merely a realisation of intrinsic demand of its social institutions;
iv) Indian bilingualism brings forward the notion of 'linguistic area' wherein linguistics features transcend genetic boundaries; and
v) the ratio of bilinguals for a given language of India is in inverse proportion to the functional value of that language as a means of wider communication.

The nature and extent of Indian bilingualism reveals that the degree of bilingualism is lower among those languages which have higher functional values. This is evident from the fact that the average percentage of bilingualism in the Hindi region is about 5.12 per cent. The major state languages also show a low proportion of bilingual population. On an average all the major state languages have less than 10 per cent bilingual population. On the other hand, the major non-state languages have 18.84 per cent bilingual population while the share of bilingual population is 42.14 per cent of the population in the case of minor languages (Apte, 1971). People belonging to major linguistic groups have less urge to learn a language other than their own. However, those belonging to minor linguistic groups, specially within the larger linguistic communities, have shown a high degree of bilingualism (Lewis 1972 : 46). In contrast, English which has more functional value represents the highest proportion (i.e., 48%) of bilingual population of India. The reason is undoubtedly because of its extensive domain as against Hindi which has a restricted domain of operation (Srivastava, 1977 : 78). Since the tribal languages of India are confined to the isolated regions and have least functional value, their speakers registered a high degree of bilingualism. On an average, there were about 31 per cent tribes who have declared themselves bilingual according to the 1981 census. About 25 per cent of them lived in rural areas while the remaining 6 per cent lived in urban centres. The bilingual tribal population in India is unevenly distributed. It varies from 5.61 per cent to 64.62 per cent. The least bilingual tribes live in two states : Uttar Pradesh (7.33%) and Rajasthan (5.61 %). The proportion of bilingual tribes varies from 10 to 20 per cent in 4 states/U.T. and from 20 - 40 per cent in another 13 states/U.T. There are 4 states/U.T.-Karnataka, Manipur, Sikkim and Mizoram in which the share of bilingual tribes ranges between 40 and 60 per cent. The highest proportion of bilingual tribes (64.6%) is in Arunachal Pradesh (Fig.25). It is interesting to note that almost the entire bilingual tribal population in the state live in rural areas. Besides, there are two states, Manipur and Sikkim, in which the share of rural bilingual tribes is also high (46.88 per cent and 52.78 per cent respectively). Rural bilingualism varies from 20 - 40 per cent in 10 states/U.T. and from 10-20 per cent in another 8 states/U.T. The least bilingual rural tribes are reported from Rajasthan, Uttar Pradesh and Lakshdweep (3.99 per cent, 5.18 per cent and 4.99 per cent respectively) (Fig. 26). The highest shares of bilingual urban tribal population have been reported from Meghalaya (19.81 %), Mizoram (15.54%), and Karnataka (14.56%). There are 5 states/U.T.-Kerala, Maharashtra, Tamilnadu, Goa, Daman & Diu and Lakshdweep in which the share of urban bilingual tribes varies from 8 to 12 per cent. The least degree of urban bilingualism was reported from Madhya Pradesh, Rajasthan, Andaman & Nicobar Islands and Arunachal Pradesh followed by Andhra Pradesh, Bihar, Himachal Pradesh, Orissa, Tripura, Uttar Pradesh, West Bengal, and Dadar & Nagar Haveli in which only 2 to 4 per cent tribes from urban areas have registered as bilingual. There are another 4 states/U.T. in which the share of urban bilingual tribes varies from 4 to 8 per cent (Table-35).

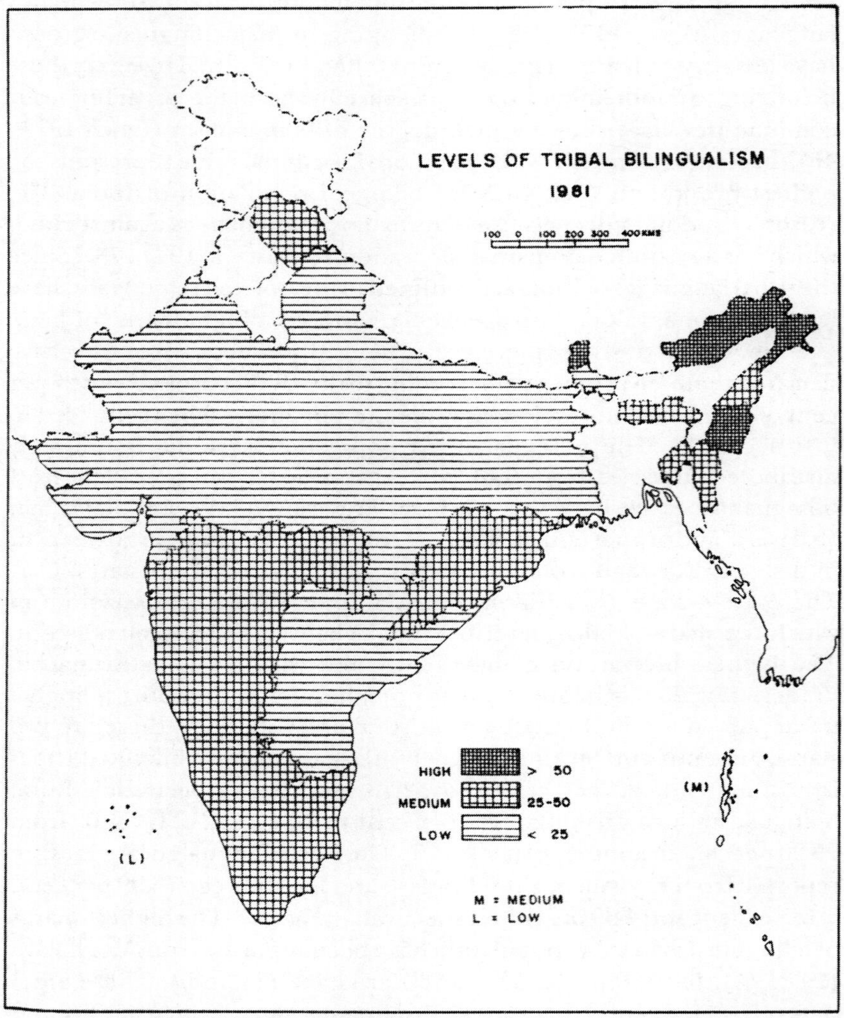
LEVELS OF TRIBAL BILINGUALISM
1981
100 0 100 200 300 400KMS
HIGH > 50
MEDIUM 25-50
LOW < 25
(M)
(L)
M = MEDIUM
L = LOW

Fig. 25

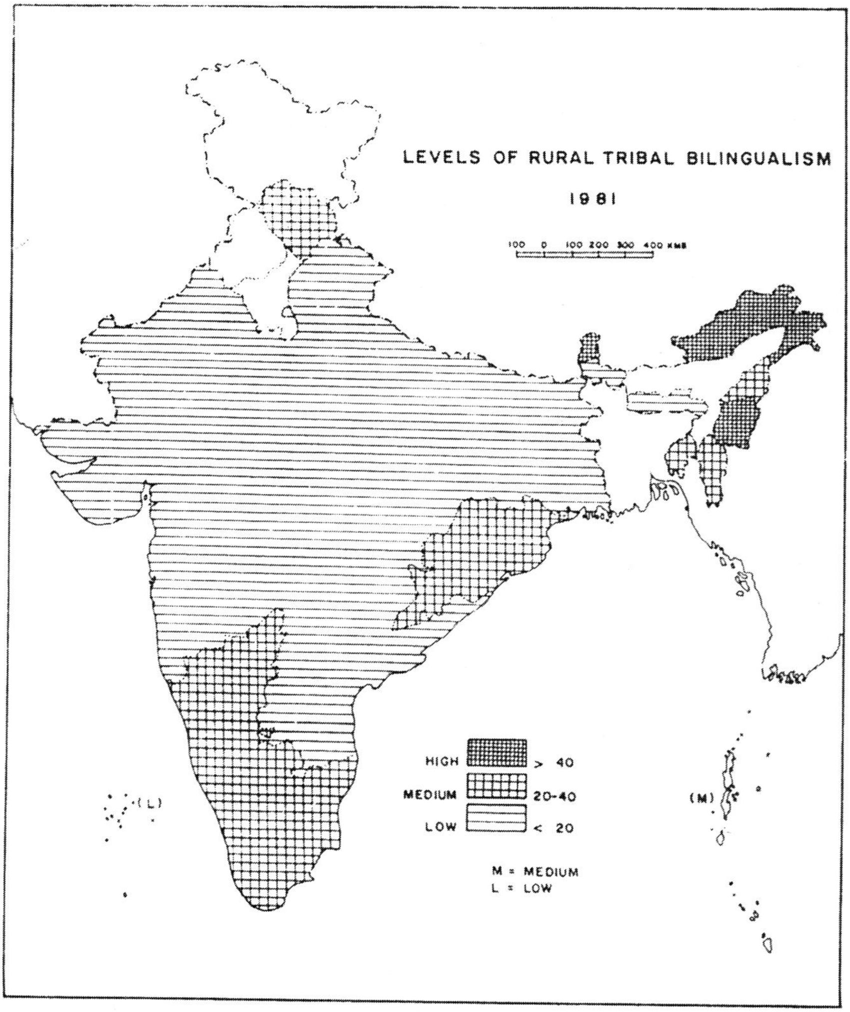
LEVELS OF RURAL TRIBAL BILINGUALISM
1981
100 0 100 200 300 400 KMS
HIGH > 40
MEDIUM 20-40
LOW < 20
M = MEDIUM
L = LOW
(L)
(M)

Fig. 26

Table-35
PERCENTAGE OF BILINGUAL TRIBAL POPULATION- 1981

States	Total	Rural	Urban
Andhra Pradesh	20.81	18.27	2.54
Bihar	19.91	16.13	3.78
Gujarat	15.66	10.69	4.97
Himachal Pradesh	28.21	25.19	3.02
Karnataka	44.86	30.30	14.56
Kerala	31.68	23.28	8.40
Madhya Pradesh	17.11	15.17	1.92
Maharashtra	27.19	16.77	10.42
Manipur	51.84	46.88	4.96
Meghalaya	33.10	13.29	19.81
Nagaland	37.45	33.08	4.37
Orissa	28.42	26.37	2.05
Rajasthan	5.61	3.99	1.62
Sikkim	59.06	52.78	6.28
Tamil Nadu	32.76	23.38	9.38
Tripura	37.18	35.17	2.01
Uttar Pradesh	7.33	5.18	2.15
West Bengal	21.81	18.24	3.57
Andaman & Nicobar Islands	36.11	35.14	0.97
Arunachal Pradesh	64.62	64.31	0.31
Dadra & Nagar Haveli	32.44	30.26	2.18
Goa, Daman & Diu	20.29	10.92	9.37
Lakshdweep	13.64	4.99	8.65
Mizoram	45.81	30.27	15.54

Source: Census of India, 1981, Sr. I, INDIA, **Special Tables for Scheduled Tribes on Mother Tongue and Bilingualism,** Pt. IX (ii)

Bilingualism has been considered to be one of the most important determinants of language shift. Language shift, in its initial stage, starts with the borrowing of words from one language to another gradually leading to the state of bilingualism which gradually leads to the shift. The process of bilingualism leading to the shift may be noticed among the tribal population in India. The study revealed that those tribes who moved out of their majority areas in search of livelihood, setting down either on marginal land or in urban centres became bilingual before switching over to the non-tribal languages.

The studies of bilingualism among the tribal population in India revealed that a little more than half of them are bilingual (Royburman, 1972 and Prasad, 1993). But it is also a fact that the nature and the patterns of bilingualism and multilingualism vary across tribes and regions. Variations between the sexes and across age groups also exist. In other words, younger sections of the population may have a higher incidence of bilingualism; it is also more prominent among the male than among the female population. The study of bilingualism among the selected tribal groups revealed that the percentage of bilingualism varies from 0 in Mirpur to 100 per cent among the Mundas of Ranchi town, the Korkus of Udaipur, Richhi, Pangra and Punasa village and the Bhils of Banswara town. The lowest share of bilingual population is reported among the Mundas of Bande village, the Korkus of Kalamkala and Kutbi villages and the Santals of Surajbeda village. In these areas, less than 25 per cent of the population is bilingual. The percentage of bilingual population varies from 25 to 50 among the Bhils of Regania, Nai Abadi and Wanera Para villages, the Mundas of Litingdih and the Santals of Dumka town. These areas are classified under 'low degree of bilingualism'. A 'fairly high' degree of bilingual population prevails among the Bhils in Umedgarhi village (Appendix- IX).

A comparative analysis of bilingualism revealed that the incidence of bilingualism among the Korkus of East Nimar district and the Mundas of Ranchi district is higher than among the Bhils of Banswara district and the Santals of Santal Parganas. On the other hand, the degree of multilingualism among the Santals and the Bhils is less than among the Mundas. On an average, the Mundas recorded 3.9 per cent multilingual population which is followed by the Santals with 1.8 per cent and the Bhils with 1.0 per cent. None of the Korku tribal population of the study area is multilingual.

6.5 **Correlates of Language Shift**

Language shift does not take place independently or in isolation-rather, it depends on a many changes in socio-economic and other cultural phenomena. In other words, it can be argued that language shift is promoted by a number of factors such as urbanization, literacy, change of work-force from primary to non-primary sectors of economy, change in traditional belief, migration, etc. The male and adult sections of population are also considered cogents in bringing about such a change. Factors which are considered to be explanatory variables for linguistic shift among the tribal population are defined and explained as follows:

Proportion of Tribal Population

It is expected that the smaller the ratio of the tribal population to total population in an area, the more likely, tribals are to switch over to non-tribal languages and to declare them as their mother tongue, abandoning their traditional languages. It is, therefore, assumed that the lower the percentage of tribal to total population, the higher the degree of language shift. On the other hand, a low degree of language shift may be associated with high concentration of the tribal population in an area.

Levels of urbanization

The development of urban centres in the tribal areas has been regarded as an important factor in bringing about language shift among the native people. In other words, there is a direct relationship between the levels of urbanization and language shift. This means that the higher the levels of urbanization in an area, the higher the degree of language shift.

Besides this, the percentage of tribes living in urban areas is considered to be another important factor leading to language shift. It has been found that those tribes who have already settled in urban centres and became part and parcel of the urban environment have already declared the non-tribal language as their mother tongue. These urban tribals have lost their cultural identity because they could not maintain contact with their traditional people who still live in hilly and forest areas and preserve their cultural identity. It is, therefore, assumed that the percentage of tribals living in urban areas may have a positive relationship with language shift.

Economic Condition

It is also found that economically well-off groups among the tribal people are more inclined to language shift than the 'low income group'. The rich tribals are more mobile and visit market centres frequently. Here they come across people of different cultures and languages. They also send their children to schools in which they are taught either in English or in the regional language. Above all, in order to maintain the hierarchy in their tribal society as well as to feel closer to the national mainstream, they consciously declare the non-tribal languages as their mother tongue. For the purpose of analysis, this variable is defined as per capita income of the tribal population. It is, therefore, expected that higher per capita income may indicate a higher degree of language shift among the tribal population.

Literacy

This is the most important vehicle of socio-economic and cultural transformation. With an increase in tribal literacy, many changes have occurred in tribal societies. One of the major changes is linguistic shift. It has been found that in most of the tribal areas, education is imparted through the non-tribal languages. Consequently, tribals of the younger generation are switching over to the non-tribal languages and declaring them as their mother tongue, abandoning their parental language. It is therefore, assumed that a higher percentage of literacy among the tribals may lead to a higher degree of language shift whereas language shift may have a negative relationship with the extent of illiteracy among the tribals.

Change in Traditional Occupation

This is another economic variable which brings about language shift among the tribal population. It has been noticed that with the growth of urban centres in tribal areas, a section of the tribal work-force has been engaged in the non-traditional economic sector, i.e., secondary and tertiary activities. This leads to a long association with the non-tribal population in these sectors which led to a number of changes including language shift. For the purpose of analysis, this variable is defined as the percentage of tribes engaged in the non-primary sectors. It is expected that the number of tribals engaged in these sectors may have a positive relationship with language shift whereas the extent of the shift may have a negative relationship with the number of tribals engaged in the primary sector.

Change in Traditional Belief

The conversion of the tribal population to Christianity and Hinduism has had a great bearing on the nature and the patterns of language shift among them. Most of the tribal population of north-east India, who embraced Christianity, have declared English as their mother tongue while the tribes of other regions registered different regional languages as a result of their conversion to Hinduism. It is, therefore, assumed here that the percentage of converted tribals may have a positive relationship with language shift. Those who preserve their tribal religion are more likely to retain their traditional languages.

Age and Sex

Age and sex are the two important demographic variables which may be studied in order to explain the variations in the magnitude of language shift among the tribal communities. It has been noticed that the young and adult sections of the tribal population who are under 45 years of age are mentally prepared to welcome such a change while the older people used to give importance to their traditional culture and old social values and did not want to accept any change. Similarly, males are more active than females in bringing about social change. It has also been found that the pace of the change among the male population is faster than among the female. For the purpose of analysis, these variables are defined as percentage of male population to total tribal population and secondly, the percentage of tribals under 45 years of age. It is expected that both these variables may have a positive relationship with language shift whereas the older generation and the female population may have a negative relationship with language shift.

An Empirical Explanation : Correlation and Regression

An examination of a scatter diagram of dependent (Y) and independent (Xs) variables revealed that there is almost a linear relationship between them. Therefore, it can be argued that a linear model of cause and effect may be employed to assess the magnitude and direction of language shift. The most suitable method to evaluate the degree of language shift through this model is stepwise regression. This is a forward addition method in which the explanatory variables are included stepwise on the basis of their partial coefficient till the R^2 starts decreasing.

Correlation Analysis

The correlation matrix given in table- 36 is based on the secondary data derived from the census at the district level. The table shows the relationship between dependent and independent variables as well as among the independent variables. From this correlation matrix, it is evident that none of the correlation coefficients between dependent and independent variables are very high. This simply implies that the relationship between dependent and independent variables is weak. Out of the 9 independent variables, 6 (percentage of urban population, percentage of tribals in urban areas, percentage of tribals engaged in non-primary activities, percentage of Hindu tribals, percentage of male tribals and percentage of tribals under 45 years of age) are positively correlated with the dependent variable (language shift). The remaining 3 independent variables (i.e., percentage of tribals to total population, percentage of literate tribals and percentage of Christian tribals) have a negative correlation with language shift. The values of the correlation coefficients vary from +0.235 to -0.257. Since these values are not close to 1, there does not exist a strong relationship between the dependent and the independent variables. It is important to note that the percentage of literate tribals and the percentage of Christian tribals are negatively correlated with language shift. In fact these two variables are important factors and are expected to have a positive correlation with the shift.

Table-36
CORRELATION MATRIX
(Based on District Level Data)

	% of Lang. shift(Y)	% of Urban pop.(X 1)	% of Tribals to total pop.(X 2)	% of Urban tribals (X 3)	% of Tribals in N.P. Sect.(X 4)	% of Tribals literate (X 5)	% of Hindu tribals (X 6)	% of Christian tribals (X 7)	% of Male tribals (X 8)	% of Tribals under 45 (X 9)
Y	1.00									
X1	0.079	1.00								
X2	-0.257*	-0.141	1.00							
X3	0.151**	0.587*	-0.172**	1.00						
X4	0.160	0.434*	-0.252*	0.690*	1.00					
X5	-0.026	0.363*	-0.066	0.563*	0.457*	1.00				
X6	0.235*	-0.061	-0.065	0.071	-0.012	-0.271*	1.00			
X7	-0.182**	0.097	0.014	0.150	0.063	0.368*	-0.882*	1.00		
X8	0.025	0.317*	-0.093	0.160	0.252*	0.130	0.013	0.008	1.00	
X9	0.115**	-0.093	0.119	0.031	0.053	0.187	0.031	0.019	-0.151**	1.00

* Significant at 0.01 level
** Significant at 0.05 level

Regression Analysis

The regression equation presented below gives the result according to the percentage of variation explained by the linear function.

$$Y = -149.96 \quad -0.7693\,X2^{*} \quad +1.18543\,X6^{*} \quad +1.9942\,X9^{**} \quad +0.21949\,X3^{**}$$

$$(-0.23702) \qquad (0.22421) \qquad (0.12359) \qquad (0.12268)$$

$R^2 = 0.1474$

* partial regression coefficient significant at 99 per cent level of confidence;

** partial regression coefficient significant at 90 per cent level of confidence; and

where Y = percentage of tribes speaking non-traditional language (Language shift);

X2 = Percentage of tribal to total population;

X3 = percentage of urban tribals to the total tribal population;

X6 = percentage of Hindu tribals to the total tribal population;

X9 = percentage of tribals under 45 years of age;

Note : The figures in parentheses are standard regression coefficients.

The analysis of the regression equation revealed that all the significant variables included here can be explained by 14.7 per cent variation in the degree of language shift. Although the power of the explanatory variables is very low, two of them are significant at 99 per cent and the remaining two are significant at 90 per cent level of confidence. The variables which emerged as significant in order of their standard regression coefficients are percentage of tribals to total population, percentage of Hindu tribals, percentage of tribals under 45 years of age and percentage of urban tribals to the total tribal population. The concentration of tribal population in an area emerged as the most important variable affecting language shift. In other words, holding all the other variables constant, the percentage of tribals to total population (X2) explained the highest proportion of variation in the dependent variable (Y) although it has a negative regression coefficient. Almost the same magnitude of variation in Y has been explained by the percentage of Hindu tribals (X6). The third position is taken by the percentage of tribals under 45 years of age (X9). This variable contributed as much as 57 per cent of the contribution of the X2 variable. Almost as large a contribution is made by the percentage of urban tribals (X3).

From the above discussion, it can be concluded that a great deal of variation in the dependent variable remains to be explained. It is also interesting to note that some of the important variables such as literacy, sex, Christianity, etc., did not play any role in explaining the magnitude of variation in the degree of linguistic shift among the tribes although they are considered effective variables. This might have happened due to the following reasons :

a) Inaccuracy in the collection of data for the tribal population: The out-of-the-way locations of the tribal villages do not encourage enumerators to collect data from door to door. Rather, in most cases, approximate figures are given in the census. These may not lead us to the proposed assumptions.
b) There may be an error in defining the tribal language with which they were traditionally attached and the non- traditional languages which have been declared by them as their mother tongue.
c) Due to the growing linguistic consciousness among the tribal population as a result of language regionalism and language politics, the collection of data for tribal languages has not only become a difficult exercise but also may lead to some erroneous conclusions.

It is to be noted here that the primary data which have been derived at the household level from the field survey have been found to be more affective in explaining the relationship between dependent and independent variables.

Correlation Analysis

The correlation matrix given in table- 37 is based on the primary data generated at the household level through field work. The table revealed that there exists a high correlation between dependent and independent variables. Out of all the independent variables, 3 (percentage of literate tribals, percentage of tribals engaged in non-primary activity, and per capita income) have been found to be positively correlated with the dependent variable. The remaining two independent variables (percentage of male tribals and the percentage of tribals under 40 years of age) have a negative correlation with the dependent variable. The values of the correlation coefficients range from +0.59 to -0.103. The relationship between the dependent variable and two independent variables (literacy and per capita income) is strong. This is evident from the values of correlation coefficients (0.59 in the case of literacy and 0.51 in the case of per capita income). The correlation between the dependent variable and the number of tribals in the non-primary sector is positive but not very strong. The value of the correlation coefficient in this case is only 0.34. The remaining two independent variables have not only weak but also negative correlations with the dependent variable. The values of their correlation coefficients are -0.26 in the case of percentage of male tribals and -0.10 in the case of tribals under 40 years of age group.

Table-37
CORRELATION MATRIX
(Based on Household Data)

	% of bilingual (Y)	**% of literate (X1)**	**% of non-primary workers (X2)**	**Per capita income (X3)**	**% of males (X4)**	**% under 45 of age (X5)**
Y	1.00					
X1	0.59*	1.00				
X2	0.34	0.33**	1.00			
X3	0.51***	0.58*	0.72*	1.00		
X4	-0.26	-0.35**	-0.06	-0.21	1.00	
X5	-0.10	-0.03	-0.17	-0.23	-0.07	1.00

* Significant at 0.01 level
*** Significant at 0.15 level

Regression Analysis

The regression equations for the field data are presented below :

$$Y = 23.23 + 0.39654\ X2^{*} + 0.03572\ X3^{***}$$
$$(0.44537) \qquad (0.25109)$$

R^2 = 0.39066

* = significant at 99 per cent level of confidence;
*** = significant at 85 per cent level of confidence;
where Y = percentage of bilingual tribals to total tribal population;
X1 = percentage of literate tribals to the total tribal population;
X3 = per capita household income of tribal population;

Note : Figures in parentheses are standard regression coefficients.

The results of the regression equation show that literacy and income are the only two important variables that caused the variation in the dependent variable Y. The former variable (X1) is significant at 99 per cent level of confidence while the latter, i.e., per capita income (X3) is significant at 85 per cent level of confidence. These two variables together explained 39.1 per cent variation in the dependent variable (Y). While excluding the second variable (X3) from the regression analysis, the contribution of X1 remained 34.9 per cent. This means that the inclusion of X3 improved explanatory power by only 4.2 per cent. This is further confirmed by the magnitude of the standard regression coefficient of these variables. This implies that at the household level, literacy has emerged as the most important and, perhaps, the only factor which explained the variation in Y.

The study of the two sets of results from regression analysis very clearly indicated that there is some inaccuracy in the secondary data particularly in the case of literacy which has a negative relationship with language shift. On the basis of the primary data, literacy shows the highest relationship with the dependent variable and emerged as the single most important variable which explained about 34.9 per cent variation in Y. It should also be noted that the regression model at the household level had much more explanatory power than the secondary data.

6.6 Explaining the Unexplained

The foregoing empirical study revealed that about 15 per cent of language shift (dependent variable) can be explained through the secondary data at the district level while 39.1 per cent is explicable through the primary data at the household level. This implies that the independent variables which have been selected for the explanation of language shift are not very effective. This means that there are certain other factors playing a dominant role which could not be included in the present model. The most important and unaccounted explanatory variables which may be suspected and deduced on theoretical grounds are the location of the tribal areas and their accessibility to the non-tribal areas, distance from urban centres, distance from communication lines, etc. In the light of the above argument; a small exercise has been attempted, basically to find out how much locational proximity explains the variations in the degree of language shift among the tribal population. In order to do this, the share of the tribal population in the villages surrounding the tribal villages has been calculated to determine if the village is predominantly tribal or non-tribal or a mixed type. A village with more than 75 per cent tribal population is predominantly tribal whereas the villages with less than 25 per cent tribal population are predominantly non-tribal. If the share of the tribal or the non-tribal population in a village varies between 25 and 75 per cent, it may be classified as a mixed type. Besides, the distance of a village from the nearest town and communication lines and the nature of the terrain of the village are also taken into account (Appendix- X).

The study of locational proximity revealed that the variation in the magnitude of language shift in the study area is, perhaps, mainly due to locational factors. Even if a village has a small tribal population but is located in the tribal dominated area, its population retains its traditional tongue while a village with a large tribal population located in the non-tribal dominated area shows linguistic shift from their traditional language to the non-traditional languages. In other words, a tribal village surrounded by predominantly non-tribal villages may show a high degree of shift in the traditional language while a tribal village (even with only a small number of tribals) in the midst of other tribal villages may have witnessed the retention of the traditional language. For example, Punasa, Richhi, Udaipur and Pangra villages are surrounded by the non-tribal villages and have shown a shift in their traditional dialect. The regional language known as Nimadi has been declared by them as their mother tongue. On the other hand, the remaining villages which are surrounded by tribal villages maintained their traditional language. The other parameters such as distance from the nearest town, communication line, and the nature of the terrain did not lead to any conclusion in explaining the degree of language shift among the tribes. It, therefore, may be concluded that nearness to the non-tribal villages is one of the most important and effective correlates emerging from this exercise.

Chapter 7

LANGUAGE SHIFT: IMPLICATIONS AND EXPLANATIONS

7.1 Introduction

Adoption of non-tribal languages by the tribal population has two basic implications: 1) assimilation or de-tribalisation and 2) integration. The first implication of language shift among the tribal communities in India indicates that these people are, gradually, being assimilated into the majority linguistic groups of the region in which they live (Doshi, 1972:465). Since language is a strong element, at least among the primitive race, of separate identity and as valuable as religion, its shift among the tribals indicates the loss of tribal identity (Census of India 1931: 231). Royburman's estimation (1972) reveals that more than half of the tribal population of the country has adopted the non-tribal languages either as the first or as the subsidiary language for their communication. Such a tendency, caused, in the opinion of some scholars, by the process of assimilation, may be either due to compulsion or due to external forces exerted by modern society on the tribal people. As a result, along with the vanishing tribal culture, the tribal dialects are also dying out while the domain of the non-tribal languages is expanding. Finally, it may be concluded that the higher the degree of cultural assimilation of the tribal society, the higher is the loss of tribal identity. On the other hand, the tribal identity would have remained intact had they clung to their traditional language.

Another important implication of language shift is integration which refers to the unification and consolidation of the tribal communities. In this process, opportunities are given to the tribals for the development of their culture. Unlike assimilation, the process of integration is not due to external forces or any compulsion-rather, it is a type of voluntary change undertaken in order to become part and parcel of the main-stream of the national culture. Barring a few tribes belonging to the north-eastern region, the majority of the central and southern Indian tribes have undergone the process of integration. The expansion of modern influence, stimulated by the process of exploitation of mineral resources and establishment of industries, commercial and administrative set-ups in the tribal areas, further accelerated the process of national integration. Besides, the Indian Constitution has given special emphasis and preferences to the tribal population. The government is also taking all possible measures to protect and safeguard as well as to promote their culture, art and their identity through both long term and short term planning. These planned interventions, through the process of developing tribal regions, have brought a number of changes including language shift. In other words, a high degree of socio-economic and cultural change indicating high levels of the development may lead to a high degree of language shift among the tribal population. Keeping this in mind, an attempt has been made to evaluate the level of development and its relationship with language shift among the tribal population of eastern India in the following section.

7.2 **Development and Language Shift**

The purpose of this exercise is to establish a relationship between the level of development and the degree of language shift among the tribal communities in the hilly and tribal districts of Bihar and Orissa. This region, a part of the Chotanagpur plateau, is known for a high concentration of the tribal population and bountiful natural resources. The region has emerged as the main focus of industries in India. Extraction of mineral resources led to the development of transport and communication, industrialisation, urbanisation, trade and commerce and migration of skilled and semi-skilled people to the region. As a result , the unplanned tribal huts at the mining centres have been replaced by planned and permanent settlements and the dark jungle has given way to electrified streets. The mining and industrial towns of the region have been linked with roadways,railways and airways in order to facilitate trade and commerce. These developments brought about many socio-economic and cultural changes through the processes of interaction and assimilation.

This region which was isolated, has now been exposed to outsiders. This is to a large extent due to mining activity. The native people (tribals) came in contact with alien people (non-tribals/ outsiders) and the process of interaction and assimilation between them has continued since. The cultural supremacy of the outsiders has left the tribals with no option but to adopt the outsiders' way of life as their own. (Bose, 1977:176). A section of tribals, specially those who were very close to outsiders, had been assimilated into the non-tribal cultural domain and thus it became difficult to distinguish between the assimilated tribals and the non-tribals. Sometimes the extent of assimilation of tribal groups reaches the stage where they do not consider themselves as tribals. On the other hand, the majority of tribals, who are much concerned with their identity and integrity, moved into the interior of the forest to preserve their tribal identity. The former group of tribes displayed almost a complete change in their socio- economic and cultural milieu (Doshi, 1972:471) whereas among the latter group, the pace of change is very slow due to certain tribal cultural restrictions. Nevertheless, the change is taking place among all tribal communities though its magnitude varies across regions and tribes (Ishtiaq, 1991:2). Developmental programmes in this region focused attention on two major issues. The first, as already mentioned, is to exploit the natural resources of the tribal region and the second is to bring the tribal people into the mainstream of the nation. Both national and international social and religious organisations such as missionaries and ashrams entered the tribal homelands to propagate their religions and to provide education, employment and medical facilities. As a result, a large section of the tribals have changed their old belief and embraced Christianity or Hinduism and also adopted English and regional languages of India as their mother tongue.

Methodological Procedure

The selection of indicators becomes very important for such studies in which a set of different social phenomena have to be compared. Indicators of the levels of development may vary for economists, sociologists, geographers, linguists, etc. because in each discipline the problem is looked at from a different angle. In this exercise the following indicators have been selected for determining the level of development.

a) percentage of urban population;
b) percentage of class I and II towns;
c) percentage of non-primary workers to total workers;
d) agricultural productivity per worker;
e) percentage of literate persons ;
f) percentage of enrollment in school/college :
   i. under 9 years of age;
   ii. between 10 - 14
   iii. between 15 - 25
g) number of primary schools per 10,000 children under 9 years of age;
h) number of secondary schools per 10,000 children between 10 and 14 years of age;
i) number of higher institution per 10,000 persons between 15 - 25 years of age;

j) number of hospital beds per 10,000 persons;
k) number of doctors per 100,000 persons.

The above variables have been used for determining the level of development. The language data for the tribal population have been classified into the following categories :

a) percentage of tribes declaring their traditional language as their mother tongue;
b) percentage of tribes declaring non-traditional language as their mother tongue.

The following methods have been applied for data analysis :

i. percentage and ratio have been calculated;
ii. the bias in the indicators has been removed through dividing these variables by the mean ($\overline{x}$) of each column;
iii. Modified Factor Analysis has been used to find out the level of development;
iv. choroplething technique has been used for preparing maps.

Linguistic Affiliation

The languages of the tribals of the region may be classified into three major linguistic groups - the Austric, the Dravidian, and the Indo-Aryan. There are more than 40 languages/dialects registered by the tribes. Out of these, 30 belong to the Austro - Asiatic branch and account for about 39 per cent of the total tribal population in the region. The Indo-Aryan groups of languages have been registered by about 41 per cent of the tribal population. Important languages among them are Hindi, Oriya, Bhojpuri, Magahi, etc. About 20 per cent of the tribes of the region declared languages belonging to the Dravidian family as their mother tongue. Kurukh Oraon, Gondi, Kui, Bhotada, Khond, are important among the Dravidian languages while Santali, Mundari, Savara, Kharia, are important languages belonging to the Austric family. The tribes in Ranchi and its surrounding areas have also declared Sadari/Sadani as their mother tongue. As already mentioned in the second chapter, linguists are yet to decide about the affiliation of this dialect which has been registered only by tribes. It has words belonging to all the three language families. Some linguists have classified it as an Indo-Aryan language because the majority of words in this dialect belong to Hindi and its dialects.

Level of Development

The level of development has been found by using the Modified Factor Analysis propounded by Kundu (1980). This method is based on the following two conditions for the determination of weights for the variables.

i) a higher weightage should be given to those which have a higher interrelationship; and

ii) a variable with a greater disparity in distribution is a more important variable for development and should therefore also be given a greater weightage.

According to this method, the factor loadings are obtained from the eigen vector corresponding to the maximum eigen value of the matrix A.

Where, $A = \frac{X' X}{N}$

Where X' = the transformed data matrix (transformation is done through the division by mean) having N observations and m variables.

After the factor loadings for the different variables have been obtained each variable is multiplied with its respective weightage and the addition of the group of weighted variable gives the composite index. The factor scores, which vary from less than one to more than seven, have been classified into three groups i.e. high, medium and low. It is interesting to note that more than half of the total number of districts in this region have low levels of development. These districts are mostly in the state of Orissa. There are two districts-Ranchi and Dhanbad with factor scores of 4.36 and 7.72 respectively. These districts are considered relatively more developed districts of the region. Factor scores vary from 2 to 4 in five districts which have been classified under medium levels of development (Table - 38 and Fig. 27).

Table-38
LEVELS OF DEVELOPMENT

Factor score	Level	No. of Districts	Districts
Above 4	High	2	Ranchi,Dhanbad
2-4	Medium	5	Hazaribagh, Singhbhum, Sambalpur, Sundargarh, Dhenkanal
Below 2	Low	8	Santal Parganas, Palamau, Kalahandi, Koraput, Bolangir, Baudhkhondmals, Keonjhar, Mayurbhanj

It is necessary to point out here that the classification adopted in this exercise is highly subjective and should not be used as the basis for the measurement of the levels of development in other regions. The classification into high, medium, and low developmental categories has been done only for this region, where not much variation was found. The classification has been done for an easy and simple explanation instead of taking each district separately. In comparison with the other regions of the country, it may be possible that almost all the districts of this region may be classified under the lowest category of development.

Degree of Language Shift

It has been found that a large number of the tribal population of the region declared non-traditional languages (regional, non-regional and other tribal languages) as their mother tongue. The degree of language shift among the tribes varies from below 30 to above 60 per cent in this region. This variation has a direct relationship with the physiographic conditions as well as the nature of the tribal groups. The shift is of a higher order in the districts in the southern part of the region. For example, in the districts of Sambalpur, Dhenkanal, Kalahandi and Bolangir , the degree of language shift is more than 60 per cent. In other words, it can be said that more than 60 per cent of the tribes in these districts have registered Oriya as their mother tongue. More than 60 per cent of the tribes in Palamau district have also declared a non-tribal language (i.e., Hindi) as their mother tongue. The highest degree of language shift has been noticed in the districts of Bolangir and Sambalpur (95% and 81% respectively). On the other hand, the degree of language shift is of a lower order in 7 districts-Ranchi, Hazaribagh, Santal Parganas, Dhanbad, Singhbhum, Baudhkhondmals, and Mayurbhanj. More than 70 per cent of the tribes in these districts retained their traditional dialect as their mother tongue. There are only three districts-Keonjhar, Koraput, and Sundargarh-in which the percentage of language shift varies from 30 to 60 (Fig.28).The degree of language shift has been classified into three categories-high, medium, and low in order to coincide with the categories of the levels of development and to establish a relationship between them (Table- 39).

Table-39
DEGREE OF LANGUAGE SHIFT

Percentage	Level	No. of Districts	Districts
Above 60	High	5	Palamau, Sambalpur, Dhenkanal Bolangir, Kalahandi
30-60	Medium	3	Koraput,Sundargarh,Keonjhar
Below 30	Low	7	Ranchi,Santal Parganas, Hazaribagh, Dhanbad, Singhbhum, Baudhkhondmals, Mayurbhanj

The classification of the degrees of language shift into three categories is again subjective. It has been done for the sake of comparative analysis. The districts in which more than 60 per cent tribes clung to their traditional language have been considered to be the areas of low linguistic shift. On the other hand, high degree of shift occurs in those districts in which more than 60 per cent tribes have declared the non-traditional languages as their mother tongue. A medium degree of language shift has been noticed in the districts in which 30 to 60 per cent tribes declared the non-traditional language as their mother tongue.

Relationship Between Development and Language Shift

The study revealed that there is no relationship between the degree of language shift and the level of development. The relationship between a high degree of language shift with high levels of development is in fact negative. This can be noticed in the following table- 40. The districts of Ranchi and Dhanbad have been classified under high levels of development but the degree of language shift among the tribes in these districts is low. On the other hand, the districts of Palamau, Kalahandi and Bolangir have been classified under low levels of development while linguistically these districts have been categorised under a high degree of language shift. It is also to be noted that the low levels of development in Santal Parganas, Mayurbhanj and Baudhkhondmals districts are

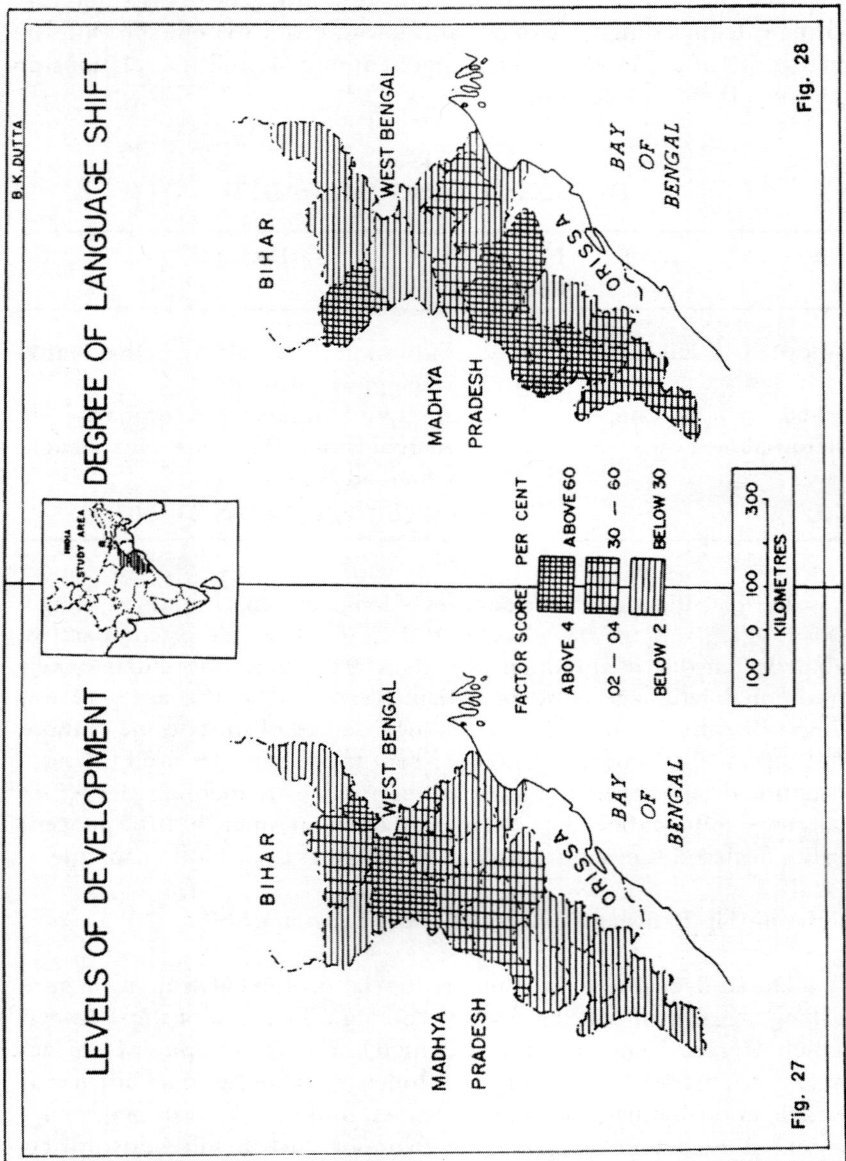
LEVELS OF DEVELOPMENT
DEGREE OF LANGUAGE SHIFT
B.K. DUTTA
INDIA
STUDY AREA
BIHAR
WEST BENGAL
MADHYA PRADESH
ORISSA
BAY OF BENGAL
FACTOR SCORE
PER CENT
ABOVE 4
ABOVE 60
02 — 04
30 — 60
BELOW 2
BELOW 30
100 0 100 300
KILOMETRES

Fig. 27

Fig. 28

related to the low degree of language shift among the tribal communities. The medium level of development is related to the medium degree of language shift only in Sundargarh district whereas it is related to a high degree of the shift in Dhenkanal and Sambalpur districts; and to a low degree of language shift in Hazaribagh and Singhbhum districts. The districts of Koraput and Keonjhar have been classified under low levels of development with a medium degree of language shift. In fact, the relationship between the levels of development and the degree of language shift among the tribes is very confusing.

Table-40
RELATIONSHIP BETWEEN PERCENTAGE OF TRIBALS, LEVELS OF DEVELOPMENT AND DEGREE OF LANGUAGE SHIFT

District	% of tribes to total pop.	Levels of development	Degree of lang. shift
Santal Parganas	38.24	low	low
Ranchi	61.61	high	low
Dhanbad	11.08	high	low
Palamau	19.24	low	high
Hazaribagh	11.30	medium	low
Singhbhum	47.30	medium	low
Kalahandi	33.19	low	high
Koraput	60.89	low	medium
Sambalpur	29.12	medium	high
Bolangir	20.67	low	high
Baudhkhondmals	40.61	low	low
Sundargarh	58. 12	medium	medium
Dhenkanal	13.94	medium	high
Keonjhar	47.14	low	medium
Mayurbhanj	61.61	low	low

7.3 Urbanisation and the Process of Language Shift

Among the various socio-economic and cultural processes promoting interaction, integration and assimilation, the role of urbanisation cannot be overlooked. As a result of urbanisation, as pointed out earlier, tribals have been drawn into the urban set-up where they have been employed as unskilled labourers. In this way, they have gradually been exposed to a new environment, social values and attitudes and have been brought into the vortex of cultural change through the process of assimilation into the non-tribal cultures. For thousands of years these primitive tribes were confined to the hilly and isolated regions. With the development of industries and the emergence of urban centres in the tribal region, they have got an opportunity to understand and to mix with the alien and relatively developed cultural groups. This has brought about a process of gradual alienation from their traditional language because of increasing frequency of the use of non-tribal languages in the transformed socio-economic milieu of the region.

The purpose of this section is to find the extent of language shift among the tribal population. It is assumed that the shift is a function of assimilation and interaction/integration resulting from urbanisation, although the impact of urbanisation is far-reaching and has transformed the entire lifestyle of the tribal people (Das, 1972: 185). Thus, urbanisation is assumed to be an agent which exposes the tribal population to the non-tribal, non-regional or non-local influences. If language shift is taken to be one of the indicators of exposure, then it can be hypothesised that :

a) With an increase in the levels of urbanisation there will be a decline in the proportion of tribes speaking their traditional languages.
b) With an increase in the levels of urbanisation there will be an increase in the proportion of tribes adopting regional languages.
c) The adoption of non-tribal non-regional languages by the tribes goes hand in hand with urbanisation. In other words, it can be said that with an increase in the levels of urbanisation, a considerable increase may be seen in the adoption of non-tribal non-regional languages among the tribal population.

The levels of urbanisation have been worked out with the help of the following variables: a) rural-urban ratio; b) percentage of urban population; c) urban population per square Kilometre; and lastly d) the percentage of tribal population to the total population. The last variable has been included as one of the indicators because the region is predominantly tribal in nature. The First Principle Component method (see page 123) has been used to determine the levels of urbanisation. The language data have been classified into: a) tribes speaking regional languages; b) tribes speaking tribal languages; and c) tribes speaking non-regional non-tribal languages.

Levels of Urbanisation

The composite score of the levels of urbanisation varies from 0.012 in Sundargarh to 67.096 in Calcutta (Appendix-XI). Calcutta, with an exceptionally high level of urbanisation, has been excluded from the list of classification of the index values into four categories, i.e., high, medium, low and very low levels of urbanisation.

The first category, in which the score varies from 0.187 to 1.126, manifests a relatively high level of urbanisation. A total of 16 districts forming 6 clusters falls under this category. Of these, Howrah, Hooghly, Nadia, and 24-Parganas along with Calcutta formed the largest urban complex. To the west lies a cluster comprising Singhbhum and Dhanbad districts. A group of three districts in central Bihar formed another cluster around Patna (Table- 41).

Table-41
DISTRICTS WITH HIGH LEVEL OF URBANISATION

State	No. of Dist.	District
Andhra Pradesh	2	Visakhapatnam, East Godavari
Assam	1	United Khasi & Jaintia Hills
Bihar	5	Patna, Bhagalpur, Monghyr, Dhanbad, Singhbhum
Madhya Pradesh	2	East Nimar,Hoshangabad
Maharashtra	1	Amravati
West Bengal	5	Nadia, Burdwan, Hooghly, Howrah, 24-Parganas

The second group of districts, in which the composite score varies from 0.115 to 0.187, has been classified under the medium level of urbanisation. Districts comprising this category are scattered all over the region (Table- 42).

Table-42
DISTRICTS WITH MEDIUM LEVEL OF URBANISATION

State	No. of Dist.	District
Andhra Pradesh	1	Srikakulam
Bihar	3	Ranchi,Gaya,Shahabad
Madhya Pradesh	4	West Nimar,Chhindwara,Dewas, Raipur
West Bengal	8	Midnapore, Bankura, Birbhum, Murshidabad, West Dinajpur, Darjeeling, Cooch Behar, Jalpaiguri

The districts with a composite score between 0.069 and 0.115 have been classified under low levels of urbanisation. The districts falling under this category formed a contiguous belt along the inter-state boundary between Bihar and Orissa and Madhya Pradesh. In a chain of another 16 districts, the composite score varies from 0.012 to 0.069. These districts may be classified under very low levels of urbanisation. Most of these districts belong to the state of Orissa and lie in a contiguous belt. The other districts in this category included Sidhi, Surguja, Bastar (M.P.), Palamau (Bihar), Garo Hills, United Mikir and North Cachar Hills (Assam) and Mizo Hills.

Correlation Analysis

An exercise on the nature of the relationship between the factors of urbanisation and the degree of language shift has been attempted. The correlation matrix in table - 43 reveals the following :

a) The concentration of the tribal population has a negative correlation with the percentage of tribes speaking regional languages and non-regional non-tribal languages. However, it shows a positive correlation with the percentage of tribes speaking tribal languages.
b) The percentage of urban population has a negative correlation with the percentage of tribes speaking tribal languages. However, it has a positive correlation with the percentage of tribes speaking regional and non-regional non-tribal languages.
c) The rural-urban ratio has a negative correlation with the percentage of tribes speaking non-regional non-tribal languages while it has a positive correlation with the percentage of tribes speaking regional as well as tribal languages.
d) The urban population per square kilometre has a negative correlation with the percentage of tribes speaking tribal languages and regional languages whereas it is positively correlated with the percentage of tribes speaking non-regional non-tribal languages.

Table-43
CORRELATION MATRIX

% of tribal pop.	% of urban pop.	Rural urban ratio	Urban Pop. p/sq. Km	% of tribe decl. reg.lang.	% of tribe decl. T.L.	% of tribe decl. NR.NT.L.
I	II	III	IV	V	VI	VII
1.000						
-0.278	1.000					
0.407	-0.431	1.000				
-0.112	0.792	-0.102	1.000			
-0.205	0.052	0.010	-0.055	1.000		
0.234	-0.078	0.045	-0.056	-0.292	1.000	
-0.091	0.346	-0.151	0.297	-0.185	-0.189	1.000

Note : The confidence level of coefficient of correlation is not found significant even at the level of 10 per cent.

To conclude, it may be pointed out that although urbanisation is one of the most important factors influencing language shift among the tribal communities, it did not show a linear positive correlation in this exercise. In some of the districts the situation is reversed. For example, the districts of Nadia, Burdwan, Hooghly, Howrah, Calcutta, 24-Parganas and the United Khasi and Jaintia Hills which have high levels of urbanisation have shown a higher incidence of speakers of tribal languages. Contrary to this, a very low level of urbanisation in the districts of Sidhi, Surguja, Palamau, Dhenkanal, Sambalpur, Bolangir, Kalahandi is associated with a high percentage of tribes adopting the regional language as their mother tongue. The low levels of urbanisation in Bastar, Purnea, Saharsa and Garo Hills were associated with a low percentage of tribes speaking regional languages. Therefore, to say that urbanisation is an important vehicle for language shift among the tribal communities may be true only in a few situations and cannot be generalised for all regions of the country.

7.4 Language Regionalism

Another important implication of the changing linguistic identity of the tribal population in India is a growing consciousness of their traditional languages. The levels of this consciousness (which is a comparatively recent phenomenon) varies among tribes (Burdhan, 1973: 53). Borrowing the idea of language consciousness from the non-tribal regions, the tribals also get inspired to demand the recognition of their languages by the VIIIth Schedule of the Constitution. The major demands are raised from the north-east region and from the Chotanagpur region. In most of the cases, language consciousness is restricted to the elite section of the population including students, teachers and industrial workers. In other words, the level of language consciousness is higher among those sections of the tribal population who are politically more conscious. Thus, it may be argued that politics is the force behind language consciousness. The language consciousness of the tribal population is quite natural and legitimate but trouble arises when the very solidarity and security of the country is threatened by this consciousness (Broker, 1969: 387 and Charlier, 1971: 371). Politics mixed with language consciousness pushes socio-economic and other considerations into the background and emerges as a force which may transcend caste, class and religious boundaries (O'Barr and O'Barr, 1976:10). For instance, the tribals of the Chotanagpur region met on a common platform to demand the Jharkhand state irrespective of their religious and linguistic affinity and socio-economic backgrounds. In north-east India, language politics mixed with ethnicity has led to many cases of bloodshed.

Language regionalism is regarded as a by-product of language consciousness. Regionalism in India has emerged due to the multilingual character of society. The hundreds of languages in India spoken in different geographical territories by people of diverse socio-economic and cultural backgrounds may be considered the most prominent obstacle to an integrated cultural identity. In this plurality lies the origin of language regionalism (Husain, 1956: 143). Each state of the Indian Republic is a linguistic unit in which the majority of people speak a cognate language (Hoijer, 1964: 455) while the linguistic minority groups, in many cases, find that their linguistic heritage is not being protected. This also leads to language regionalism. Since most of the tribal languages are the languages of the minority linguistic groups in one or the other state of India, the incidence of language regionalism among these linguistic groups is becoming more prominent. Language regionalism in the tribal regions of India, as pointed out earlier, is a recent phenomenon which has arisen only in the last few decades. The constant pressure exerted on the government by the tribal and non-tribal minority linguistic groups for the inclusion of their languages in the VIIIth Schedule of the Constitution has brought about many untoward and unholy situations. The inclusion of Manipuri, Nepali and Konkani in the VIII th Schedule only recently has given an impetus to the other linguistic groups to continue their demands with renewed hope. At present, Bhojpuri, Maithili, Dogri, Santali, Marwari, Bodo, etc. are some of the linguistic groups spear-heading the struggle and demanding their languages also be recognised national languages under the constitutional provision.

7.4.1 Language Revivalism

Factors such as education, employment, urbanization, etc. are considered important variables in bringing about language shift. But it is not necessary that they always function in the same direction. It is observed that though, in some cases, these factors in their early stages undoubtedly play a positive role in bringing about language shift, at the later stage they become instrumental in bringing about cultural consciousness/ regionalism. Such a revivalism glorifies the traditional cultural ethos. As a result, the primitive people tend to preserve their cultural heritage and reject any sort of imposition of new cultural values belonging to the alien group of 'superior' people. The stages of language revivalism (which is a part of cultural revivalism/ consciousness) have been shown through a schematic diagram (Fig.29)

It is interesting to note that some of the tribals of India who declared the non-tribal languages as their mother tongues during the 1961 census have, for a number of reasons, changed their affiliation back to their traditional languages in the successive censes. This kind of situation may generally be noticed in those tribal regions in which the non-tribals have settled. The example may be cited here is that of from the Mundas of Murhu Block (Ranchi District) where a section of the Mundas had declared English as their mother tongue in 1961: during the next census the entire Munda population had returned back to Mundari.

The given schematic diagram represents a situation in which the non-tribals, in search of natural resources or in administrative or business capacity, have settled in tribal regions. But the situation becomes quite different if the tribals migrate to non-tribal regions. In that case the migrant tribals get assimilated into the non-tribal culture and communicate in the language of the non-tribals. It has been noticed that these tribals have no intention of going back to their traditional languages, rather, they prefer to continue with the non-tribal languages. For example, the Korkus of Khandwa Tehsil (East Nimar District) who have already switched over to Nimadi, consider Korku as an inferior language. This change has been brought about by the processes of interaction and assimilation which have been shown in the following unidirectional diagram (Fig.30).

Language revivalism is a typical phenomenon not only in the tribal areas but also in the non-tribal regions of the country. It is necessary to

STAGES OF LANGUAGE SHIFT

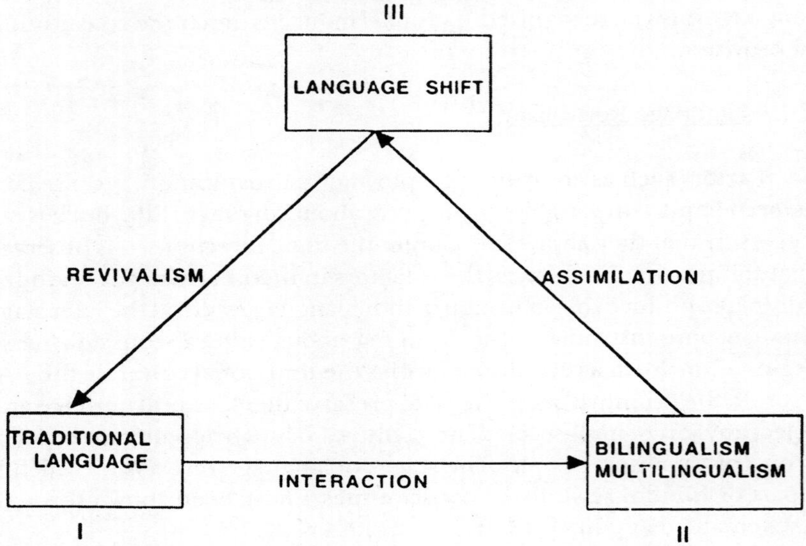

Fig. 29

UNIDIRECTIONAL LANGUAGE SHIFT

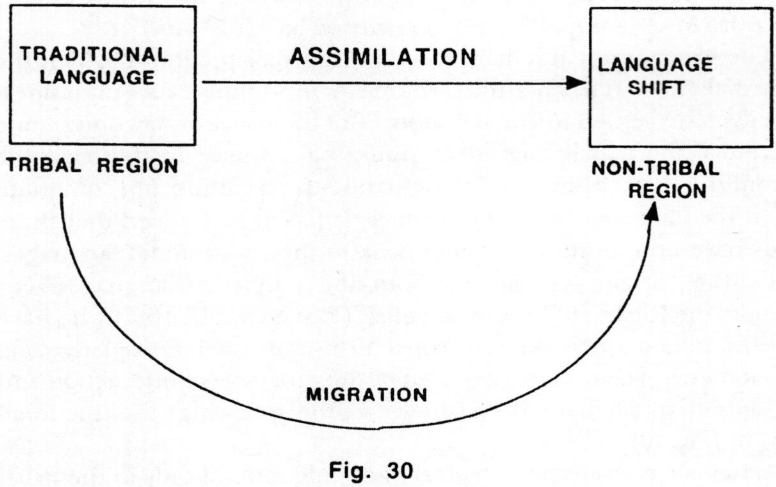

Fig. 30

mention here that no proper attention has been paid to the study of language revivalism and its processes . The studies of Kachru (1977), Mitra (1974), Khubchandani (1972 and 1992), Ahmad and Ishtiaq (1994) are, basically, on language dynamics and the changing attitude to linguistic identity among the Indian population may also be referred to understand the nature of linguistic revivalism. It is also necessary to point out that in India quantitative/ statistical change is not necessarily a clue to actual change in language which often aims at achieving the socio-political advantages (Kachru, 1977:20). This tendency is not only confined to the tribal people of India but may also be noticed among the ethnic groups of the United States of America. Many subordinate groups have separated themselves from the dominant group and formed social bonds to preserve their distinctive traditions in the spheres of language, religion, recreation, etc. They do not want to abandon their cultural distinctiveness-rather, they want access to goods and services and also to the institutional privileges held by the English speaking middle class people (Paulston and Paulston, 1980: 79).

7.4.2 Demand for Separate Tribal Territory

The tribals of India have constantly been demanding territories of their own language. An example may be cited from the Chotanagpur region in which the tribes have been demanding a separate state of Jharkhand. Besides the major tribal groups such as the Santals, the Mundas, the Oraons, the Bhumij and the Kharias, the other smaller tribal groups have also joined this movement and have claimed 21 districts spread over the states of Bihar, Orissa, West Bengal and Madhya Pradesh. The other regions which have witnessed such struggles include the western, the central and the north-east regions of the country. In the early twenties the Bhils attempted to start a movement for a Bhil Raj but it was quickly suppressed by the British administration. There were many similar mass movements by the Bhils in the post independence period, specially during the sixties, but the government promptly took control of the situation and successfully suppressed the movement. The Gonds, who live in an area known as Gondwanaland (roughly spread over the districts of Bastar, Mandla, Chhindwara, Raigarh and Surguja) may also demand secession after the consolidation of the tribes. (Kluyev, 1981: 152).

North-east India has a different history of its own owing to its strategic location. The region, specially Nagaland, has been prone to such struggles. In fact, insurgents in the north-east states of India, particularly those in Nagaland have never considered their region a part of India. The insurgency crisis has been further aggravated by the bloody boundary disputes between Assam on one side and Meghalaya, Arunachal Pradesh, Mizoram and Nagaland on the other, each party claiming more territories (Hindustan Times, December 14, 1989). The Naga secessionist movement, the Mizo, Manipuri and the Khasi movements and presently, the Bodo movement in Assam have taken a violent turn on many occasions. The Hindustan Times, Nov. 22, 1989 also reported that the Manipuri Demand Coordinating Committee had called for a 24-hour Manipur Bandh to draw the Centre's attention to the demand for inclusion of the Manipuri language in the VIIIth Schedule of the Constitution-a demand which has finally been granted in 1992.

Besides secessionist demands by tribal people in different parts of the country, there has also been a constant demand for the inclusion of their languages in the VIIIth Schedule of the Constitution. The tribal people of India are also demanding education through their own languages and the development of suitable script for their languages which they feel would be achieved only after they are granted territories of their own.

The above are a few examples of the demand for a separate tribal territory based on language and ethnicity as well as on cultural identity. In some cases, these struggles are mild whereas in others they are violent. But such demands are continuing though efforts have been made by the state as well as by the central government to suppress these struggles.

7.4.3 Geographic Dimension of Language Regionalism

The geographical dimension of the language regionalism brings to light the fact that language regionalism is much more limited and restricted in nature and scope in the tribal areas than in the non-tribal regions. It is confined mostly to two regions of the country: the central and the north-eastern regions. The intensity of language regionalism is higher in the north-east due to the ethnicity factor whereas in central India the degree of language regionalism is of a comparatively low order. Such variations in language regionalism in these two regions are also due to the difference in the nature of geographical entity. The former region is located in the strategic areas of the country whereas the latter is surrounded by areas in which the highly cultivated and advanced Indo-Aryan and Dravidian languages are spoken. It is because of the above reasons that the demand for a separate administrative unit on the basis of language was fulfilled in the north-east whereas similar demands by the tribals living in central and eastern India were not.

Language consciousness among the tribal people is growing day by day and it is an ongoing process. After the achievement of a certain level of socio-economic upliftment, demands for the recognition of each tribal language will emerge. It is to be noted that till today no scientific attention has been paid to the solution to tribal language regionalism as far as the major central Indian tribal languages are concerned. Before the situation worsens, an appropriate solution should be found. The creation of the council of representation for minority linguistic groups (as has been done in the case of Gorkhaland in West Bengal) may be a good solution. The Jharkhand Autonomous Council in Bihar, conceived almost on the same lines for the Chotanagpur people has also come into operation very recently.

7.4.4 What do the Tribals Feel ?

The following paragraphs deal with the response of the tribal people to the shift in their traditional dialect and how they feel about the development of their tribal languages. Will they go back to their own traditional dialect on account of language revivalism/regionalism ? If no, why do they want to continue with the non-tribal language instead of their own ? These were some of the questions/queries formulated in the questionnaire in order to gather first hand information which may serve as a useful guideline to the educational planners for the region.

It was found that none of the Korku respondents from Khandwa Tehsil were in favour of studying through their traditional dialect except one, a school teacher, who explained that Hindi is the main reason for their children drop out of school. He emphasised the need for primary education through the Korku medium. In contrast, a compounder belonging to the same tribe highlighted the importance of Hindi and suggested that Hindi must continue as the medium of instruction at all levels. It was noticed that all those Korkus who have switched over to Nimadi, a regional language, had no urge to revive their traditional language-rather, they regarded Korku as the language of the inferior group of people residing in the jungles and hills of the Satpuras.

The situation was more or less the same as far as Bhils of Banswara district were concerned. The rural Bhils did not show any concern for the recognition of Bhili while the urban Bhils supported the idea of its retaining the status of a community language. None of the respondents from Banswara district wanted Bhili to be the medium of instruction at any level. They supported education through the medium of Hindi. Unlike the Bhils and the Korkus, the Mundas and the Santals were much more conscious about their traditional language. The people belonging to both these tribal groups in the Chotanagpur region have always been in favour of the recognition of their language as the regional as well as the state language. Some of them, specially the educated persons from the Munda tribe also asserted that their language is the oldest in India and, therefore, must be recognised at the national level. As a result they insisted that education must be imparted in their own mother tongue up to higher levels.

The choice of Hindi among the Bhils and the Korkus is basically due to social and economic reasons. The zeal to enter the mainstream of national culture led to the Bhils of Banswara district and the Korkus of East Nimar district opting for Hindi while the Mundas and the Santals of Chotanagpur (Bihar) regarded this phenomenon as a sign of the disintegrating of their language, culture and tribal identity. They feel proud of their tribal culture and language and do not want to lose them in any event. In fact, they want to preserve them at all costs.

Chapter 8

PLANNING FOR THE PRESERVATION OF TRIBAL LANGUAGES

The study of the previous chapters highlights the need for urgent planning not only to preserve and develop tribal languages but also to stop from dying a natural death in the peripheral areas of the tribal heartlands and in those areas where the Indo-Aryan and Dravidian languages have made encroached irreparably. Thus, the purpose of planning is two fold: first, to understand the mechanisms through which these languages are dying out and secondly, to evolve some suitable methods to check their complete elimination from their homelands and to suggest ways through which written scripts may be evolved for all these languages and means of introducing them as the media of education at the primary level, especially in those areas where they are spoken overwhelmingly. It is to be noted that these two purposes of planning are not independent-rather, they are complementary to each other. For example, one of the reasons for abandoning the tribal languages is that they do not have scripts of their own. Therefore, there is a need to develop suitable scripts for these languages. Through this example it becomes easy to understand how one purpose is related to the other. But in nature, they are quite different from one another. The former may be described as investigative and the latter as suggestive. As far as the investigation of the problem is concerned, chapter-6 has been completely devoted to determining the possible socio-economic and other factors responsible for the dying out of the tribal languages. These variables have already been tested by applying correlation and regression techniques. Besides, an exercise in locational proximity has also been done in the last section of the same chapter to understand how far this factor in terms of location, site, terrain and nearness to towns explains the nature and magnitude of linguistic shift. Historical and demographic factors seem to be the most important variables to understand the reasons for the gradual abandonment of the tribal languages. The second chapter presents a detailed study of these processes.

As far as the suggestive part of the planning of the tribal languages is concerned, the following steps need to be taken care of :

Classification

The first and the foremost step to planning for saving and developing of the tribal languages is the careful scrutiny of all these tribal languages and their classification by a group of experts including linguists, anthropologists, sociolinguists, and other social scientists. Proper care must be taken in those cases where twin mother tongues have been reported by tribes (see chapter-3). The variant dialects of a language have also been categorised, in some cases, as distinct tribal languages which have multiplied the number of tribal languages creating unnecessary confusion in planning and implementation. In most cases, the tribal dialects and groups bear the same name. But the problem arises when the tribal name and the names of their languages are categorised as separate languages. The Mundari and Munda languages may be cited as an example. They have been classified as distinct languages. In fact these two should be clubbed as one language, i.e., Mundari. Besides, the fact that some tribes have also reported their occupation in place of their languages should also be taken care of during the process of classification. Although the task of scrutiny and proper classification is very difficult and painstaking, its relevance in the process of planning cannot be ignored.

Script

A language which has no literary tradition may not survive long, specially in this modern age when all the isolated patches in the tribal areas have been exposed to the non-tribals through the process of regional development. As a result, contact between the speakers of folk-languages and the speakers of the advanced neighbouring languages is increasing at a fast pace. Young tribals who intend to study, find that their languages are of little help compared to the alien languages. Such a situation invariably leads to language shift. Had they had scripts of their own, and had education been imparted in their own tribal languages, such a situation would not have arisen. A mention has to be made here of the Santali and Khasi languages for which scripts have been developed only in the last century. These have shown less linguistic change than other tribal languages for which scripts have not been evolved.

The question of script is a debatable one. Some may favour the Devanagri while others favour the scripts of the regional languages of the country. A group of scholars have already advocated the adoption of the Roman script. Since many of the tribal languages are transcend the regional or state boundaries, the script of the regional language will not be a viable solution. Then the choice is between the Devanagri and

Roman scripts. Since the central and eastern Indian tribes are quite familiar with Hindi and many of them have already switched over to Hindi, it would be appropriate for them to adopt Devanagri as their script while the Roman script should be assigned to all those tribal languages spoken in the north-eastern region of India. Those tribal groups who are confined to one state may have achoice between the script of regional languages or Devanagri.

Medium of Instruction

The survival of a language depends not only on its having a literature of its own but also on its being spoken by a sufficiently large population. It must be able to convey and exchange of ideas easily and to incorporate changes in step with new develpments. Sanskrit, though a highly cultivated and rich language, is considered a dead language while Santali, a tribal language with no literary tradition, is an active one. But unless it is used as a medium of instruction, it cannot be carried on for long. Through the medium of instruction, a language formally passes from one generation to another and, therefore, chances of its growth and development multiply.

Another positive aspect of imparting education through the medium of tribal languages is the achievement of a higher level of literacy among the tribal population. The studies on education among the tribals clearly indicated that their high drop-out rate and low literacy level have a positive relationship with the medium of instruction which, invariably, is the non-tribal language. For this purpose a group of teachers, preferably from each tribal group must be trained to take up this challenge.

Identification of Linguistic Area

Identification of the linguistic area for each tribal language becomes an important aspect of planning. It is argued that the tribal linguistic area coincides with the tribal area, although this may not be true for all tribes. For example, almost all the Korkus of Khandwa Tehsil (East Nimar District) declared Nimari, a dialect of Hindi, as their mother tongue. This means that the tribal linguistic area for the Korkus is obviously smaller than the tribal area. The area of the Savara language may be taken as another example. This language is confined mostly to the hilly parts of Baudhkhondmals, Koraput, Ganjam and Srikakulam districts while the Savara tribe is distributed over 20 districts. Such a situation may occur in many cases where the typical tribal dialect is squeezed into the interior and hilly parts of the tribal areas. Without the proper identification of tribal linguistic areas, it would be difficult and unwise to plan for all the tribal population because a substantial proportion of the tribals, in many cases, have already switched over to the non-tribal languages and do not have any urge to revive their traditional language.

Role of the Government

In planning, the role of the government becomes very important at least to meet the expenditure and to maintain law and order, if needed. Planning for the tribal languages may not draw the attention of many of the voluntary non-governmental organizations because it requires not only a huge sum of capital but also may continue for years together. The work of Christian missionaries, especially the works of the Scandinavians among the Santals in this regard need to be mentioned here with the highest regard (Chatterji, 1973: 67). Besides missionaries, some native organisations such as Bhartiya Adim Jati Sewak Sangh and Adivasi Sewa Mandal are also engaged in this type of work and have had major contributions. These works need augmentation and further extension with the full cooperation of and proper attention from the government to achieve higher success.

As far as human resources are concerned, the services of retired government officers and retired teachers may be utilised for this cause. In fact, there is no dearth of such persons who would like to dedicate themselves to social service after retirement. A group of such dedicated persons should be asked to take up charge of any one tribal group familiar to them. The objectives of planning should not be diversified-rather, they should be restricted and emphasis should be laid only on the development of education among the tribal population, evolving written scripts and preparing text books and imparting education through the media of tribal languages.

To achieve these goals, each tribal dialect region must have its own office headquarter with all accessories required for the office to pursue the above tasks effectively. To begin with, a tribal group should be selected. There should be a time bound programme which will be based on the size of the tribal population and the area over which they are spread. The achievement of this project will give a new direction to other projects of this nature.

The Tribals' Involvement

The success of planning also depends on the involvement of the masses. Language is a symbol of cultural identity and can be used as a tool to achieve social, economic and political goals. It also transcends caste and religious boundaries and can push the social and economic factors into the background. Since people are sentimentally attached to their languages, it would be difficult to exclude them from the planning process. Therefore, their active participation is needed for a better understanding of their languages and of related problems and also to know how and in what way they want their languages developed. Their active participation would also be of great help in finding the areas of pure and corrupt languages. This would be an asset in developing the script and in preparing a dictionary.

Finally, we may conclude that planning for the tribal languages needs dedicated persons with a zeal for social service. They must have the courage to work in the inhospitable tribal regions. Inspiration may be drawn from the works of the Christian missionaries. For this planning, personal as well as group involvement are much more important than material assets.

Chapter 9

SUMMARY AND CONCLUSIONS

Language shift is a universal phenomenon and is occurring among almost all the tribal communities of India but its magnitude varies across tribes as well as within the same tribal group. Regional variation is basically due to either the migration of tribals to the non-tribal regions or of the non-tribals to the tribal areas for harnessing natural resources. In the former case they get assimilated, in most cases, into the non-tribal cultures and became part and parcel of the non-tribal society for all practical purposes while in the latter, the process of language shift takes place through the process of bilingualism/ multilingualism.

The findings of the present study reveal that the scheduled tribes of India may, broadly, be classified into two groups on the basis of their linguistic affiliations. One group includes those who continue to be identified with their traditional language and have registered it as their mother tongue. The other group consists of those tribes who have discarded their traditional language and have declared non-traditional languages as their mother tongue. The case in which the traditional language is maintained is one of language maintenance while language shift has occurred in the latter group.

The Austric speaking tribal people of India display a high degree of multiplicity in their mother tongues. But their traditional languages continue to hold sway in remote, forested and hilly areas while the minor groups among the tribals have been assimilated into the dialectal regimes of the major groups. The process of language shift is most vigorous on the periphery of the tribal home lands. There are 12 districts (see chapter-4) in which more than 80 per cent of the Austric tribes have switched over from their traditional language and declared regional languages as their mother tongue. In another 7 districts the degree of the shift varies from 60 to 80 per cent. The Austric tribes have also declared the non-tribal non-regional languages and the languages of the other tribal groups as their mother tongue but the share of the speakers of these languages did not exceed 50 per cent except in one or two cases. It has been found that the majority of them have retained their traditional language as mother tongue. More than 80 per cent of the Austric tribes in 24 districts of the region maintained their linguistic identity while this share varies from 60 to 80 per cent in other 16 districts.

Unlike the Santals and the Korkus, the other Austric tribes have shown a greater tendency to shift their linguistic affiliation especially towards the regional languages. The shift is highest among the Savaras followed by the Kharias, the Mundas and the Hos.

It has been found that out of a total of 53 districts, there are 32 districts in which cent per cent Bhils have declared non-traditional languages as their mother tongue. Out of the remaining 21 districts, there are 16 in which the degree of the shift is high (i.e., more than 50 per cent Bhils have switched over from their traditional language) while moderate and low degrees of the shift are found in only 4 districts. Almost cent per cent Bhils of Dungarpur district have maintained their linguistic identity.

Out of a total of 10 districts, there are 3 in which cent per cent Korkus have switched over to the non-traditional languages. Out of the remaining 7 districts, 2 are classified as areas of a high degree of language shift, one district as moderate (i.e. 25 to 50 per cent shift) and 4 districts as areas of a low degree (i.e. less than 25 per cent) of the shift.

Almost all the Mundas in 13 districts have discarded their traditional language while in another 21 districts the degree of the shift is of a higher order. Out of the remaining 7 districts 4 are classified as areas of moderate shift and 3 as areas of a low degree of language shift. Unlike the Mundas, Korkus and Bhils, a large number of the Santals have maintained their linguistic identity. There are only 2 districts (with a very small Santali population) in which almost all the Santals have shifted away from their old language. Out of the remaining 35 districts, there are 5 with a high degree of language shift: 7 with moderate and 19 with a low degree of the shift. There are 4 districts in which cent per cent Santals have maintained their linguistic identity.

Linguistic shift among the tribal population is multi-dimensional, varying for the regional, the other tribal and the non-tribal non-regional languages. It is interesting to note that language shift among the tribes in India is, mostly, towards the regional languages. More than 90 per cent Bhils in 23 districts have switched over to the regional languages while more than 88 per cent Korkus have declared the regional languages as their mother tongue in 5 districts. As many as 80 per cent of the Mundas in 9 districts and between 60 and 80 per cent Mundas in another 5 districts have registered the regional language as their mother tongue. Besides, they have also adopted the languages of the other tribal groups and the non-tribal non-regional languages but the share of the speakers of these languages remained very low with a few exceptions such as the districts of Balasore (Orissa) and Jalpaiguri (West Bengal) in which more than 90 per cent Mundas have declared the languages of the other tribal groups as their mother tongue.

A study of the typology of language shift and maintenance among the selected tribes of India revealed that the areas of very high degree of language shift are associated with a low grade of maintenance, high degree of the shift with moderate maintenance; moderate degree of the shift with high maintenance and low degree of the shift with very high maintenance for all these tribal groups.

The analysis of household data revealed that the entire Bhil population of Wanera Para, Umedgarhi, Nai Abadi and Regania villages (Bagidora Tehsil) and the Bhils of Banswara town have maintained Bhili, their traditional mother tongue. On the other hand the Korkus of Punasa, Richhi and Udaipur villages (Khandwa Tehsil) have already switched over to the regional language and declared Nimadi as their mother tongue. In contrast, cent per cent Korkus of Mirpur, Kalamkala and Kutbi villages (Hersud Tehsil) retained their traditional language as their mother tongue. The Santals of Surajbeda village (Littipara Block) and of Dumka town have also registered Santali as their tongue.

The study among the Mundas in Ranchi town revealed that more than 90 per cent of them have switched over from their traditional language and have declared Sadari as their mother tongue. But the situation in the rural areas, altogether, is different. Cent per cent Mundas in Kula Buru and Litingdih villages (Bundu Block) and Bande village (Murhu Block) have declared Mundari as their mother tongue. In short, the household level study revealed that the Mundas of Ranchi town and the Korkus of Khandwa Tehsil (East Nimar District) have changed their linguistic identity while the Bhils of Banswara district, the Santals of Santal Parganas, the Korkus of Khalwa Tehsil (East Nimar District) and the Mundas residing in the rural areas of Ranchi district have shown resistance to language shift. Since the study areas fall under the Hindi region, an attempt has also been made to find out the degree of exposure of the tribes to Hindi. It has been found that the Mundas of Ranchi town, the Bhils of Banswara town and the Korkus of Pangra, Punasa, Udaipur and Richhi villages are overwhelmingly exposed to Hindi whereas the Bhils of Umedgarhi and the Mundas of Litingdih villages are exposed significantly. The Santals of Dumka town and the Korkus of Kalamkala and the Bhils of Regania, Nai Abadi, Wanera Para villages are fairly exposed. The Korkus of Kutbi and Mirpur and the Mundas of Bande and Kula Buru are least exposed to Hindi.

The study of bilingualism among these tribes revealed that bilingualism is highly concentrated in rural areas, specially in the north-east and the southern states of India. It is noticed that a higher incidence of bilingualism is found among the young people as well as among the male population. Almost all the Bhils of Banswara town and the Korkus of Pangra, Punasa, Richhi and Udaipur villages are bilingual. The Bhils of Nai Abadi, Wanera Para and Regania villages , the Korkus of Kalamkala and Kutbi villages, the Mundas of Bande, Kula Buru and Litingdih villages and the Santals of Dumka town have a low incidence of bilingualism. The Bhils of Umedgarhi village have fairly high levels of bilingualism. Although there has been a decline in the trend of tribal bilingualism in recent decades, it is an undeniable fact that the pace of bilingualism among these communities is gaining momentum. Since bilingualism is susceptible to change according to variations in social, political and economic scenarios, its fluctuations may not reflect a real change.

The correlation matrix shows that the percentage of urban tribals, tribals engaged in non-primary occupations, tribals who embraced Hinduism and per capita income are positively correlated with language shift whereas the percentage of tribal to total population is negatively correlated with language shift. It is important to note that literacy, which is negatively correlated at the district level, shows a high positive correlation at the household level. Both age and sex groups are positively correlated at the district level while they have a negative correlation at the household level. The findings of the regression analysis revealed that all the significant variables together could explain only about 15 per cent variation in the degree of language shift at the district level whereas at the household level they could explain upto 39 per cent.

On the basis of the regression result, it was assumed that there might be some other factors other than the above mentioned which have played a vital role in bringing about linguistic shift among these tribes. In search of these, site and locational factors in terms of terrain, nearness to communication lines and urban centres and population characteristics of the surrounding villages were studied. This study revealed that a tribal village surrounded by villages with a predominantly tribal culture has witnessed the retention of its traditional language; if surrounded by non-tribal villages, it tends to show a change in linguistic identity. Areas where the tribal culture has been assimilated into the alien culture are areas of language shift.

Finally, it may be concluded that the majority of the Austric tribes of India, by and large, maintain their linguistic identity except for those who have occupied the periphery of the tribal heartlands or those who have migrated to urban centres. The Bhils, linguistically, are the most exposed tribal groups followed by the Mundas, the Korkus and the Santals. The anomaly results at the district and the household level is mainly because of the fact that the study area is selected on the basis of high concentration of these tribes. Because of this limitation, the findings of the household study have a limited application in the areas of high concentration and should not be generalised for all tribal areas or for the other tribes of the country because of inter-tribal and intra-tribal variations across regions.

It is interesting to note that the process of regional development and the process of urbanisation in the tribal areas/study area do not play a significant role to bring linguistic shift although they play a major role in bringing about socio-economic changes. The degree of language shift among the tribal communities may indicate the degree of cultural assimilation into the majority linguistic groups as one way of preserving cultural identity is to maintain their traditional languages. In the north-east and the central regions of the country the mix of language consciousness and ethnicity have led to tribal unrest as demands for the inclusion of their tribal languages in the Eighth Schedule of the Indian Constitution became interwined with secessionist movements.

Policy Implications

Changing linguistic identity in a multilingual country like India sometimes does not represent a real index of shift in language. Rather, it is a change in people's perception which compels them to declare their mother tongue differently in different periods of time. Such a flexibility in language declaration has, in many cases, been more due to political factors than to economic and social causes. An example may be cited here from the state of Bihar in which Hindi as a mother tongue was dropped by about 35 per cent of its speakers in 1961 and by about 9 per cent in 1971 (Khubchandani,1972:432 and Kachru,1977:21). Besides, the tremendous growth in some of the regional and tribal languages including Marwari, Nepali, Konkani, Maithili, Bhojpuri, Dogri, and some other tribal languages such as Santali, Bhili, Gondi, etc. is merely due to political consciousness about their linguistic identity. Language has always been a victim of politics and has been used as an effective tool in almost all the multilingual countries of the world to achieve political goals. In India too, language and politics interact with each other to push economic, social and other issues into the background and transcend the caste and religious boundaries (O'Barr and O'Barr, 1976). Thus, before arriving at any conclusion, linguistic shift must be examined from a political perspective. This may be more useful and relevant to language planners in a country like ours. The census data may not be taken as conclusive for the purpose of the analysis and for policy programmes. These data must be verified with the data generated through extensive field- work at the household or at the village level. The study must be conducted separately for each tribe in the different regions of the country because there exist a large amount of socio-economic and regional variations within the tribal group itself.

The tribal languages of India represent valuable relics of the country's past cultural heritage in the form of oral tradition and folk-lore and must not be allowed to be destroyed. Rather efforts should be made to preserve this pristine heritage. All possible assistance should be given for their proper development. These languages may serve a better purpose if they are assigned uniform scripts irrespective of their regional variations and are also made the media of education upto the primary level in those areas in which they are spoken overwhelmingly. Some valuable work has been started in this direction by a number of tribal welfare organisations such as Bhartiya Adim Jati Sewak Sangh, Adivasi Sewa Mandal, and Christian missionaries. Their work needs to be further augmented and expanded. Integrating the tribal people into the main stream of the national culture should not involve the destruction of their precious historic culture and language. Rather, they should be given priority in the country's planning and programmes before the tribal languages vanish from our land.

Appendix- I

SAMPLE DESIGN FOR FIELD WORK

Village/Town	Tribal Group	No. of Households Surveyed
Banswara District		
1. Regania	Bhil	28
2. Nai Abadi	Bhil	11
3. Umedgarhi	Bhil	5
4. Wanera Para	Bhil	25
5. Banswara Town	Bhil	10
Ranchi District		
6. Bande	Munda	41
7. Litingdih	Munda	7
8. Kula Buru	Munda	11
9. Murhu	Munda	8
10. Ranchi Town	Munda	35
Santal Parganas District		
11. Suraj Beda	Santal	18
12. Dumka Town	Santal	22
East Nimar District		
13. Mirpur	Korku	15
14. Kutbi	Korku	35
15. Punasa	Korku	25
16. Pangra	Korku	28
17. Udaipur	Korku	23
18. Richhi	Korku	29
19. Kalamkala	Korku	21

Appendix - II

MOTHER TONGUES CONSIDERED AS TRIBAL LANGUAGES IN 1961

Languages	No. of Speakers	Languages	No. of Speakers
Abor/Adi	3912 (13)	Korwa	17720 (5)
Agaria	98	Kota	956 (2)
Aimol	108	Koya	140,777 (2)
Aka/Hrusso	81	Kuki-Unspec.	28,943 (3)
Anal	5522 (2)	Kurukh/Oraon	1,141,804 (9)
Andamanese	17 (2)	Lakher	9,531
Angami	42,770 (2)	Lalung	10,576
Ao	57,745 (3)	Lamgang	1,866
Asuri	4,540	Lepcha	23,760
Beriya	144	Lotha	26,611
Bhili	2,439,611 (36)	Lushai/Mizo	222,202 (2)
Bhumij	142,003 (7)	Makware	769
Birhor	590	Mao	28,873 (2)
Birjia/Binjhia	2,395 (2)	Maram	4,928
Bodo	361,801 (3)	Maring	7,745
Chang-Naga	11,329	Mikir	154,893 (2)
Chiru	3,590 (2)	Miri	136,598 (2)
Chote	1,035	Mishmi	669 (4)
Dafla	1,380 (3)	Mru	48
Deori	9,103	Munda-Unsp.	261,653 (8)
Dimasa	32,708 (2)	Mundari	737,037 (2)
Gadaba	40,193	Naga-unsp.	33,333 (3)
Garo	307,040 (3)	Nicobarese	13,936
Gondi	1,501,431 (13)	Nocte	66
Hakki			
Pakki	81	Onge	131
Halam	17, 243 (12)	Paite	18,612
Hengna	2	Parji	109,401 (3)
Hmar	25,530	Pawi	6,866
Ho	648,359 (2)	Phom	13,390 (2)
Jatapu	19,467	Pochury	18,500 (3)
Juang	15,795	Purum	82
Kabui	30,089 (2)	Rabha	44,432 (2)
Kacha-Naga	9,734 (3)	Ralte	170
Kanauri	28,630 (6)	Rangkhol	4,651 (3)
Kharia	177,159 (5)	Rengma	5,935 (2)
Khasi	632,443 (6)		

Khawathlang	1		Santali	3,247,058	(11)
Kherwari	647		Savara	265,721	
Khezha	8,828	(2)	Sema	47,464	
Khiemnungam	12,435	(2)	Shompen	70	
Khoirao	406		Simte	9,583	(3)
Khond	168,027		Singpho	819	
Kisan	50,378		Tangkhul	44,020	
Koch	8,225	(2)	Tangsa	460	(2)
Koda/Kora	31,724	(4)	Thado	31,974	(12)
Kolami	51,055	(3)	Toda	765	
Kom	5,478		Tripuri	299,643	(6)
Konda	12,298		Uchai	768	
Konyak	57,119	(3)	Vaiphei	8,657	
Korku	220,242	(4)	Wancho	2,713	
			Yimchungre	12,673	(2)
			Zemi-Naga	490	(3)

Source : Census of India, 1961 INDIA, Vol. I, **Language Tables** Pt. II C (ii)

Note : Figures in Parentheses against languages are number of mother tongues.

Appendix- III

AUSTRO-ASIATIC LANGUAGES OF INDIA

Mother Tongues	No. of Speakers	
	1961	1981
Munda Branch		
*Mother Tongues Attested**		
1. Kherwari	647	1434
2. Santali	3130829	4208304
3. Har	9	-
4. Karmali	90849	40069
5. Mahili	19697	102695
6. Manjhi	2296	-
7. Pahariya	2287	39270
8. Mundari	736524	1101522
9. Bhumij	131258	50284
10. Kurmi	351	-
11. Birhor	590	5950
12. Koda/Kora	13277	21983
13. Khaira	18325	-
14. Ho	648066	802434
15. Turi	1562	-
16. Asuri	4540	7783
17. Agariya	98	-
18. Birjia/Brijia	2391	4057
19. Korwa	16286	28386
20. Koraku	53	-
21. Singli	7	-
22. Korku	208165	363148
23. Muwasi	9829	11012
24. Nihali	1167	-
25. Kharia	171269	197840
26. Juang	15795	18469
27. Savara	265721	234811
28. Gadaba	40193	27567
29. Munda Unspec.	167159	included in Mundari
30. Kol	64465	4234
31. Thar	15595	-
Mother Tongues Tentatively Classified		
1. Gayari	16	
2. Gora	1	

3.	Lohari Santali	130	-
4.	Mura	513	-
5.	Bhuiya/Bhuyan	10	-
6.	Larka	32	-
7.	Rahiya	1029	-
8.	Mirdha Koda	76	-
9.	Udangmudria	46	
10.	Lohara	293	169089
11.	Makari	1081	1005
12.	Baiti	5	-
13.	Dhelki	58	-
14.	Lodha	5	-
15.	Mirdha-Kharia	5822	-
16.	Adibhasa-Munda	13140	-
17.	Lohari-Munda	123	-
18.	Mahto	7	-
19.	Parenga	767	-
20.	Parhaiya	397	3745

Mother Tongues Reclassified

1.	Kamari-Santhali	903	-
2.	Kisan-Santhali	41	-
3.	Kisan-Bhumij	4569	-
4.	Parsi-Bhumij	4754	-
5.	Pahari-Birjia	4	-
6.	Jangali-Korwa	35	-
7.	Manjhi-Korwa	1339	-

Mon-Khmer Branch

Mother Tongues Attested

1.	Khasi	289650	632443
2.	Pnar/Synteng	55113	29
3.	War	3854	-
4.	Nicobarese	13936	21424

Mother Tongues Reclassified

1.	Jaintia	14673	-
2.	Nongtung	122	-
3.	Bhoi-Khasi	651	-

* Mother tongues of India have been classified into 3 groups according to the Linguistic Survey of India (LSI) scheme 1961. They are— 'Mother Tongues Attested', 'Mother Tongues Tentatively Classified', and 'Mother Tongues Reclassified'.

Appendix - IV

TIBETO-BURMAN LANGUAGES

Mother Tongues	No. of Speakers	
	1961	1981
Tibeto-Himalayan Branch		
Bhotia Group		
Mother Tongues Attested		
1. Tibetan	33931	55138
2. Lama	59	-
3. Balti	33570	47718
4. Ladakhi	50146	72587
5. Budhi	2764	-
6. Champa	1	-
7. Sham	1	-
8. Lahuli	11412	20110
9. Spiti	33	-
10. Jad	306	1221
11. Sherpa	1673	12607
12. Sikkim Bhotia	36760	31438
13. Bhutani	422	-
14. Dukpa	1116	-
15. Kagate	44	-
16. Bhotia-Unspecified	29371	-
17. Zanskari	6	-
Mother Tongues Tentatively Classified		
1. Gazai	30	-
2. Girdu	1	-
3. Khama	7	-
4. Khamba	23	342
5. Kongbo	281	5
6. Konyo	14	-
7. Memba	66	-
8. Monpa	296	33187
9. Sherdukpen	10	2096
10. Taiphaikial	1	-
11. Tangbo	9	-
12. Yora	2	-
13. Askardi	1	-
14. Tumbal	1	-
15. Adibhasha-Bhotia	26	-
16. Marchha	470	-

Himalayan Group

Mother Tongues Attested

1.	Lahuli of Chamba	3021	-
2.	Kanashi	563	-
3.	Malani	562	-
4.	Kanauri	28495	47913
5.	Samchu	4	-
6.	Jangali	13	-
7.	Dhimal	11	-
8.	Limbu	5418	18320
9.	Khambu	25	-
10.	Rai	3313	-
11.	Gurung	82	-
12.	Tamang	4939	-
13.	Sunwar	297	-
14.	Mangari	1136	-
15.	Newari	284	-
16.	Lepcha	23706	26078
17.	Kami	5	-
18.	Toto	383	-

Mother Tongues Tentatively Classified

1.	Baudh	2	-
2.	Chini Pahari	9	-
3.	Jangi	119	-
4.	Pahari Chamang	1	-
5.	Banbhasha	7	-
6.	Rawati	91	-

North Assam Branch

North-East Frontier Group

Mother Tongues Attested

1.	Aka/Hrusso	81	2947
2.	Dafla	1175	140986
3.	Bangni	28	-
4.	Abor/Adi	705	125371
5.	Miri	103188	5201
6.	Mishing	33410	-
7.	Mishmi	279	24059
8.	Chulikata/Idu	183	5869
9.	Digaru	100	3992
10.	Miju	107	4085

Mother Tongues Tentatively Classified

1.	Apatani	177	16580
2.	Ashing	46	-
3.	Bokar	80	-
4.	Bori-Abor/Adi	58	1884
5.	Gallong	883	8998
6.	Milang	21	706
7.	Minyong	1228	3573
8.	Padam	610	6708
9.	Pailibo	18	535
10.	Pangi	15	-
11.	Pasi-Abor/Adi	11	-
12.	Ramo	8	818
13.	Simong	1	26
14.	Tagin	228	27122

Bodo Group

Mother Tongues Attested

1.	Bodo/Boro	286339	27887
2.	Kachari	65259	7212
3.	Mech	10203	26959
4.	Lalung	10576	-
5.	Dimasa	32507	1371
6.	Garo	307026	408111
7.	Achik	4	-
8.	Dalu	10	-
9.	Koch	7698	16682
10.	Banai	527	-
11.	Rabha	44410	19270
12.	Rangdania	22	-
13.	Tripuri	215624	490464
14.	Jamatia	14522	44501
15.	Reang	65004	84004
16.	Deori	9103	3608
17.	Mikir	154786	11206
18.	Arleng	107	-

Mother Tongues Tentatively Classified

1.	Hairamba	201	-
2.	Kok Barak	3	-
3.	Murasing	22	-
4.	Noatia	4468	7182

Assam-Burmese Branch

Naga Group

Mother Tongues Attested

1.	Angami	34431	78398
2.	Sema	47464	93869
3.	Rengma	5931	15036
4.	Khezha	7324	15908
5.	Ao	56385	105610
6.	Monsang/Mongsen	1359	1139
7.	Lotha	26611	57913
8.	Tableng	14	-
9.	Chang Naga	11329	23133
10	Kacha Naga	4119	16033
11.	Kabui	17360	53142
12.	Khoirao	406	918
13.	Mao	31030	57435
14.	Maram	4928	6544
15.	Tangkhul	44020	79058
16.	Maring	7745	11532
17.	Konyak	46701	83261
18.	Naga-Unspecified	13563	17569

Mother Tongues Tentatively Classified

1.	Chakru	8339	-
2.	Meluri-Rengma	4	-
3.	Poma	1504	-
4.	Nokpu	1	-
5.	Lemei	2728	-
6	Liangmei	2887	-
7.	Upama Naga	58	-
8.	Urima Naga	58	-
9.	Zemi Naga	374	11414
10.	Rongmei	12720	-
11.	Paomata	7843	-
12.	Shamnyuyangan	9461	-
13.	Tabu	957	-
14.	Phelungre	252	-
15.	Pochury	2736	-
16.	Sangtam	15512	28838
17.	Orangkong	5	-
18.	Phom	13385	24265
19.	Tikhir	2486	3588
20.	Yimchungre	10187	27360
21.	Khiemnungam	12434	-

22.	Pangsha	1	-
23.	Nocte	66	27569
24.	Wancho	2713	32169
25.	Makware	769	612
26.	Tangsa	165	16396
27.	Tikhak	295	-
28.	Chakesang	10310	60771
29.	Zeliang	9460	21085

Kuki-Chin Group

Mother Tongues Attested

1.	Manipuri/Meithei	621244	904353
2.	Thado	24213	59274
3.	Changsen	338	-
4.	Chongloi	2	-
5.	Hangseen/Hansing	16	-
6.	Haokeep/Haokup	2676	-
7.	Khongzai	4111	-
8.	Kipgen	77	-
9.	Langtung	5	-
10.	Ralte	170	109
11.	Paite	18612	32670
12.	Tlangtlang	3	-
13.	Lakher	9531	15738
14.	Lushai/Mizo	221985	384747
15.	Bete	2964	-
16.	Rangkhol	1517	-
17.	Halam	5481	18853
18.	Khelma	722	-
19.	Shekasip	98	-
20.	Langrong	175	-
21.	Aimol	108	1862
22.	Chiru	3059	3744
23.	Koireng	531	948
24.	Kom	5478	-
25.	Hmar	25530	34170
26.	Lamgang	1866	-
27.	Chote	1035	1687
28.	Purum	28	447
29.	Anal	4875	10780
30.	Vaiphei	8657	16311
31.	Khami	1	-
32.	Kuki-Unspecified	28943	46271

33.	Chin-Unspecified	60	-
34.	Matu	212	-
35.	Poi	2	-

Mother Tongues Tentatively Classified

1.	Moyol	4	-
2.	Baite	204	-
3.	Hangui	4	-
4.	Indoi	3	-
5.	Kilong	10	-
6.	Lhouvum	1	-
7.	Lumhao	12	-
8.	Mate	60	-
9.	Shongthu	15	-
10.	Singson	24	-
11.	Tezang	2	-
12.	Thangngen	201	14
13.	Pawi	6886	-
14.	Pang	217	-
15.	Hadem	170	-
16.	Banshi	69	-
17.	Bongcher	6	-
18.	Charichong	213	-
19.	Kaipang	1977	-
20.	Kalai	2050	-
21.	Karbong	72	-
22.	Mursum	4486	-
23.	Rupini	2028	-
24.	Saimal	41	-
25.	Moyon	647	1642
26.	Gangte	4877	7891
27.	Neisel	10	-
28.	Khawathlang	1	-
29.	Simte	2818	5034
30.	Tidim	4	-
31.	Zou	6761	12466
32.	Darlong	817	-
33.	Mulsom	289	-

Mother Tongue Reclassified			
1.	Bisnhupuriya	15182	-
Burma Group			
Mother Tongues Attested			
1.	Mru	48	1231
2.	Arakanese	16	-
3.	Kaman	1	-
4.	Mogh	10424	17116
Kachin Group			
Mother Tongues Attested			
1.	Kawri	6	-
2.	Singpho	819	2353

Appendix - V

DRAVIDIAN TRIBAL LANGUAGES OF INDIA

Languages		No. of Speakers	
		1961	1981
Southern Dravidian			
1.	Coorgi/Kodagu	79127	93116
2.	Tulu	934849	1376306
3.	Koraga	192	16665
4.	Malekudi	2	2434
5.	Parava	48	-
6.	Udipi	17	-
7.	Toda	765	-
8.	Kota	862	720
9.	Ko Bhashai	94	-
Central Dravidian			
10.	Kui	1254	507639
11.	Pengu	510907	-
12.	Kolami	46065	78500
13.	Manne	4982	-
14.	Naiki-Kolami	8	-
15.	Gondi	1384321	1954693
16.	Dorli	35455	-
17.	Galki	24	-
18.	Kalari	47	-
19.	Kandra	4	-
20.	Kokadi	17	-
21.	Maria	65371	-
22.	Nagarchi	74	-
23.	Pankhali	1	-
24.	Pardhan	453	132942
25.	Parsi Gondi	14990	-
26.	Raj Gondi	335	-
27.	Thoti	339	1625
28.	Parji	84607	33091
29.	Dhurwa	24641	8612
30.	Koraputi	153	-
31.	Koya	140776	242534
32.	Dorachuttam	1	-
33.	Khond/Kondh	168027	204501
34.	Konda	12298	11062
35.	Kisan	50378	155283

Northern Dravidian			
36.	Adibhasha-Kurukh/Oraon	2101	-
37.	Adibhasha Nagesia	9	124
38.	Dhangri	4377	included in Dhanwari
39.	Dhanwari	23	69809
40.	Kisan-Kurukh/Oraon	102	-
41.	Kurukh/Oraon	1132931	1264590
42.	Lohari-Kurukh/Oraon	707	included in Kurukh/ Oraon
43.	Malhar	77	-
44.	Nagesia	1484	-
45.	Malto	88645	94614
46.	Sauria	31	4283
47.	Semi-Dravidian Hybrids	554	-
48.	Bharia	249	1022
49.	Ladhodi	305	-

Appendix - VI

INDO-ARYAN TRIBAL LANGUAGES OF INDIA

Languages		No. of Speakers	
		1961	1981
Bhili Group			
1.	Adivasi-Bhili	7	-
2.	Baglani	2	-
3.	Baori	2080	1884
4.	Barel	173479	-
5.	Bavchi	3	4129
6.	Bhilali	349312	included in Bhili
7.	Bhili	828583	4450771
8.	Bhilody	59243	included in Bhili
9.	Bhimchaura	129	-
10.	Byadha	49	-
11.	Charani	192	-
12.	Chodhari	59732	219897
13.	Dhanki	375	-
14.	Dhodia	30571	473906
15.	Dubli	14	16019
16.	Dungari	162	-
17.	Gamti/Gavit	38168	361709
18.	Kokna/Kokni/Kukna	84776	217322
19.	Kotali	455	-
20.	Kotvali	2794	-
21.	Magari	21	-
22.	Mawchi	42837	-
23.	Naikadi	1494	-
24.	Neelishikari	223	-
25.	Padvi	216	-
26.	Panchali	459	-
27.	Paradhi	10253	98353
28.	Pawri	38593	-
29.	Pittala Bhasha	131	-
30.	Ranati	8	-
31.	Tadavi	4097	55881
32.	Takankari	9	-
33.	Takari	101	-
34.	Basava	12905	-
35.	Wagdi	756786	-
36.	Walvi	595	-

Khandeshi Group			
1.	Ahirani	363780	-
2.	Chitodi	22	-
3.	Dangi	60584	-
4.	Dhedgujari	48	-
5.	Khandeshi	3692	1186921
Halabi/Halbi Group		299660	524758

Appendix - VII

DISTRIBUTION OF AUSTRIC SPEAKERS IN THE TOTAL TRIBAL POPULATION - 1961

% Category	No. of Dist./UT.	Name of the Dist./UT.
> 80	11	United Khasi and Jaintia Hills, (Assam); Monghyr, Santal Parganas, Dhanbad, Singhbhum (Bihar); Amravati (Maharashtra); Malda, Burdwan, Birbhum, Bankura (W.Bengal); Nicobar Islands.
65-80	8	Bhagalpur, Saharsa, Hazaribagh (Bihar); Mayurbhanj (Orissa); West Dinajpur, Murshidabad, Hooghly, Midnapore (W. Bengal).
50-65	4	Purnea (Bihar); East Nimar (M.P.); Ganjam (Orissa); Purulia (W.Bengal).
30-50	5	Ranchi (Bihar); Keonjhar, Cuttuck, Balasore (Orissa); Calcutta (W.B.).
20-35	7	Srikakulam (Andhra) ; Patna (Bihar) ; Betul (M.P.) ; Sundargarh (Orissa) ; Jalpaiguri, Nadia, Howrah (W.B.).
5-20	6	Koraput, Baudhkhondmals, Dhenkanal (Orissa); Darjeeling, Cooch Behar, 24-Parganas (W.B.).
1-5	8	Visakhapatnam (Andhra) ; United Mikir and North Cachar Hills (Assam); Gaya, Palamau (Bihar) ; Hoshangabad, Chhindwara (M.P.) ; Bolangir (Orissa); Tripura.
< 1	15	East Godavari (Andhra); Garo Hills, Mizo Hills (Assam); Shahabad, Champaran (Bihar); Sidhi, Dewas, West Nimar, Balaghat, Bilaspur, Raipur, Bastar (M.P.); Kalahandi, Puri (Orissa); Nagaland.

Appendix - VIII

LINGUISTIC EXPOSURE AMONG THE TRIBALS

Age groups	**0 - 19**		**20 - 39**		**40 - 59**		**60 +**	
Sex groups	**M**	**F**	**M**	**F**	**M**	**F**	**M**	**F**
1. Dumka Town	62.0	74.5	76.0	41.0	82.8	54.5	39.0	26.0
2. Ranchi Town	95.4	100	98.6	100	97.0	100	70.3	78.0
3. Bande	54.9	36.0	60.3	47.0	52.9	40.0	38.7	21.0
4. Litingdih	93.7	100	92.4	81.5	95.3	55.5	-	-
5. Kula Buru	23.5	0.00	45.4	0.00	29.3	0.00	-	-
6. Mirpur	24.0	15.0	23.7	21.0	34.0	-	-	-
7. Kalamkala	62.4	52.0	60.5	60.0	56.0	-	61.5	-
8. Kutbi	53.8	38.0	49.9	34.8	51.0	15.2	18.6	18.4
9. Wanera Para	65.7	51.0	85.0	55.0	73.6	48.0	74.6	-
10. Umedgarhi	87.5	-	76.5	-	100	75.0	48.0	-
11. Nai Abadi	72.1	33.0	79.0	54.0	74.0	-	74.3	-
12. Regania	56.4	30.8	74.1	39.5	75.0	60.0	78.0	-

The above data have been divided by 100 to bring the unity and then they have been squared.

1.	0.38	0.56	0.58	0.17	0.69	0.30	0.15	0.07=	2.9
2.	0.91	1.00	0.97	1.00	0.94	1.00	0.49	0.61=	6.9
3.	0.30	0.13	0.36	0.22	0.28	0.16	0.15	0.04=	1.6
4.	0.88	1.00	0.85	0.66	0.91	0.31	-	0.00=	1.6
5.	0.06	0.00	0.21	0.00	0.09	0.00	-	- =	0.36
6.	0.06	0.02	0.11	0.04	0.12	-	-	- =	0.35
7.	0.39	0.27	0.37	0.36	0.31	-	0.38	- =	2.08
8.	0.29	0.14	0.25	0.12	0.26	0.02	0.03	0.03=	1.14
9.	0.43	0.26	0.72	0.30	0.57	0.23	0.56	- =	3.04
10.	0.77	-	0.59	-	1.00	0.56	0.23	- =	3.15
11.	0.52	0.11	0.62	0.29	0.55	-	0.55	- =	2.64
12.	0.32	0.09	0.55	0.16	0.36	0.56	0.61	- =	2.65

The row total is divided by 'n' (n is the number of observation under different age - sex groups)

1. 2.9/8 = 0.36
2. 6.92/8 = 0.86
3. 1.64/8 = 0.21
4. 4.0/7 = 0.66
5. 0.36/6 = 0.06
6. 0.35/5 = 0.07
7. 2.08/6 = 0.35
8. 1.14/8 = 0.14
9. 3.04/7 = 0.43
10. 3.15/5 = 0.63
11. 2.64/6 = 0.44
12. 2.65/7 = 0.38

These values were subtracted from 1 to get the index value.

1.	1 - 0.36	=	0.64	7.	1 - 0.35	=	0.63
2.	1 - 0.86	=	0.14	8.	1 - 0.14	=	0.86
3.	1 - 0.21	=	0.79	9.	1 - 0.43	=	0.57
4.	1 - 0.66	=	0.34	10.	1 - 0.63	=	0.37
5.	1 - 0.06	=	0.94	11.	1 - 0.44	=	0.56
6.	1 - 0.07	=	0.93	12.	1 - 0.38	=	0.62

Appendix - IX

PERCENTAGE OF BILINGUAL TRIBAL POPULATION

Age group	0 - 19		20 - 39		40 - 59		60 +		Average (%)
Sex groups	M	F	M	F	M	F	M	F	
Dumka Town	26	8	22	6	18	12	4	4	40.65
Surajbeda	36	-	18	9	36	-	-	-	11.00
Ranchi Town	100	100	100	100	100	100	100	100	100.0
Murhu	-	100	-	100	-	100	-	-	100.0
Bande	34	-	46	5	15	2	-	-	20.47
Litingdih	35	12	29	-	24	-	-	-	44.73
Kula Buru	-	-	48	-	-	-	-	-	4.78
Udaipur	100	100	100	100	100	100	100	100	100.0
Richhi	100	100	100	100	100	100	100	100	100.0
Mirpur	-	-	-	-	-	-	-	-	0.00
Kalamkala	-	-	1	-	-	-	-	-	1.39
Pangra	100	100	100	100	100	100	100	100	100.0
Kutbi	30	4	33	1	29	-	-	-	22.96
Wanerapara	30	-	46	-	22	-	2	-	27.54
Umedgarhi	42	16	26	-	16	-	-	-	57.58
Nai Abadi	15	-	50	-	34	-	-	-	34.21
Regania	24	6	49	-	20	-	-	-	31.61
Punasa	100	100	100	100	100	100	100	100	100.0
Banswara Town	100	100	100	100	100	100	-	-	100.0

Appendix - X

PROXIMITY OF THE VILLAGES UNDER STUDY

Village	% of Tribals	Terrain	Distance from Town	Distance from Road	Village Type	L. Shift/ Maintenance
Regania	90	Plain	32 Km	2.0 Km	Tribal dominated	Maintenance
Wanerapara	87	do	35 Km	0.5Km	do	do
Umedgarhi	75	do	33 Km	0.5Km	do	do
Nai Abadi	100	do	35 Km	0.5Km	do	do
Punasa	10	do	50 Km	0.0Km	Non-tribal dominated	Shift
Richhi	60	do	55 Km	1.0Km	do	do
Udaipur	75	do	48 Km	0.0Km	do	do
Mirpur	88	do	45 Km	0.0Km	Mixed Type	Maintenance
Kalamkala	34	do	45 Km	0.0Km	do	do
Kutbi	98	Hilly & forested	82 Km	30 Km	Tribal dominated	do
Pangra	45	Plain	35 Km	7.0Km	Non-tribal dominated	Shift
Litingdih	95	Hilly & forested	35 Km	5.0Km	Tribal dominated	Maintenance
Kula Buru	100	do	34 Km	4.0Km	do	do
Bande	78	Plain	50 Km	0.0Km	do	do
Surajbeda	78	do	80 Km	0.0Km	do	do

Appendix - XI

THE COMPOSITE SCORE OF THE LEVELS OF URBANISATION

District	Factor Score	District	Factor Score	District	Factor Score
Srikakulam	0.234	Dewas	0.172	Keonjhar	0.057
Visakhapatnam	0.240	West Nimar	0.173	Cuttuck	0.113
East Godavari	0.286	East Nimar	0.254	Mayurbhanj	0.039
Garo Hills	0.047	Hoshangabad	0.217	Balasore	0.098
U.K.& J.Hills	0.254	Betul	0.097	Darjeeling	0.131
U.M.& N.C.Hills	0.026	Chhindwara	0.145	Jalpaiguri	0.130
Mizo Hills	0.064	Balaghat	0.070	Cooch Behar	0.119
Patna	0.440	Surguja	0.053	W. Dinajpur	0.118
Gaya	0.122	Bilaspur	0.103	Malda	0.076
Shahabad	0.119	Raigarh	0.072	Murshidabad	0.169
Champaran	0.086	Raipur	0.138	Nadia	0.369
Monghyr	0.195	Bastar	0.034	24-Parganas	0.931
Bhagalpur	0.187	Amravati	0.517	Calcutta	67.09
Saharsa	0.068	Kalahandi	0.039	Howrah	1.126
Purnea	0.100	Koraput	0.064	Hooghly	0.984
S.Parganas	0.081	Sambalpur	0.084	Burdwan	0.386
Palamu	0.060	Bolangir	0.062	Birbhum	0.122
Hazaribagh	0.110	Baudhkhondmal	0.062	Bankura	0.115
Ranchi	0.124	Ganjam	0.113	Midnapore	0.134
Dhanbad	0.281	Sundargarh	0.012	Purulia	0.104
Singhbhum	0.291	Dhenkanal	0.058		
Sidhi	0.018	Puri	0.101		

REFERENCES

Ahmad, A. and M. Ishtiaq (*1994*) : "Dialect Regions of Bihar Plain : Some Issues in Methodology" in SPATIAL ASPECTS OF LANGUAGE (ed.) by N.H. Itagi, Central Institute of Indian Languages, Mysore, pp.111-122.

Apte, M.L. (*1962*) : "Linguistic Acculturation and Its Relation to Urbanisation and Socio-economic Factors", INDIAN LINGUISTICS,Vol. 23, pp. 5-25.

——(*1971*) : "Some Socio-linguistic Aspects on Interlingual Communication in India" ANTHROPOLOGICAL LINGUISTICS, Vol. 12, No. 3, PP. 63-82.

Blount, B.G. and M. Sanches (*1977*) : SOCIO-CULTURAL DIMENSIONS OF LANGUAGE CHANGE, Academic Press, New York.

Bonvillain, N. (*1978*) : "Linguistic Changes in Akwesasne Mohawk: French and English Influences",INTERNATIONAL JOURNAL OF AMERICAN LINGUISTICS, Vol. 44, No. 1, pp.31-39.

Bose, A. (*1969*) : "Some Aspects of Linguistic Demography of India", in LANGUAGE AND SOCIETY IN INDIA, Indian Institute of Advanced Study, Simla, pp.37-51.

Bose, N.K. (*1977*) : CULTURE AND SOCIETY IN INDIA, Asia Publishing House, Mumbai.

Bottiglioni, G. (*1954*) : " Linguistic Geography: Achievements, Methods and Orientations", WORD, Vol. 10, No. 2-3, pp. 375-387

Breton, R.J.L. (*1971*) : "The Geography of Languages as a Basis for the Geography of Ethics", in POPULATION AND SETTLEMENT GEOGRAPHY, Selected Papers of the International Geography Congress(ed.) by S.P.Chatterji and S.S. Dasgupta, pp. 66 - 70.

Broker, G. (*1969*) : "Language and Regionalism" in LANGUAGE AND SOCIETY IN INDIA, Indian Institute of Advanced Study, Simla, pp. 387-394.

Burdhan, A.B. (*1973*) : THE UNSOLVED TRIBAL PROBLEM, Communist Party Publication, New Delhi.

Chambers, J.K. and P. Trudgill (*1980*) : DIALECTOLOGY, Cambridge University Press, Cambridge,U.K.

Charlier, R.H. (*1971*) : "Linguistic Minorities, Enclaves and Enclaves in Belgium" in POPULATION AND SETTLEMENT GEOGRAPHY, Selected Papers of the International Geographical Congress, India, 1969, (eds) S.P. Chatterji and S.P. Dasgupta, pp. 321-388.

Chatterji, S.K. (*1963*) : LANGUAGES AND LITERATURES OF MODERN INDIA, Bengal Publications, Calcutta.

————(*1969*) : "Inaugural Address" in LANGUAGE AND SOCIETY IN INDIA, Indian Institute of Advanced Study, Simla, pp. 11-23.

————(*1973*) : "Tribal Languages", in THE TRIBAL PEOPLE OF INDIA, Publications Division, Government of India, New Delhi, pp. 63-70.

———— *and S.M. Katre* (*1973*) : "Languages", in GAZETTEER OF INDIA, Ministry of Information and Broadcasting, Government of India, New Delhi, Vol. 1, pp. 367-411.

Chumaceiro, R.M. (*1983*) : "Language Maintenance and Shift among Jerusalem Sephardim", INTERNATIONAL JOURNAL OF SOCIO-LINGUISTICS, Vol.37, pp.25-39.

Crystal, D. (*1971*) : LINGUISTICS, Penguine Books, England.

Dalton, E.T. (*1872*) : DESCRIPTIVE ETHNOLOGY OF BENGAL, Office of the Superintendent of Government Printing Press, Calcutta.

Das, N. (*1972*) : " The Tribal Situation in Orissa", in TRIBAL SITUATION IN INDIA, (ed.) by K.S.Singh, Indian Institute of Advanced Study, Simla, pp. 185-193.

Dasgupta, J. (*1970*) : LANGUAGE CONFLICT AND NATIONAL DEVELOPMENT, University of California Press, Berkeley, USA.

Diebold, A.R. Jr. (*1964*) : "Incipient Bilingualism", in LANGUAGE IN CULTURE AND SOCIETY : A READER IN LINGUISTICS AND ANTHROPOLOGY, (ed.) by D. Hymes, Allied Publishers, New Delhi, pp.495-508.

Dorian, N.C. (*1982*) : "Language Loss and Maintenance in Language Contact Situations", in THE LOSS OF LANGUAGE SKILLS, (ed.) by R.D. Lambert and B.F. Freed, Newbury House Publishers, Rowley Mass, pp.44-59.

Doshi, S.L. (*1972*) : "Tribals: An Assimilationist Society and National Integration", in TRIBAL SITUATION IN INDIA, (ed.) K.S. Singh, Indian Institute of Advanced Study, Simla, pp. 462-467.

————(*1985*) : " Tribals: An assimilationist Society and National Integration", in TRIBAL SOCIETY IN INDIA, (ed.) by K.S. Singh, Manohar, New Delhi.

Fierman, W. (*1982*) : " The Shifting Russian and Uzbek Language Balance in Pre-World War II Uzbekistan", INTERNATIONAL JOURNAL OF LANGUAGE, Vol. 38, pp.125-150.

Fishman, J.A. (*1976*) : "The Sociology of Language", in ADVANCES IN SOCIOLOGY OF LANGUAGE, (ed.) by J.A. Fishman, Vol. 1, Mouton, The Hague.

Gait, E. (*1970*) : "Introduction", in S.C.Roy's MUNDAS AND THEIR COUNTRY, Asia Publishing House, Mumbai.

Gal, S. (*1979*) : LANGUAGE SHIFT:SOCIAL DETERMINANTS OF LINGUISTIC CHANGE IN BILINGUAL AUSTRIA, Academic Press, New York.

Ghurye G.S. (*1963*) : THE SCHEDULED TRIBES, Popular Prakashan, Mumbai.

Gill, H.S. (*1977*) : "Indian Bilingualism", in INDIAN BILINGUALISM (ed.) by P.G. Sharma and S. Kumar, Kendriya Hindi Sansthan, Agra, pp. 17-20.

Gopal, R. (*1966*) : LINGUISTIC AFFAIRS OF INDIA, Asia Publishing House, Mumbai.

Greenberg, J.H. (*1956*) : "The Measurement of Linguistic Diversity", LANGUAGE, Vol. 32, pp. 109-115.

Grierson, G.A. (*1967*) : LINGUISTIC SURVEY OF INDIA, (reprint), Motilal Banarsidass, Delhi, Vols. I, II, IV, and IX.

Gupta, S.K. (*1977*) : "Traditional and Emerging Political Structures", in TRIBAL HERITAGE OF INDIA, (ed.) by S.C. Dube, Vikas Publishing House, New Delhi, pp.161-186.

Haugen, E. (*1972*) : "The Ecology of Language", in THE ECOLOGY OF LANGUAGE (ed.) by Anwar S. Dil.Standford University Press, California, pp. 325-339.

Hoijer, H. (*1948*) : "Linguistic and Cultural Change", LANGUAGE, Vol. 24. No.4, pp.335-345.

————(*1964*) : "Linguistic and Cultural Change", in LANGUAGE IN CULTURE AND SOCIETY : A READER IN LINGUISTICS AND ANTHROPOLOGY, (ed.) by D.Hymes, Allied Publishers, New Delhi, pp. 455-466.

Hunter, N.W. (*1877*) : STATISTICAL ACCOUNT OF SANTAL PARGANAS.

Husain, S.A. (*1956*) : THE NATIONAL CULTURE OF INDIA, National Book Trust of India, New Delhi.

Hutton, J.H. (*1933*) : CENSUS OF INDIA, 1931, Vol. I-A, Pt. I, Manager of Publications, Delhi.

Ishtiaq, M. (*1982*) : "Linguistic Mobility among the Santals of the Chotanagpur Region (Bihar)", NATIONAL GEOGRAPHER, Vol. 17, No.1, pp. 59-68.

——————— (*1985*) : "Language Shift among the Tribal Communities: A Case Study of Santals, Mundas and Oraons in Bihar", THE GEOGRAPHER, Vol.32, No.2, pp.69-78.

——————— (*1991*) : "Dialectal/Linguistic Change among the Scheduled Tribes in India and Its Correlates : A Geographical Analysis" Unpublished, Ph.D. Thesis submitted to J.N.U., New Delhi.

Itagi, N.H. et. at (*1986*) : COMMUNICATION POTENTIAL IN THE TRIBAL POPULATION OF ASSAM AND MADHYA PRADESH, Central Institute of Indian Languages , Mysore, India.

Johnson, L. (*1976*) : "A Rate of Change Index for Language", LANGUAGE IN SOCIETY, Vol. 5, pp. 165-172

Joseph, B.D. (*1983*) : "The Language Use in the Balkans : The Contributions of Historical Linguistics", ANTHROPOLOGICAL LINGUISTICS, Vol. 25, No. 3, pp. 275-287.

Kachru, B.B. (*1977*) : "Linguistic Schizophrenia and Language Census: A Note on the Indian Situation", LINGUISTICS, Vol. 186, pp.17-32.

Khubchandani, L.M. (*1972*) : Distribution of Contact Languages in India: A Study of the 1961 Bilingual Returns, Indian Census Centenary Seminar, New Delhi. Also in ADVANCES IN THE STUDY OF SOCIETAL MULTILINGUALISM (ed) by J. Fishman, 1978, Vol. 2, Mouton, The Hague.

——————(*1972*) : "Mother-tongue in Multi-lingual Societies", in ECONOMIC AND SOCIO-CULTURAL DIMENSIONS OF REGIONALISATION, Census Centenary Monograph, No. 7, Registrar General of India, New Delhi, pp.427-445.

—————(*1992*) : TRIBAL IDENTITY: A LANGUAGE AND COMMUNICATION PERSPECTIVE, Indian Institute of Advanced Study, Shimla.

Kluyev, B.I. (*1981*) : INDIA: NATIONAL AND LANGUAGE PROBLEM, Sterling Publishers, New Delhi.

Kochar, V. (*1970*) : SOCIAL ORGANISATION AMONG THE SANTALS, Editions India, Calcutta.

Kundu, A. (*1980*) : MEASUREMENT OF URBAN PROCESSES: A STUDY IN REGIONALISATION, Popular Prakashan, Mumbai.

Labov, W. (*1972*) : SOCIOLINGUISTIC PATTERNS, University of Pennsylvania Press, Philadelphia.

Lewis, E.G. (*1972*) : MULTILINGUALISM IN SOVIET UNION, Mouton, The Hague, Paris.

Liberson, S. (*1970*) : LANGUAGE AND ETHNIC RELATIONS IN CANADA, Wiley, New York.

———— (*1977*) : "A Social Theory of Race and Ethnic Relations", in MAJORITY AND MINORITY: THE DYNAMICS OF RACIAL AND ETHNIC RELATIONS, (ed) by N.R. Yetman and C.H. Steele, Allyn and Bacon, Inc., Boston, pp. 45-53.

———— *and E. J. Mc Cabe,* (*1978*) : " Domains of Language Usage and Mother Tongue Shift in Nairobi", INTERNATIONAL JOURNAL OF SOCIOLOGY OF LANGUAGE, Vol. 18, pp.69-81.

Mackinnon, K.M. (*1977*) : "Language Shift and Education Conservation of Ethnolinguistic Culture amongst School Children of a Gaelic Community", INTERNATIONAL JOURNAL OF SOCIOLINGUISTICS, Vol. 14, pp.31-55.

Majumdar, D.N. (*1958*) : RACES AND CULTURES OF INDIA, Asia Publishing House, Mumbai.

Mamoria, C.B. (*1957*) : TRIBAL DEMOGRAPHY IN INDIA. Kitab Mahal, Allahabad.

Marten (*1913*) : CENSUS OF INDIA, 1911, Vol. 1, Pt. 1, Calcutta Superintendent Goverment Printing, India, p. 332

Mazumdar, S.N. (*1970*) : MARXISM AND LANGUAGE PROBLEM IN INDIA, People's Publishing House, New Delhi.

Milroy, J. and L. Milroy (*1985*) : "Linguistic Change, Social Network and Speaker Innovation", JOURNAL OF LINGUISTICS, Vol. 21, pp. 339-384.

Misra, B. G. (*1977*) : STUDIES IN BILINGUALISM, Central Institute of Indian languages, Mysore.

Mitra, A. (*1974*) : USING MOTHER TONGUE DATA COLLECTED IN POPULATION CENSUSES FOR SOCIO-LINGUISTIC STUDIES, Memeographed, Census of India.

Nigam, R.C. (*1971*) : LANGUAGE HANDBOOK ON MOTHER TONGUE IN CENSUS, Census Centenary Monogarph, No. 10, Census of India, New Delhi.

O' Barr, W.M. and J.F. O' Barr (*1976*) : LANGUAGE AND POLITICS: CONTRIBUTIONS TO SOCIOLOGY OF LANGUAGE, The Hague, Paris.

Pandey, S. (*1977*) : "Socio-linguistics and Language Change", INDIAN LINGUISTICS, Vol. 38, No. 1,pp. 43-50

Paulston, C.B. and R.G. Paulston (*1980*) : "Language and Ethnic Boundaries", LANGUAGE SCIENCES, Vol. 2, No. 1, pp. 69-101.

Peng, F.C.C. (*1979*): "Sound Change and Language Change: A Socio-linguistic Interpretation", LANGUAGE SCIENCES, Vol. 1, No. 1, pp.94-123.

Prabhoo, L.R. (*1980*): "Dative Case in Indo-Aryan and Dravidian : Contact and Interference in the Indian Sub-Continent", INTERNATIONAL JOURNAL OF DRAVIDIAN LINGUISTICS, Vol.9, pp. 252-273.

Prasad, K.N. (*1993*) : "Bilingualism among the Chotanagpur Tribes" in SOCIAL STRUCTURE AND REGIONAL DEVELOPMENT : A SOCIAL GEOGRAPHY PERSPECTIVE, (ed.) by A. Ahmad, Rawat Publications, Jaipur, pp. 115-127.

Rajora, S.C. (*1987*) : SOCIAL STRUCTURE AND TRIBAL ELITES, Himanshu Publications, Udaipur, India.

Raza, M. and others (*1977*): "Tribal Population of India : Spatial Patterns of Clustering and Concentration", OCCASIONAL PAPER, No. 5, CSRD, Jawaharlal Nehru University, New Delhi.

Risley, H.H. (*1915*) : PEOPLES OF INDIA, Oriental Books Reprint Corporation, New Delhi.

Roy, N.C. (*1962*) : FEDERALISM AND LINGUISTIC STATES, Firma K.L. Mukhopadhyay, Calcutta.

Roy, S.C. (*1970*) : THE MUNDAS AND THEIR COUNTRY, Asia Publishing House, Mumbai.

Royburman, B.K. (*1972*) : "Tribal Demography: A Preliminary Appraisal", in TRIBAL SITUATION IN INDIA, (ed.) by K.S.Singh, Indian Institute of Advanced Study, Simla, pp. 39-50.

Rubenstein, H. (*1957*) : "The Recent Conflict in Soviet linguistics", LANGUAGE, Vol. 27, No. 3, pp.281-287.

Russell, R.V. (*1916*) : THE TRIBES AND CASTES OF CENTRAL PROVINCES OF INDIA, Vol. 2, MacMillan and Company, London.

Sachchidananda, (*1972*): "The Tribal Situation in Bihar", in TRIBAL SITUATION IN INDIA, (ed.)by K.S.Singh, Indian Institute of Advanced Study ,Simla,pp. 169-184.

Schmidt, P. (*1933*) : "Introduction" in SANTALI-ENGLISH, ENGLISH-SANTALI DICTIONARY, (ed.) by A. Campbell.

Scotton, C.M. (*1983*) : "Tongzhi in China: Language Change and Its Conversational Consequences", LANGUAGE IN SOCIETY, Vol. 12, pp.477-494.

Sharma, P.G. (*1977*) : "Indian Bilingualism" in INDIAN BILINGUALISM, (ed.) by P.G. Sharma and S. Kumar, Kendriya Hindi Sansthan, Agra, pp.3-16.

Singh, J.D. (*1977*) : "Aspects of Indian Bilingualism" in INDIAN BILINGUALISM, (ed.) by P.G. Sharma and S. Kumar, pp. 88-96.

Southworth, F.C. (1974) : "Linguistic Stratigraphy of North India" INTERNATIONAL JOURNAL OF DRAVIDIAN LINGUISTICS, Vol. 3, No. 1, pp. 201-223.

Srivastava, R.N. (1977) : "Indian Bilingualism : Myth and Reality", INDIAN BILINGUALISM (ed.) by P.G. Sharma and S. Kumar, pp.57-87.

Trudgill, P. (1974): "Linguistic Change and Diffusion : Description and Explanation in Sociolinguistic Dialect Geography", LANGUAGE IN SOCIETY, Vol. 2, pp. 215-246.

Volchok, B.Ya. (1964) : "The Interaction of Caste and Tribal Communities in Central India", JOURNAL OF SOCIAL RESEARCH, Vol. 7, Nos. 1 and 2.

Weinreich, U. (1953) : LANGUAGE IN CONTACT: FINDINGS AND PROBLEMS, Publications of Linguistic Society, New York.

————, *W. Labov and M.I. Herzog (1968)* : "Empirical Foundations for a Theory of Language Change", in DIRECTIONS FOR HISTORICAL LINGUISTICS, (ed.) by W.P. Lehmann and Y. Malkiel, University of Texas Press, Austin, pp. 95-188.

Census of India, 1911, Vol. I.

Census of India, 1961, Vol. I, INDIA, LANGUAGE TABLES, Pt. II c(ii).

Census of India, 1971, Sr. 1, INDIA, SOCIAL AND CULTURAL TABLES, Pt. II c(ii).

Census of India, 1971, Sr. 1, INDIA, SPECIAL TABLE FOR SCHEDULED TRIBES Pt. V-A (ii).

Census of India, 1981, Sr. INDIA, SPECIAL TABLE FOR SCHEDULED TRIBES ON MOTHER TONGUE AND BILINGUALISM, Pt. IX (II).

Census of India, 1981, Sr. 1. INDIA, HOUSEHOLDS AND HOUSEHOLD POPULATION BY LANGUAGE MAINLY SPOKEN IN THE HOUSEHOLD, Pt. B(i).

Census of India, 1981, Sr. 1 INDIA, PRIMARY CENSUS ABSTRACT : SCHEDULED TRIBES, Pt. II B (iii).

INDEX

Adi 5, 62
Adivasi Sewa Mandal 142
Agariya 51
Ahmad 8, 135
Amerindian 16
Anal 25
Angami 25
Ao 5, 25, 63
Apparent change 10
Apte, M.L. 17, 103
Aravalli hills 22
Assam-Burmese language 24
Assimilation 14, 119, 121
Asuri 51
Australoid 16
Austro-Asiatic 5, 22
Austronesian 22

Bagidora 2
Balti 25
Bande 2, 101, 107
Banswara 2, 100
Bhartiya Adim Jati Sewak Sangh 142
Bhili 5, 27, 63
Bhilodi 5
Bhil Raj 135
Bhils 2, 76, 84, 135
Bhojpuri 133, 149
Bhotia 25
Bhumij 11, 23, 44
Bilingualism/Multilingualism 101, 106, 145
Bilinguals 13
Birhor 61
Birjia 51
Blount, B. G. and M. Sanches 12, 17
Bodo 2, 25, 63, 133
Bonvillain, N. 16
Bose, N.K. 17, 120
Broker, G. 132
Bundu 2, 82
Burdhan, A.B. 2, 14, 132

Campbell 29
Chamber, J.K. and P.Trudgill 10
Chang 25
Charlier, R.H. 132
Chatterji, S. K. 16, 17, 19, 20, 29, 142
Chumaceiro, R. M. 16
Colonization 13
Convergent 7
Coorgi/Kodagu 26
Creole 12
Crystal, D. 10
Cultural change 14

Dalfa 5, 25
Dalton, E.T. 17, 29
Das, N. 128
Dasgupta, J. 14, 16, 98
Detribalisation 119
Diachronic 10, 16
Diebold, A.R.Jr. 7
Divergent 7
Dogri 133, 149
Dorian, N.C. 16
Doshi, S.L. 1, 16, 28, 61, 119, 121
Darvidian 5, 19, 26
Dumka 2, 4, 82, 101, 107

Fierman, W. 16
Finnish-American language 12
Fishman, J.A. 7, 13, 17
Folk language 16

Gadaba 9, 23, 47
Gait, E. 29

Gal, S. 16
Garo 5, 25, 63
Ghurye, G.S. 16
Gill, H.S. 102
Gondi 5, 26, 63, 149
Gondwana land 135
Gopal, R. 16
Greenberg, J.H. 99
Grierson, G.A. 16, 29, 35, 41, 43, 47
Gupta, S.K. 8

Halabi/Halbi 5, 27, 64
Halam 25
Hansda 35
Haugen, E. 102
Hersud 4, 82
Himalayan languages 25
Hmar 25
Ho 5, 10, 23, 36, 64
Hoijer, H. 7, 14, 16, 61, 132
Hunter, W.W. 29
Husain, S.A. 132
Hutton, J.H. 17

Indo-Aryan 5, 19, 27
Integration 119
Ishtiaq, M. 17, 97, 121, 135
Isolating language 23
Itagi, N.H. 61

Jharkhand 135
Johnson, L. 16
Joseph 17
Juang 50

Kabui 25
Kacha Naga 25
Kachru, B.B. 17, 135, 149
Kalam Kala 2, 82, 100, 107
Kannada 26
Karmali 51
Kera 35
Khaira 51
Khalwa 2
Khandeshi 5, 27, 64
Khandwa 82
Kharia 5, 23, 41, 43, 64
Khasi 5, 23, 37, 64
Kherwari 51
Khezha 25
Khiemnungam 25
Khondh/Khond 5, 26, 65
Khubchandani, L.M. 14, 76, 135, 149
Kinuari 25
Kisan 5, 65
Kluyev, B.I. 135
Koch 25
Kochar, V. 31
Koda/Kora 23, 47, 50
Kol 51
Kolarian language 29
Konda 26
Konkani 132, 149
Koraku 51
Korku 2, 5, 23, 39, 41, 65, 77, 86
Koya 5, 26, 65
Kui 5, 26, 65
Kuki 25
Kula Buru 2, 82, 101
Kundu, A. 123
Kurmi 51
Kurukh/Oraon 5, 26, 65
Kutbi 2, 82, 100, 107

Labov, W. 16
Ladakhi 25
Lahuli 25
Lakher 25
Language consciousness 132, 133, 136
Language contact 12
Language maintenance 145
Language regionalism 131, 133, 136
Language revivalism 133
Language shift 7, 10, 11, 16, 145
Language typology 83
Lepcha 25
Lewis, E.G. 103
Liberson, S. 12, 17
Limbu 25
Linguistic diversity 98
Linguistic exposure 99
Linguistic indentity 51, 135
Litingdih 2, 82, 107
Littipara 2
Lotha 25
Lushai/Mizo 5, 25, 66
Lyngngam 39

Mackinnon, K.M. 17
Mahali 51
Maithili 133, 149
Majumdar, D.N. 29
Malayalam 26
Malto 26
Mamoria, C.B. 20
Manjhi 51
Mao 25
Maring 25
Marten 17
Marwari 133, 149
Max Muller 29
Mazumdar, S.N. 16
Meithei/Manipuri 23, 25, 132, 136
Mikir 5, 26, 66
Milroy, J. and L. Milroy 7, 17
Mirpur 2, 82, 100, 107
Mishmi 25
Misra, B.G. 102
Missionary 142
Mitra, A. 17, 135
Mohawk 16
Monkhmer 22, 37
Monolingual 13
Muasi 41, 51
Mukhia 4
Multilinguals 13
Munda/Mundari 5, 23, 33, 66
Mundas 2, 11, 79, 90
Murhu 2, 82, 101

Naga 25
Nagpuri 35
Nai Abadi 2, 100, 107
Nepali 132, 149
Nicobarese 23, 50
Nigam, R.C. 18, 23
Nihali 51
Nimadi 4
Nissi/Dafla 5, 66
Nocte 25
Non-traditional language 10
Non tribal, Non regional language 11

O'Barr, W.M. and J. F. O'Barr 132, 149
Oraon 11

Paharia 51
Pandey, S. 17
Pandit, M.L. 18
Pangra 2, 100, 107
Paite 25
Parji 26
Paulston, C.B. and R.G. Paulston 135
Peng, F.C.C. 16
Phom 25
Pidgin 12
Pnar/Synteng 51
Prabhoo, L.R. 12
Prestigious language 13
Proto-Australoids 29
Punasa 2, 82, 100, 109

Rabha 25
Rajora, S.C. 12
Raza, Moonis 8
Real change 10
Regania 2, 100, 107
Regional language 11
Rengma 25
Richhi 2, 82, 100, 107
Risley, H.H. 29
Ray, N.C. 6, 13, 17
Royburman, B.K. 17, 119
Roy, S.C. 29
Rubenstein, H. 7
Russell, R.V. 16, 28

Sachchidananda 16
Sadari/Sadani 12
Sanskrit 14
Sanskritization 16
Santali 5, 23, 30, 67
Santal Parganas 2
Santals 2, 4, 80, 91
Savara 5, 23, 43, 67
Schmidt, P. 29
Scotton, C.M. 16, 61
Sema 25
Sharma, P.G. 102
Sherpa 25
Shift 10
Siamese-Chinese language 24
Singh, J.D. 102
Sino-Tibetan 19, 23
Social setting 13

Sothworth, F.C. 13
Srivastava.R.V. 102, 103
Sub-ordinate 12
Sumerians 16
Super-ordinate 12, 13
Surajbeda 2, 4. 82, 101, 107
Synchronic 10
Synteng/Pnar 39

Tamari 35
Tamil 26
Tangkhul 25
Tangsa 25
Tehsil 2, 4
Telugu 26
Thado 25
Thar 51
Tibetan 25
Tibeto-Burman 5, 24
Tone language 23
Traditional language 10
Tribal identity 119
Tribal language 19
Tribal territory 135
Tripuri 5, 25, 67
Tulu 5, 26, 67
Turi 51

Udaipur 2, 82, 100, 107
Umedgarhi 2, 100, 107
Urdu 14

Vaiphei 25
Volchok, B.Ya. 15

Wancho 25
Wanerapara 2, 100, 107
War 39, 51
Weinreich, U. 12, 17, 102

Yimchungre 25

Zemi Naga 25